Collins

AQA GCSE 9-1
English Language
& Literature

Revision Guide

Paul Burns

About this Revision & Practice book

Revise

These pages provide a recap of everything you need to know for each topic.

You should read through all the information before taking the Quick Test at the end. This will test whether you can recall the key facts.

Practise

These topic-based questions appear shortly after the revision pages for each topic and will test whether you have understood the topic. If you get any of the questions wrong, make sure you read the correct answer carefully.

Review

These topic-based questions appear later in the book, allowing you to revisit the topic and test how well you have remembered the information. If you get any of the questions wrong, make sure you read the correct answer carefully.

Mix it Up

These pages feature a mix of questions for all the different topics, just like you would get in an exam. They will make sure you can recall the relevant information to answer a question without being told which topic it relates to.

Test Yourself on the Go

Visit our website at **collins.co.uk/collinsGCSErevision** and print off a set of flashcards. These pocket-sized cards feature questions and answers so that you can test yourself on all the key facts anytime and anywhere. You will also find lots more information about the advantages of spaced practice and how to plan for it.

Workbook

This section features even more topic-based questions as well as practice exam papers, providing two further practice opportunities for each topic to guarantee the best results.

ebook

To access the ebook, visit collins.co.uk/ebooks and follow the step-by-step instructions.

QR Codes

Found throughout the book, the QR codes can be scanned on your smartphone for extra practice and explanations.

A QR code in the Revise section links to a Quick Recall Quiz on that topic. A QR code in the Workbook section links to a video working through the solution to one of the questions on that topic.

Contents

Reading Task

Read the text below and answer the questions that follow.

From *Little Women* by Louisa May Alcott

'Christmas won't be Christmas without any presents,' grumbled Jo, lying on the rug.

'It's so dreadful to be poor!' sighed Meg, looking down at her old dress.

'I don't think it's fair for some girls to have plenty of pretty things, and other girls nothing at all,' added little Amy, with an injured sniff.

'We've got Father and Mother, and each other,' said Beth contentedly from her corner.

The four young faces on which the firelight shone brightened at the cheerful words, but darkened again as Jo said sadly, 'We haven't got Father, and shall not have him for a long time.' She didn't say perhaps never, but each silently added it, thinking of Father far away, where the fighting was.

Nobody spoke for a minute; then Meg said in an altered tone, 'You know the reason Mother proposed not having any presents this Christmas was because it is going to be a hard winter for everyone; and she thinks we ought not to spend money for pleasure, when our men are suffering so in the army. We can't do much, but we can make our little sacrifices, and ought to do it gladly. But I am afraid I don't.' And Meg shook her head, as she thought regretfully of all the pretty things she wanted.

'But I don't think the little we should spend would do any good. We've each got a dollar, and the army wouldn't be much helped by our giving that. I agree not to expect anything from Mother or you, but I do want to buy *Undine and Sintram* for myself. I've wanted it so long,' said Jo, who was a bookworm.

'I planned to spend mine in new music,' said Beth, with a little sigh, which no one heard but the hearth brush and kettle holder.

'I shall get a nice box of Faber's drawing pencils. I really need them,' said Amy decidedly.

1 At the start of the extract which of the girls seems the happiest?

Support your answer with evidence from the text.

_____

_____ [3

2 Why is the girls' father not living with them?

_____ [1

3 a) What is it that the girls all think about their father but do not say?

_____

b) Why do you think they do not say it?

_____ [2

4 What is meant by the following expressions?

a) Little sacrifices

_____

b) A bookworm

_____ [2]

5 Using your own words, explain Jo's argument for spending the money.

_____

_____ [2]

6 Why does the writer use the past tense ('I planned') when Beth is talking about what she would like, and the future ('I shall') when Amy speaks?

_____

_____ [3]

7 What do we learn about the characters and situation of the four girls?

Think about:
- the situation of the family as a whole
- how they behave and what they are interested in
- what they say and how they speak.

_____

_____

_____ [5]

Writing Task

Thank-You Letter

Your grandfather lives abroad and was not able to come home for your birthday. However, he sent you a present. Here is part of the letter that came with it. You now want to reply to him, thanking him for the present and telling him all about your birthday.

I decided to send you money because I don't really know what you like now and I want you to get something you really want. Please let me know what you decided to spend the money on – and send me one of those lovely letters full of news, that I so enjoy reading.

Looking forward to hearing from you,

Love, Grandad

Write your letter on a separate piece of paper. [20]

Spelling

You must be able to:

- Spell basic and regular words
- Spell complex and irregular words.

Quick Recall Quiz

Spelling Rules

- A lot of English spelling is regular, meaning it follows rules or patterns. Here are some of the most useful rules.

'i' before 'e' except after 'c'

- achieve
- receive

Changing the 'y' to 'ie'

- Change the 'y' to 'ie' when adding 's' to a word ending in 'y'.
  - berry – berries
  - pity – pities

  but only if there is a **consonant** before the 'y'. If there is a **vowel** before the 'y', you just add 's'.
  - boy – boys
  - say – says
- Follow the same rule when you add 'ed'.
  - pity – pitied
  - play – played

- To form the **plural** of words that end in 'o', add 'es' (potatoes), except for words taken from Italian (pianos).
- If a word ends in 's' or a 'buzzing' or 'hissing' sound, add 'es' (glasses, dashes).
- You can also learn when to double a letter before 'ing' or 'ed'.
- Look for other patterns and rules that will help your spelling and learn them.

> **Key Point**
>
> Spelling matters: it helps you to make your meaning clear. You can – and should – work at improving your spelling.

Homophones

- **Homophones** are words that sound the same but have different meanings. These cause a lot of problems. Here are some of the most common:
  - 'Here' means 'in this place': 'It's over here.'
  - You hear with your ears: 'I can hear you.'
  - 'There' means 'in that place': 'I put it over there.' It is also used in phrases such as 'there is' and 'there are'.
  - 'They're' is a **contraction** of 'they are': 'They're not really friends.'
  - 'Their' means 'belonging to them': 'They took all their things with them.'
  - 'Where', like 'here' and 'there', refers to place: 'Where do you think you're going?'

- 'Wear' is used about clothes etc.: 'You wear your earrings on your ears'.
- 'We're and 'were' are not homophones but they often get mixed up:
  * 'We're' is a contraction of 'we are': 'We're in the same class.'
  * 'Were' is the **past tense** of 'are': 'We were very happy there.'
- 'To' indicates direction: 'He went to the cinema.' It is also used as part of a **verb**: 'I want to do this now.'
- 'Too' means excessively: 'Too much' or 'too many'.
- 'Two' is the number 2: 'There were two questions to choose from.'

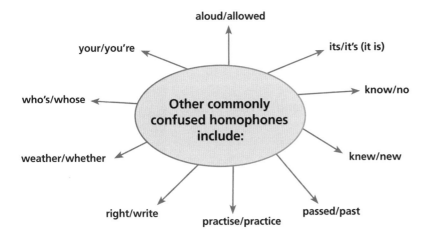

aloud/allowed
your/you're
its/it's (it is)
who's/whose
know/no
weather/whether
knew/new
right/write
practise/practice
passed/past

Other commonly confused homophones include:

Key Point

Identify the words you tend to get wrong. Make a list of them and set about learning them.

- If you're not sure about any of these, look up their meanings and practise using them in sentences. You might be able to think of others that give you trouble.

Spelling Strategies

- **Mnemonics** are ways of remembering things. It can be useful to learn a phrase where the first letters of the words spell out the word you are trying to spell:
  - Big Elephants Can Always Upset Small Elephants (**because**).
- Another useful trick is to **isolate** the part of the word that causes you trouble:
  - There is **a rat** in sep**arat**e.
- Or you might **associate** the spelling with the meaning of the word:
  - **Necessary** – it is necessary to wear one collar, two socks
- Some letters are not pronounced clearly, if at all (**silent letters**).
- Try splitting up the word and saying it slowly and carefully to yourself:
  - **en-vir-on-ment**
  - **k-now-ledge**.

Quick Test

Identify the correct spelling from the alternatives given in the following sentences:
1. We had know/no idea wear/where we were going.
2. Its/it's Monday today.
3. I can't decide weather/whether to/two/too buy it or not.
4. Hurry up or you'll miss football practice/practise.

Key Words

consonant
vowel
plural
homophone
contraction
past tense
verb
mnemonic
isolate
associate
silent letter

Punctuation

Quick Recall Quiz

You must be able to:

- Clearly demarcate sentences
- Accurately use a range of punctuation.

Ending Sentences

- **Full stops** separate sentences. A common mistake students make is to use **commas** instead of full stops.
- **Question marks** can be used in direct speech or at the end of rhetorical questions (i.e. questions which do not require a reply):
  - 'Do you really want to do that?' she asked.
  - Are we ready to meet the challenge?
- **Exclamation marks** are used to show surprise, shock and other extreme emotions:
  - What a monstrosity!
  - That's amazing!

Commas

- Commas are used to separate subordinate clauses from main clauses. Subordinate clauses give extra information but are not necessary for the sentence to make sense:
  - Mina, having run the marathon, was exhausted. ← 'having run the marathon' is the subordinate clause
  - After eating two puddings, Ali was full. ← 'After eating two puddings' is the subordinate clause
- They are used in lists:
  - I ordered fish, chips, mushy peas and a fizzy drink.
- Commas are also used to introduce and to end direct speech:
  - He shouted, 'Leave me alone!'
  - 'Nobody move,' ordered the policeman.

Colons and Semi-colons

- **Colons** are used before an explanation:
  - It took two hours: it was a difficult job.
- They introduce quotations:
  - Mercutio plays down his injury: 'Ay, ay, a scratch, a scratch.'
- They introduce lists:
  - The collection was wide and varied: historic manuscripts; suits of armour; ancient bones; and hundreds of old coins.
- Note that **semi-colons** are used to separate the items in the list above. Semi-colons separate items in a list that consist of more than one or two words. The semi-colon helps with clarity.
- Semi-colons are also used to show that two clauses are closely related, when the writer does not want to use a connective or a full stop:
  - The flowers are blooming; the trees are green.

> ### Key Point
>
> Commas must not be used to link clauses (statements which could stand alone as sentences) unless a connective or relative pronoun is used:
>
> I fed the cat, although it had already eaten.
>
> I fed the cat, which had already eaten.

Brackets, Dashes and Ellipsis

- Brackets go around a bit of extra information:
  - A huge man (he was at least seven feet tall) dashed across the road.
- Dashes can be used to show an interruption in the train of thought:
  - I finished the meal – if you could call it that – and quickly left.
- Ellipsis (...) indicates the omission of words from a sentence:
  - 'We left... in a hurry' rather than 'We left the old rickety building in a hurry'.

    It can also be used to show a thought trailing off or to make the reader wonder what comes next:
  - I realised that I was not alone...

Inverted Commas

- **Inverted commas** can also be referred to as **speech marks** or **quotation marks**.
- Speech marks surround the actual words spoken:
  - 'Never again!' she cried.
- Similarly, when quoting from a text, you put the inverted commas (quotation marks) around any words taken from the original:
  - Tybalt refers to Romeo as 'that villain'.
- Inverted commas are also used for titles:
  - Shelley's 'Ozymandias' is about power.

Apostrophes

- **Apostrophes** are used to show **omission** (also called contraction), or **possession**.
- Only use apostrophes for omission when writing informally. In formal writing you should write all words in full. When you do use an apostrophe, put it where the missing letter or letters would have been:
  - You **shouldn't** have done that.
  - **Malik's** finished but **Rachel's** still working.
  - Let's go home.
- Apostrophes for possession show ownership. If the owner is singular, or a plural that does not end in 's', add an apostrophe and an 's' to the word that indicates the 'owner':
  - the cat's tail
  - the class's teacher
  - the children's toys
  - James's hat.
- The only time you have to do anything different is for a plural ending in 's'. In this case, simply add an apostrophe:
  - the cats' tails
  - the boys' team.

> **Key Point**
>
> Punctuation matters because writing does not make sense without it. Incorrect punctuation can change the meaning of your writing or even turn it into nonsense, confusing the reader.

> **Key Words**
>
> full stop
> comma
> question mark
> exclamation mark
> colon
> semi-colon
> ellipsis
> inverted commas
> speech marks
> quotation marks
> apostrophe
> omission
> possession

> **Quick Test**
>
> Insert the correct punctuation:
> 1. Wheres my hamster Leo cried
> 2. He had gone there was no doubt about it
> 3. Maureen who lived next door searched her bins
> 4. Maureens son found Hammy in the kitchen

Sentence Structure

You must be able to:

- Use sentence structures accurately
- Use a variety of sentence structures for effect.

Quick Recall Quiz

Simple Sentences

- Every sentence must contain a **subject** and a main verb. The subject is the person or thing (a **noun** or **pronoun**) that the sentence is about. The verb is the doing, feeling or being word:

  Ronnie ate

  subject | verb

- **Simple sentences** often include an **object** (also a noun).

  Ronnie ate an apple

  subject | verb | object

  'An apple' is the direct object. You can also use an indirect object:

  Ronnie ate at the table

  subject | verb | preposition | object

  The **preposition** explains Ronnie's relationship to the table.

- You can vary simple sentences, and other sentence forms, by changing the verb from the **active** to the **passive voice**:

  The apple was eaten by Ronnie

  subject | verb | preposition | agent

  Here the apple, by being put at the start of the sentence, becomes the subject.

Minor Sentences

- A **minor sentence**, also known as a **fragment**, is not really a sentence at all because it does not contain a main verb. Minor sentences are very short and are used for effect. They are often answers to questions or exclamations:
  - Oh my word!
  - Just another boring day.
- They should be used rarely or they will lose their impact.

Compound Sentences

- To make a **compound sentence** you join together two **clauses** of equal importance using a **conjunction**. Clauses are phrases that could stand alone as simple sentences.
- You can use 'and', 'but' or 'or' to form compound sentences:
  - Lucia left the room and [she] went to the shops.
  - Lucia left the room but Mark stayed in the house.

Key Point

Try to vary the length and type of sentences you use. The examiner is looking for a range of sentence types being used correctly and effectively.

- You can join more than two clauses in this way, though the result often appears clumsy:
  - Lucia left the room and went to the shops and bought a banana.

Complex Sentences

- A **complex sentence** also has two or more clauses joined together. The main clause should make sense on its own but the **subordinate clause**, which adds detail or explanation, does not need to.
- Some complex sentences are formed by joining two clauses with a conjunction. In these sentences the two clauses are not equal. Examples of conjunctions you might use are:

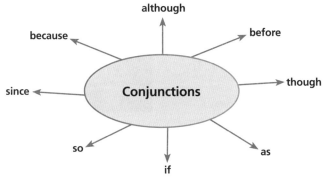

- The conjunction tells you what the relationship between the two clauses is:
  - Charlie left school **because** he had moved house.
  - Charlie left home **after** he had moved house.

  In the first sentence moving house is the reason for Charlie leaving school, whereas the second simply tells us the order in which the events happened.
- Sometimes the conjunction is placed at the beginning of the sentence rather than between the two clauses:
  - Although he felt ill, Atif ate an apple.
- Conjunctions are not needed to form complex sentences:
  - Maria, who loved shopping, left the house immediately.
  - Having left the house quickly, Maria went shopping.
- The first of these examples uses a **relative pronoun** (who) to connect the clauses, while the second changes the verb form to a past participle (having left).
- You can build even longer sentences by using several clauses and joining them in an appropriate way:
  - Atif was ill for several days so he stayed in bed, sometimes reading and sometimes watching television, but mostly bored and grumpy.

> **Key Point**
>
> Complex sentences can give more information and express more complex ideas.

> **Key Words**
>
> subject
> noun
> simple sentence
> object
> preposition
> active voice
> passive voice
> minor sentence
> fragment
> compound sentence
> clause
> conjunction
> complex sentence
> subordinate clause
> relative pronoun

> **Quick Test**
>
> Which of the following is (a) a simple sentence, (b) a compound sentence, (c) a complex sentence and (d) a minor sentence?
> 1. Never again.
> 2. The hamster was found safe and well.
> 3. She liked sheep but she hated cows.
> 4. Although she had been there before, the girl could not remember where she was.

Text Structure and Organisation

You must be able to:

- Organise your writing in coherent paragraphs
- Use a range of discourse markers.

Quick Recall Quiz

Paragraphs

- The traditional way of starting a new **paragraph** is to **indent** the first line of the new paragraph, that is, start a centimetre or two in from your margin. This is usual in most books, and in handwritten work. Try to do it in your exams.
- There is no set length for paragraphs. Try to vary the length of your paragraphs. You might use long paragraphs for a detailed description or explanation and short paragraphs for impact.

Starting a New Paragraph

- When you start writing about something new, you should start a new paragraph. This could be a change of:
  - **speaker** – when using direct speech, start a new paragraph when a new person speaks:

    'I didn't see anything,' added Marco.

  - **person** – introducing a new character:

    Julie was quite the opposite…

  - **place**:

    Toppington is also worth a visit…

  - **time**:

    A week later, Roland realised that all was not well…

  - **topic or idea** – moving from one aspect of your subject to another or introducing a different opinion:

    Another cause of concern is the local bus shelter…
    Some residents disagree with this view…

- Paragraphs often start with **topic sentences**, which introduce the topic or subject of the paragraph:

  When we left, there was nobody else on the boat.

  Laurie Grantham, 17, has her own take on fashion.

Key Point

Paragraphs help you to organize your text so that it makes sense, follows a logical order and is easier to read.

← The topic of the paragraph is the boat and whether or not it was empty.

← This paragraph is about Laurie's attitude to fashion.

Opening and Closing Paragraphs

- Opening and closing paragraphs can make a big difference to the impact of your writing. How you approach them depends on the form and purpose of your writing.
- Beginnings and endings in descriptive and narrative writing are dealt with on pages 40–43. Beginnings and endings in non-fiction are dealt with on page 30 and pages 53–55.

Discourse Markers

- **Discourse markers** connect sentences and paragraphs. They guide readers through the text, showing how one sentence relates to another and how one paragraph relates to another.
- They can be single-word **connectives**, such as 'however', or phrases, such as 'in addition to this'. A discourse marker can also be a phrase which picks up on an idea from the previous paragraph:
  - This kind of behaviour is common throughout Europe.
- Not all discourse markers (for example, 'however' and 'therefore') have to be used at the beginning of a sentence. They can be more effective a little way in.
- Discourse markers have many different purposes:

To add information or ideas	In addition; As well as; Furthermore; Moreover	The new building, moreover, will ruin the view from Huntington Hill.
To point out a similarity	Similarly; In the same way	Similarly, the owl hunts at night.
To introduce a contrasting idea or point of view	Nevertheless; On the other hand; In spite of; Alternatively	Some good points have been made in favour of the plan. Nevertheless, I still think it's a bad idea.
To express cause and effect	As a result; Consequently; In order to; Therefore	I have had no objections so far. I will, therefore, continue as planned.
To give order or to sum up	Firstly; Finally; In conclusion; Basically	Finally, I'd like to thank Josh for making all this possible.
To express passing time	Subsequently; Later; As soon as; Meanwhile	The police took an hour to arrive. Meanwhile, Archie had escaped.

> **Key Point**
>
> You do not have to use a discourse marker in every sentence or even every paragraph, especially in descriptive and narrative writing.

> **Quick Test**
>
> Identify the discourse markers in the following sentences and explain their purpose.
> 1. First, I will consider Ken's proposal.
> 2. Tom's idea, on the other hand, is ridiculous.
> 3. Before the bus shelter was built, there was no vandalism.
> 4. I suggest, therefore, that we demolish the bus shelter.

> **Key Words**
>
> paragraph
> indent
> topic sentence
> discourse marker
> connective

Standard English and Grammar

You must be able to:

- Use Standard English
- Use correct grammatical structures.

Standard English

- **Standard English** is the version of English that is widely accepted as being correct.
- You may not always have to write in Standard English. Characters in a story might use **dialect** or **slang** to reflect their background and character. If you are writing for teenagers or children, you might use the sort of language they would use with their friends.
- For all other purposes write in Standard English, using correct **grammar** and spelling.

Personal Pronouns: First Person

- The most common misuse of **personal pronouns** is the confusion of 'I' and 'me'. 'I' is the subject of the sentence; 'me' is the object:
  - 'Ikram and me were late' is clearly wrong because you would not say: 'Me was late.' You would say: 'I was late.' So, logically, it must be: 'Ikram and I were late.'
  - Similarly you should not say: 'They gave prizes to Lucy and I.' The correct form is: 'They gave prizes to Lucy and me.'

Personal Pronouns: Second Person

- 'You' is both the **singular** and **plural** form of the second person. You could say, 'Thank you for coming' to one person or to hundreds. There is no such word as 'yous'.
- Do not use the Americanism 'you guys'. 'Guys' is not Standard English.

Words and Phrases to Avoid

- Be aware of any words or phrases that are common in your area but are not Standard English, and avoid using them in formal writing.
- The same applies to current slang used by young people (such as 'sick' for 'good') and Americanisms, for example, using 'lay' instead of 'lie' or 'period' rather than 'full stop'.

Modal Verbs

- Do not use the word 'of' instead of 'have' after **modal verbs** such as would, could, should and might:
  - If I'd known, I would **have** told you.

Key Point

Standard English is the form of English which is most widely understood. You need to be able to use it so that your audience can understand what you are saying.

Verbs: Agreement and Tenses

- There are three basic tenses – past, **present** and future. This section focuses on the past tense because that is where most errors occur.
  - A common error is to confuse the first and **third person** of the verb, for example, using 'you was' instead of 'you were'.
  - Another is the confusion of the **simple past tense** and the **perfect tense**, which expresses a completed action (for example, using 'done' instead of 'did' or 'has done'). The perfect tense is formed by adding the past participle to 'have' or 'has'.
- Most verbs follow this pattern:

	Singular	Plural
Simple past	I/you/he/she/it walked.	We/you/they walked.
Perfect	I/you have walked. He/she/it has walked.	We/you/they have walked.

- Many of the most commonly used verbs are irregular, among them the verb 'to be'. These are its correct forms:

	Singular	Plural
Simple past	I was.	We were.
	You were.	You were.
	He/she/it was.	They were.
Perfect	I/you have been.	We/you have been.
	He/she/it has been.	They have been.

- Some other irregular verbs which cause problems are shown here.

Simple Past	Perfect	Simple Past	Perfect
ate	have/has eaten	sang	has/has sung
did	have/has done	saw	have/has seen
drove	have/has driven	spoke	have/has spoken
gave	have/has given	taught	have/has taught
got	have/has got	went	have/has gone
lay	have/has lain	woke	have/has woken

- If you are writing in the past tense and you want to refer to something that happened before the events you are describing, use the **past perfect tense**, which is formed using 'had' and the past participle:
  - She had eaten before she arrived.
- If you are writing about an event in the past which continued for some time, use the **past continuous**, formed by the past tense of the verb 'to be' and the present participle:
  - She was eating for the whole journey.

Key Words

Standard English
dialect
slang
grammar
personal pronoun
singular
plural
modal verb
present tense
third person
simple past tense
perfect tense
past perfect tense
past continuous tense

Quick Test

Rewrite the following sentences in Standard English:
1. Me and Jay was put on detention.
2. I seen you guys on Saturday.
3. You was the bestest player we had.
4. After we had sang the first number, we done a dance.

1 The following paragraph includes 10 incorrect spellings. Find them and rewrite them correctly.

> We where hoping for good whether for Sports Day. Unfortunately, on Friday morning it was poring with rain. Luckily, by ten o'clock it was clear and sunny. I was very exited when I got to the stadium but I had a long weight for my race, the 200 meters. Their were eight of us in the final. I was in the inside lane, witch I don't usually like, but I ran well round the bend and was second comming into the straight. As I crossed the line I was neck and neck with Jo. It wasn't until the teacher congratulated me that I knew I had definately won.

_____

_____ [10]

2 The following five sentences have been written without punctuation.
Insert the correct punctuation.

a) Peter Kowalski who was the tallest boy in the class easily won the high jump.

_____

b) What are you doing in the sand pit shouted Miss O'Connor get out of there at once.

_____

c) Francesca won medals for the long jump the high jump and the relay.

_____

d) I wasnt entered in any of the races because Im hopeless at running.

_____

e) Jonathan finished last however he was pleased with his time.

_____ [5]

3 **a)** Change each of the following pairs of sentences into single sentences, using conjunctions.

  i) Uzma stayed off school. She had a stomach ache.

  _____

  ii) He might be in the changing rooms. He might have already left.

  _____

b) Change the following pairs of sentences into single sentences using relative pronouns.

  i) Michael announced the results. He has a really loud voice.

  _____

  ii) The form with the best results won a cup. The cup was presented by Mr Cadogan.

  _____

c) Turn the following three sentences into a single sentence.

   i) Maria had won the discus competition. She went home early. She was feeling sick.

   _____ [5]

4 Rewrite the following sentences using Standard English.

a) Me and Noora is going to town tomorrow.

   _____

b) You guys can come wiv us if youse want.

   _____

c) We was well chuffed with what we bought.

   _____

d) I don't know nothing about what they done at school.

   _____

e) I aint skiving off again coz I wanna get my GCSEs.

   _____ [5]

5 Insert each of the following five connectives or discourse markers in the text below to help it to make sense.

however   as well as   also   as a result of   consequently

I am disgusted by the plan to close our library. (1)_____ having a massive impact on our community, this act of vandalism shows how little interest the council has in education. (2) _____ this attitude, our children are being deprived of a wonderful resource. Adults, especially older people, (3) _____ benefit greatly from the library. The council says we can use Hartington Library, but that is much too far away for most pensioners. (4) _____, they will lose what has become for many a real lifeline, making them feel part of the community. (5) _____, it does not have to be like this. There are other ways for the council to save money: we could start with cutting down on the Mayor's free trips to America!   [5]

6 Rewrite the following paragraph on a separate piece of paper, correcting errors in spelling, punctuation and grammar.

My first experiance of Bingley Park Library was when I was five. My grandmother, who were an avid reader, visitted the library every week and always borrowed four books. She read more or less anything but she especially liked detective story's, gardening books, and film star's biografies. Naturally, she wanted the rest of her family to be as enthusiastic as she was about books therefore, as soon as I could read, me and her marched down to bingley park. It was an imposing and rather frightening edifice for a child of five, the librarian, Miss Maloney, was just as imposing and twice as intimidating.   [10]

Explicit Information and Ideas

Quick Recall Quiz

You must be able to:

- Identify and interpret explicit information and ideas.

Explicit Information

- **Explicit** information is information that is openly stated. You will find it in the text.
- When answering questions it does not matter whether you think what the writer says is true or plausible. You are required to find the information and repeat it, either in the writer's words or in your own.
- Questions about explicit information normally ask you to list a number of things you can find in the text, for example:
  - List four things the writer tells you about the garden.
  - What do you learn about butterflies from the text?
- Read the text below and list four things the writer tells us about Griselda the cat:

> There were only two places where Griselda would sit in the garden: in the middle of the lawn (to catch the sun) and (if the sun was too hot) in the shade of the plum tree. She sometimes hunted at night and would return in the morning with little presents for us, mice or birds, which she always left in the middle of the kitchen floor to make sure we got them.

- You could say:
  - She would only sit in two places in the garden.
  - She liked to sit in the middle of the lawn.
  - If it was hot she sat under the plum tree.
  - She hunted at night.
  - She brought back mice and birds.
  - She left mice and birds in the kitchen.
    There are six points made here. You can get marks for any four of them but if you put more than four you will not get any extra marks.
- You would not get marks for:
  - She was a cat – you are told this in the question, not in the text.
  - She was friendly – there is no mention of this in the text.
  - There was a plum tree in the garden – true, but it is not about Griselda. It would be a good answer if you were told to 'list four things about the place where Griselda lived'.

> **Key Point**
>
> You may be directed to a section of the text. Make sure you take your information only from that part of the text.

Explicit Ideas

- Explicit ideas are ideas and **opinions** that are openly stated.
- You could be asked, for example:
  - List four ways in which people react to the news.

– List four reasons given for the start of the war.
- Read the text below and **identify** four ideas that, according to the writer, would improve the park:

> Bilberry Recreation Ground is an eyesore. It is time for radical action. Let's start by getting rid of the graffiti – it's not art; it's vandalism. The Victorian benches are also in a sad state – let's restore them. There used to be beautiful flower beds. It's time we planted some new ones. Let's encourage families to return by building a new and exciting playground. What about a kiosk selling cups of tea and ice cream? Finally, may I suggest a change of name? 'Recreation Ground' sounds old-fashioned and dreary. Let's call it Bilberry Park from now on.

- You would get marks for:
  - Get rid of the graffiti.
  - Restore the park benches.
  - Plant new flower beds.
  - Build a playground.
  - Build a refreshment kiosk.
  - Change the name.
- You would not get marks for:
  - It is an eyesore – this is not an idea for improvement.
  - Put a fence round the park – you might think this is a good idea but the writer does not mention it.
  - Take radical action – this is too vague.

Key Point

It does not matter whether you agree with what the writer says. You are being asked to identify the writer's ideas, not yours.

Quick Test

1. What does 'explicit' mean?
2. Can you quote from the text?
3. Can you put the answer in your own words?
4. If you are asked to list four points, do you get an extra mark for giving five?

Key Words

explicit
opinion
identify

Quick Recall Quiz

Implicit Information and Ideas

You must be able to:

- Identify and interpret implicit information and ideas.

Implicit Information

- **Implicit** information is not stated openly. It is **implied**, so you have to 'read between the lines' to **infer** it from the text.
- Sometimes information is implied by saying what is not true:
  - He was not a happy child.
  This implies that he was sad.
- One piece of information can be implied by giving another:
  - They painted their garden shed blue.
  We can infer from this that they had a garden. Otherwise it would not be a 'garden' shed.

Key Point

To imply something means to suggest something without expressly stating it. If you infer something you understand something which has been implied.

Implicit Ideas

- Similarly, writers can make their views and feelings clear without openly stating them:
  - I would rather stick pins in my eyes than sit through another maths lesson.
  This implies that the writer does not like maths.
- When you infer meaning and explain what you have inferred, you are **interpreting** implicit information or ideas.
- Sometimes we infer a writer's views or feelings by putting together a number of pieces of **evidence**. Read the following text:

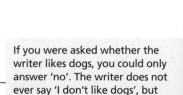

One thing that really annoys me is the way they constantly scratch themselves. And every dog I've ever met has had smelly breath. As for the constant barking and yapping! Give me a nice quiet cat or hamster any day.

If you were asked whether the writer likes dogs, you could only answer 'no'. The writer does not ever say 'I don't like dogs', but gives three negative opinions about them and no positive ones.

True or False?

- You might get a question in the form of a tick box exercise, for example: 'Choose four statements below that are TRUE'.
- Read the following passage:

I Left My Heart on Bilberry Rec

by Mary Goodenough

Bilberry Rec is a part of my past. It didn't have wonderful facilities or beautiful vistas. There were no rose gardens or tea shops, no adventure playgrounds and certainly no 'wild meadows'. There were a few trees and hedges, the 'swing park' and a football pitch.

It was what it said it was: a recreation ground, a place where people of all ages went for recreation. Small children played on the swings and didn't often bash their heads on the concrete floor. Bigger children played football or cricket – or just fought. Courting couples walked hand in hand along the muddy paths or snogged on the broken benches. Pensioners walked their dogs and everyone used it as a short cut.

I know times have changed. And my head tells me the new Bilberry Park will be much nicer (and cleaner and safer) than the old Rec, but my heart wants it left just as it is. It's a sure sign of getting older – an attack of illogical nostalgia.

- Which of the following statements are true?
  1. Mary Goodenough has happy memories of Bilberry Rec.
  2. There was a rose garden in Bilberry Rec.
  3. The new park will have better facilities than the old Rec.
  4. Goodenough didn't feel safe in the Rec.
  5. Bilberry Rec was a beautiful place.
  6. Sometimes there were accidents in the swing park.
  7. Goodenough understands why things should change.
  8. Bilberry Rec is going to be built on.
- Numbers 1, 3, 6 and 7 are true.
  - 1 is implied by references to her 'heart' and nostalgia.
  - 3 is implied by referring to what the old Rec didn't have and calling the new park 'nicer...cleaner and safer'.
  - 6 is implied by saying that it didn't happen 'often'.
  - 7 is implied by saying that her 'head' tells her it will be better and that her nostalgia is 'illogical'.

 Key Point

When completing a 'true or false' exercise, make sure you fill in the correct number of boxes.

Quick Test

1. Who implies, the writer or the reader?
2. Who infers?
3. Should you give your opinion?
4. What happens if you tick/shade too many boxes?

Key Words

implicit
imply
infer
interpret
evidence

Synthesis and Summary

You must be able to:

- Select and synthesise evidence from different texts
- Summarise the content of texts.

Synthesis

- **Synthesis** is the bringing together of parts to make a whole. In exams this usually takes the form of writing about two different texts.
- In Paper 2 of the English Language exam (Question 2) you will have to compare the **content** of two non-fiction texts.
- The texts will be about similar subjects but one will have been written in the nineteenth and one in the twenty-first century, so it is likely that there will be differences in attitudes as well as in the things and people described.

> **Key Point**
>
> Remember to look for both explicit and implicit information and ideas.

Summary

- A **summary** is a shortened version of something, keeping the main points but leaving out unnecessary detail.
- When you write a summary do not add your own thoughts or comment on the writers' style or techniques. You will have an opportunity to compare the writers' techniques in your answer to Question 4.
- You should use evidence from the text in the form of short quotations but most of the answer should be in your own words. Do not copy out huge chunks of the text.
- You may write about one text and then about the other, but to gain high marks you should write about both throughout your answer, summarising different aspects of the texts.

Approaching the Question

- Read the question carefully. It will not just ask you to summarise the texts; it will have a particular focus, for example:
  - Write a summary of the differences between Mary and Jordan.
  - Summarise the different feelings of the writers about school.
- **Skim read** both texts.
- Underline or highlight the main points in the texts.
- You might want to do a (very quick) plan, listing **differences** (and **similarities** if asked for).
- Focus on the question.
- Don't repeat yourself.
- Don't waste time on an introductory and concluding paragraph.
- Write in proper sentences and paragraphs, using connectives.

Example

- Below are two short extracts from texts about sea voyages. Think about what you would include if you were asked to write a summary of the differences between the voyages:

Daily Southern Cross, 21 October 1859

The *Mermaid* […] arrived in harbour on Wednesday at 4 a.m. She left Liverpool on 11th July at 5 p.m. Passengers have been very healthy during the voyage; three infants died, and one birth occurred. The passengers speak highly of Captain White and officers.

Southern Star, 19 July 2014

After three weeks the luxury liner *Ariadne* finally arrived home and the passengers disembarked from the journey one of them described as 'a floating nightmare'. For the last week almost a quarter of the passengers had been confined to their cabins with mild food poisoning and many are now demanding their money back.

- You could pick out the following differences:

Mermaid	Ariadne
Journey over three months	Three-week journey
Passengers 'healthy' – three infants died	Food poisoning
Passengers praise captain and crew	Passengers demand money back

- A paragraph summarizing the differences might read:

The **Mermaid's** journey lasted over three months; **Ariadne's** took three weeks. The **Mermaid's** passengers are 'healthy' but the **Ariadne's** have food poisoning. However, 'three infants died' on the **Mermaid**, suggesting that not everyone was healthy. Nevertheless, it would seem that the Victorian passengers were happier than the modern ones, as they 'speak highly' of the crew rather than complaining.

> **Key Point**
>
> Bear in mind that this is a short answer question, attracting only 8 marks of the total of 80 for the paper, so you should aim to spend no more than 9 minutes on it.

Quick Test

1. Should the summary be shorter than the original text?
2. Should you use quotations in your summary?
3. Can you write about just one of the texts?
4. Should you discuss the writers' use of language in your answer?

> **Key Words**
>
> synthesis
> content
> summary
> skim read
> difference
> similarity

Referring to the Text

Quick Recall Quiz

You must be able to:

- Select appropriate and relevant examples from texts
- Use textual references to support and illustrate your interpretation of the texts.

Referring to the Text

- You can **refer** to a text by **paraphrasing** the text or by **quoting** from the text.
- For all Language questions and some Literature questions, you will have a text in front of you from which you can take your examples.
- For other Literature questions you will have to rely on your memory, so it is a good idea to learn some significant quotations.

Paraphrasing

- Paraphrasing means putting something into your own words. It is useful for summing up, for example:

> *The writer gives us a number of examples of cruelty to animals such as neglect and physical violence, which he describes in very vivid terms.*

- When you are writing about a longer text, such as a novel, you might not need to quote because you are writing about events or feelings and the exact wording is not important:

> *Lydia clearly does not think much about her family's reputation. When she returns from London she does not express any shame at her behaviour but boasts about being married.*

> **Key Point**
>
> It is very important to refer to the text in your answers, both in English Language and English Literature exams.

Using Quotations

- A **quotation** is a word or phrase taken directly from the text. Indicate that you are quoting by putting inverted commas (or quotation marks) around the quotation.
- There are three main ways to set out your quotations.
- If your quotation consists of just a few words (or even one word) and fits naturally into your sentence, you simply put it into inverted commas (quotation marks):

> *At the start of the soliloquy Juliet refers to 'love-performing night' but later it becomes a 'sober suited matron all in black'.*

This is called **embedding**. Examiners like you to embed and it should be the method you use most often.

- If the quotation will not fit easily into your sentence but is fairly short (no more than 40 words of prose or one line of verse), put a colon (:) before it, continue on the same line and use inverted commas:

> Benvolio passionately asserts that he is not lying: 'This is the truth or let Benvolio die.'

- If you want to use a longer quotation, leave a line and indent. You must indent the whole quotation. When quoting verse, end the lines where they end in the original. Do not use inverted commas:

> This opposition will inevitably cause problems for the lovers and Juliet expresses her dilemma:
>
>> My only love sprung from my only hate!
>> Too early seen unknown and known too late!
>
> The use of paradox emphasises her confusion.

> **Key Point**
>
> Only put words taken directly from the text inside the quotation marks. Spell and punctuate exactly as in the text.

Using PEE

- Remember to use PEE: Point, Evidence, Explanation (or Exploration).
- First make your **point**, saying what you want to say about the text.
- Then give your **evidence**, either in the form of a paraphrase or a quotation.
- Finally, **explain** or explore the evidence you have given.

> The writer is very concerned about what he sees as widespread cruelty to domestic animals. He mentions the 'heartless neglect' of some dogs by their owners. The use of this emotive adjective paints the owners as villains and appeals to the compassion of the readers.

← Here the first sentence makes the point, the second gives the evidence in quotation marks, and the third explains/explores the evidence.

Quick Test

1. What are the two different ways of using evidence from the text?
2. When you quote, what goes inside the inverted commas?
3. When should you not 'embed' a quotation?
4. What does PEE stand for?

> **Key Words**
>
> refer
> paraphrase
> quote (verb)
> quotation (noun)
> embed

Analysing Language 1

Quick Recall Quiz

You must be able to:

- Explain, comment on and analyse how writers use language
- Use relevant subject terminology to support your views.

Diction and Register

- **Diction** and **register** both refer to the writer's choice of words or **vocabulary**.
- Most texts you read will be in Standard English. Sometimes, however, you will come across a text that uses a lot of non-standard words, for example slang and dialect words (see pages 14–15).
- Their use can tell you something about the identity, background and character of the writer, the narrator, certain characters or the audience at which the text is aimed.
- Writers might use specialized diction: for example, a lot of scientific or medical terms. The use of such language shows that the text is aimed at people who are interested in the subject and probably already know quite a lot about it.
- Writers might use words and expressions associated with a particular subject – for example, war or nature – for rhetorical or figurative purposes. Sometimes their word choice is referred to as a **semantic field**. We can often infer their attitude to the subject from their choice of semantic field.

Parts of Speech (Word Classes)

- **Nouns** are naming words.
  - **Concrete** (or **common**) nouns name objects (chair, mountain).
  - **Abstract nouns** name ideas and feelings (love, suspicion).
  - **Proper nouns** have capital letters and name individual people (Jelena), places (Warsaw), days of the week (Saturday), months (April) etc.
  - A 'noun phrase' is a group of words built around a noun.
- **Adjectives** describe or define nouns (the **red** house; his **undying** love).
- **Verbs** are doing, feeling and being words. You might comment on whether verbs are:
  - in the past tense (she walked; he was thinking; they had walked)
  - in the present tense (she is walking; he thinks)
  - or in the future tense (we are going to walk; you will go).
- **Adverbs** describe verbs, telling us how something is being done, for example, she spoke **slowly**; he writes **carefully**.
- **Pronouns** stand in for nouns. Whether the writer uses first person (I/we), second person (you) or third person (he/she/they) can make a difference to how we read the text. 'I' makes the text more personal to the writer. 'We' and 'you' aim to involve the reader more in the text. There are different types of pronouns.

> ### Key Point
>
> When we talk about 'parts of speech' or 'word class' we are referring to what words do in sentences. It is important that you can identify these so that you can refer easily to them in a way that shows you understand their function: for example, 'The writer uses a lot of adjectives associated with war to describe the scene.'

Personal pronouns	Relative pronouns
I/me	who
we/us	whom
you	whose
he/him	that
she/her	which
it	
they/them	

- **Prepositions** are used to express the relationship between nouns (or noun phrases) and other parts of the sentence or clause:
  - We went **to** the cinema.
  - The cat is **under** the table.
- **Conjunctions** join words, phrases and clauses: for example, 'and', 'but', 'although', 'because'. A conjunction is a type of connective but the two words are not interchangeable. Other types of word and phrase, including relative pronouns and adverbs, can also act as connectives (see Sentence Structure, pages 10–11).
- **Determiners** come before nouns and help to define them. The most common are the definite article (the) and the indefinite article (a/an). Other examples of determiners are 'this', 'both' and 'some'.

Key Words

diction
register
vocabulary
semantic field
noun
concrete noun
abstract noun
proper noun
adjective
verb
adverb
pronoun
preposition
conjunction
determiner

Quick Test

Read this sentence:
The old horse was munching thoughtfully on his oats.
Identify:
1. Two nouns
2. A verb
3. An adjective
4. A preposition
5. An adverb

Analysing Language 2

You must be able to:

- Explain, comment on and analyse how writers use language
- Use relevant subject terminology to support your views.

Connotation

- A **connotation** is an implied meaning. Words can have associations other than their literal meanings. For example, red can indicate danger or anger. 'Heart' has connotations of love and sincerity.

> **Key Point**
>
> Writers use language to affect and influence their readers.

Emotive Language

- Writers often seek to arouse certain feelings or emotions in the reader, for example, pity or anger. This can be done by using **emotive language**: words and phrases that have certain connotations.
- A reporter writing about a crime could write:

  Burglars stole some jewellery from Mr Bolton's house.

This just tells us the facts. A writer who wanted to influence our emotions might write:

  Heartless burglars stole jewellery of great sentimental value from frail pensioner Albert Bolton. ←

The adjective 'heartless' makes the burglars sound deliberately cruel, and 'frail' emphasizes the weakness of the victim, while the phrase 'of great sentimental value' tells us how important the jewellery was to Mr Bolton. This increases our sympathy for him.

Rhetorical Language

- **Rhetoric** is the art of speaking. Effective speakers have developed ways of influencing their audiences. Writers also use rhetorical techniques to affect readers.
- **Hyperbole** is another word for exaggeration:

  Councillor Williams is the most obnoxious man ever to disgrace this council chamber.

- Lists of three are used to hammer home a point:

  Friends, Romans, countrymen.

- **Repetition** is used to emphasize the importance of the point being made:

  Victory at all costs, victory in spite of all terror, victory however long and hard the road may be; for without victory there is no survival.

- **Rhetorical questions** are questions which do not need an answer. Sometimes the writer gives an answer:

  Can we do this? Yes, we can.

Sometimes they are left unanswered to make the reader think about the answer:

  What kind of people do they think we are?

Sound

- The sound of words can make a difference to their meaning and effect.
- **Onomatopoeia** is the use of words which sound like their meaning:

  > The door creaked open and clunked shut.

- **Alliteration**, the use of a series of words starting with the same sound, is common in newspaper headlines as well as in poetry and other literary texts:
  - Brave Bella battles burglars.
  - Storm'd at with shot and shell.
- When you see alliteration, think about why the writer uses a particular sound. Some consonants ('d', 'k', 'g') are hard. Others ('s', 'f') are soft. 'P' and 'b' have an explosive quality.
- The repetition of 's' sounds is also referred to as **sibilance**.
- **Assonance** is the use of a series of similar vowel sounds for effect:

  > From the bronzey soft sky…Tipples over and spills down.

Imagery

- Literal **imagery** is the use of description to convey a mood or atmosphere. A description of a storm might create an atmosphere of violence and danger.
- Figurative imagery uses an image of one thing to tell us about another.
  - **Similes** compare one thing to another directly, using 'like' or 'as':

    > Straight and slight as a young larch tree.

  - **Metaphors** imply a comparison. Something is written about as if it were something else:

    > Beth was a real angel.

  - **Personification** makes a thing, idea or feeling into a person:

    > At my back I always hear
    > Time's winged chariot hurrying near.

  - The personification of nature, giving it human qualities, is also called **pathetic fallacy**:

    > The clouds wept with joy.

    This term can also be applied to a literal description in which nature or the weather reflects the feelings of characters.
  - A **symbol** is an object which represents a feeling or idea, for example a dove to represent peace.

> **Key Point**
>
> Imagery is usually associated with literary texts, such as poems. However, non-fiction texts also use imagery to paint pictures in the readers' minds.

> **Key Words**
>
> connotation
> emotive language
> rhetoric
> hyperbole
> repetition
> rhetorical question
> onomatopoeia
> alliteration
> sibilance
> assonance
> imagery
> simile
> metaphor
> personification
> pathetic fallacy
> symbol

> **Quick Test**
>
> Of which literary techniques are the following examples?
> 1. Macbeth doth murder sleep.
> 2. Ill met by moonlight.
> 3. I wandered lonely as a cloud.
> 4. You were sunrise to me.

Analysing Form and Structure

Quick Recall Quiz

You must be able to:

- Explain, comment on and analyse how writers use form and structure
- Use relevant subject terminology to support your views.

Form and Structure

- The structure of a text is the way in which it is organized: for example, the order in which information is given or events described.
- The terms 'structure' and 'form' are both used to describe how a text is set out on the page.

Openings

- The beginning (opening) of a text is very important as it has to draw in the readers and encourage them to continue reading.
- Some texts begin by giving an overview of the subject, indicating what the text is going to be about:

> There are thousands of varieties of butterfly. In this article I will discuss some of the most common.

- A writer might explain why he or she has decided to write:

> Lewis's views about youth unemployment are fundamentally wrong.

- Fiction writers can use their openings to introduce characters or settings:

> 'I shall never forget Tony's face,' said the carrier.

- Texts can also start with dramatic statements, designed to shock, surprise or intrigue:

> It was a bright cold day in April, and the clocks were striking thirteen.

Endings

- Fiction writers might give a neat conclusion: for example, with the solving of a crime or a marriage:

> Reader, I married him.

- They might prefer to leave us with a sense of mystery or suspense:

> 'Who are they?' asked George [...]
> *'Wolves.'*

- Writers of essays and articles usually end by drawing together their main points and reaching a conclusion.
- Some texts end with a question or even an instruction:

> Get out there now and use your vote!

Key Point

You should consider why the writer has decided to arrange things in a particular way and the effect of this on the reader.

Chronological Order

- **Chronological order** gives events in the order in which they happened. This is the most common way of ordering fiction, and non-fiction texts such as histories, biographies and travel writing.
- Writers might, however, start at the end of the story or somewhere in the middle before going back to recap previous events in 'flashbacks'.
- **Reverse chronological order** means starting with the latest event and working backwards. You will see this in blogs and discussion forums.

Other Ways of Ordering Texts

- Some texts start with general information and move on to more detailed information and explanation.
- A text giving a point of view might build up to what the writer thinks are the most persuasive arguments.
- Information can be arranged in **alphabetical order**, as in dictionaries and encyclopaedias.
- Texts sometimes rank things or people in order of importance or popularity, as in a music chart, either starting with the best and working down or starting with the worst and working up.

Divisions

- Books are usually divided into **chapters**, sometimes with titles or numbers.
- Most prose is arranged in **paragraphs** (see pages 12–13), while verse is often divided into **stanzas** (see pages 102–103). Make sure you use the correct terminology.
- Other devices used to divide up text include **bullet points**, numbering and **text boxes**. Headlines and subheadings help to guide readers through the text.

Analysing Structure

- When analysing a short text, or an extract from a longer text, think about how and why the writer changes focus from one paragraph or section to another, perhaps moving from a general description to something more detailed, from a group of people to a particular character, or from description to action or speech.

Revise

Key Point

Texts, especially longer texts, are often divided into sections. These give order to their contents and help readers find their way through the text.

Key Words

opening
conclusion
chronological order
reverse chronological order
blog
alphabetical order
chapter
paragraph
stanza
bullet point
text box

Quick Test

Put the following in:
1. chronological order
2. reverse chronological order
3. alphabetical order
   a) December 2022
   b) January 2012
   c) April 2020
   d) November 2020

1 Insert the correctly spelled word in each of the following pairs of sentences.

    a) except/accept

        I did them all _____ the last one.

        I _____ your apology.

    b) affect/effect

        The weather seemed to have a bad _____ on everyone's mood.

        I don't think the weather will _____ the result.

    c) aloud/allowed

        Nobody is _____ in here at lunchtime.

        Mo really likes reading _____ in class.

    d) write/right

        Nobody got the _____ answer.

        I'll _____ a letter and explain.

    e) who's/whose

        He couldn't return it because he didn't know _____ coat it was.

        Tell me _____ going and then I'll decide.   **[5]**

2 Rewrite the following passage on a separate piece of paper using the correct punctuation.

> dont you think we should wait for him asked Eve
>
> not at all Henry replied he never waits for us
>
> well that's true Eve replied but he doesn't know the way

    [10]

3 Rewrite the following passage on a separate piece of paper, using a variety of simple, compound and complex sentences (and adding words if necessary) to make it more effective.   **[10]**

> Henry and Eve waited for another ten minutes. Joel did not arrive. They left without him. They walked to the bus stop. There was no-one there. This suggested they had just missed the bus. Henry was very annoyed with Joel. Eve told him to calm down. She told him to forget about Joel. The journey was uneventful. They got off the bus by the lake. It looked eerie in the moonlight. They sat down on a grassy bank. They took their sandwiches and drinks out of the bag. Henry felt a hand on his shoulder.

    [10

4 Pick the five sentences in which the correct forms of the verb are used.

    a) You was really good tonight. ☐

    b) Ms Ahmad taught me how to boil an egg. ☐

c) They've gotten two more kittens. ☐

d) I knew the song because we had sung it in class. ☐

e) I rung the bell twice but nobody come. ☐

f) She lay on the sofa until she felt better. ☐

g) I done my homework at break. ☐

h) He says he won't come because he's already seen it. ☐

i) I have done what you asked. ☐

j) I'm going to lay down here for a while. ☐ [5]

5 Put the following nouns into their plural forms.

a) pizza _____ **f)** stadium _____

b) latch _____ **g)** quality _____

c) mosquito _____ **h)** church _____

d) sheep _____ **i)** woman _____

e) donkey _____ **j)** hypothesis _____ [5]

6 Rearrange the following paragraphs so that the whole letter makes sense.

a) The next thing I knew two young girls were leaning over me. I'm sorry to say I thought the worst when I saw the rings through their noses. But they asked me if I was all right and very gently helped me to stand up. One of them stayed with me while the other went into the shop and fetched a chair. Then I noticed there were two boys carefully collecting all my shopping and bagging it up.

b) When it was all collected in, they called a taxi to take me home. I'm sorry to say I didn't ask their names, so I'd like to give them a big thank you through your newspaper. Whoever you are, you're a real credit to Bilberry and to your generation!

c) I was in town on Wednesday to do my usual shop in the supermarket. I got a little more than usual so my bags were rather heavy. As I came out of the shop I lost my balance and keeled over, spilling all my shopping.

d) I wasn't badly hurt but it was quite a shock. I just sat there on the pavement, stunned and not knowing what to do.

e) I am writing to express my thanks to a group of young people I met last week. It isn't often we hear good things about teenagers. We read so much about crime and vandalism, drinking and bad manners that we can easily end up thinking the worst of all teenagers.

a) ☐ **b)** ☐ **c)** ☐ **d)** ☐ **e)** ☐ [5]

1   Read the passage below. List four reactions that people have to Scrooge.   [4]

From *A Christmas Carol* by Charles Dickens

Nobody ever stopped him in the street to say, with gladsome looks, 'My dear Scrooge, how are you? When will you come to see me?' No beggars implored him to bestow a trifle;[1] no children asked him what it was o'clock; no man or woman ever once in all his life inquired the way to such and such a place, of Scrooge. Even the blindmen's dogs appeared to know him; and when they saw him coming on, would tug their owners into doorways and up courts; and then would wag their tails as though they said, 'No eye at all is better than an evil eye, dark master!'

[1] *bestow a trifle* – to give a small amount

_____

_____

_____

_____

2   How does Dickens use language to give us an impression of Scrooge's character? You could comment on his use of:
* words and phrases
* language feature and techniques
* sentence forms.   [8]

Write your answer on a separate piece of paper.

3   Read the passage below.

From a letter written by Charles Lamb to William Wordsworth

London, January 30, 1801

I ought before this to have replied to your very kind invitation into Cumberland. With you and your sister I could gang[1] anywhere. But I am afraid whether I shall ever be able to afford so desperate a Journey. Separate from the pleasure of your company, I don't much care if I never see a mountain in my life. I have passed all my days in London […] The lighted shops of the Strand and Fleet Street, the innumerable trades, tradesmen and customers, coaches, waggons, playhouses, all the bustle and wickedness round about Covent Garden, the very women of the Town, the Watchmen, drunken scenes, rattles;[2] — life awake, if you awake, at all hours of the night, the impossibility of being dull in Fleet Street, the crowds, the very dirt & mud, the Sun shining upon houses and pavements, the print shops, the old *Book* stalls, […] coffee houses, steams of soup from kitchens, the pantomimes, London itself a pantomime and a masquerade, all these things work themselves into my mind and feed me without a power of satiating me. The wonder of these sights impels me into night walks about the crowded streets, and I often shed tears in the motley Strand from fullness of joy at so much *Life*. — All these emotions must be strange to you. So are your rural emotions to me […]

     My attachments are all local, purely local. — I have no passion […] to groves and valleys. — The rooms where I was born, the furniture which has been before my eyes all my life, a book case which has followed me about (like a faithful dog, only exceeding him in knowledge) wherever I have moved, old tables, streets, squares, where I have sunned myself, my old school, — these are my mistresses. Have I not enough, without your mountains?

[1] *gang* – a dialect word for 'go'
[2] *rattles* – constant chatterers

Which of the following statements are TRUE? Tick the correct boxes.

    a) Charles Lamb hates London. ☐

    b) He has always lived in London. ☐

    c) He finds life in the city exciting. ☐

    d) He does not like going out after dark. ☐

    e) He thinks Wordsworth will find it strange that he does not like the countryside. ☐

    f) He likes to spend time with Wordsworth and his sister. ☐

    g) He loves climbing mountains. ☐

    h) He is thinking of buying some new furniture. ☐ [4]

4   Now read this article and write a summary of the differences between Weston's and Lamb's attitudes to city life. [8]

I'm a City-Hater – Get Me out of Here!

by Malcolm Weston

I've had enough. I'm leaving. Who was it who said that when a man is tired of London he's tired of life? Well, I don't think I'm tired of life – I'd like to go on living as long as I can – but I'm fed up to the back teeth with London. It's dirty. It's noisy. You can barely move in Oxford Street sometimes. Everything's expensive (how can anyone afford to live here?). And everyone is so bad-tempered. I know it's meant to be terribly lively and exciting but, frankly, I'm bored with it. Sorry, Londoners. It's nothing personal: I don't really like any cities – or towns. So I'm off home. And this time next week you'll find me (if you can – it's a bit off the beaten track) halfway up a mountain somewhere in the Lake District, looking up at the sky and listening to the sound of silence.

Creative Reading 1

You must be able to:

- Read and understand a range of literature
- Critically evaluate literature texts.

Story Structure

- Most novels and stories begin by 'setting the scene', introducing characters or places and giving us a sense of the world we are entering.
- That world might be very like our own world but it could be unfamiliar, perhaps because the story is set in a different country or a different time.
- The writer might even, like Tolkien, have invented a complete fantasy world.
- This part of a story is called **exposition** and can take a chapter or more, or maybe just a few lines.
- The event that really gets the story going is sometimes called the **inciting incident**. This can be dramatic and shocking, like Pip's encounter with the convict at the beginning of *Great Expectations*, or it can be a seemingly ordinary event, like Darcy coming to stay with Bingley in *Pride and Prejudice*.
- Inciting incidents change the lives of the protagonists (the main characters) for ever.

> **Key Point**
>
> Every story has a beginning, a middle and an end. The extracts you will be given might come from any part of the story.

- During the course of a story there are usually several **turning points**. Turning points are events which change the direction of the story for good or ill. Sometimes we can see them coming; sometimes they are unexpected and surprising 'twists' in the plot.
- Towards the end, most stories reach a **climax**, or denouement, when things come to a conclusion, sometimes happily as in a fairy tale, sometimes not. This is the event the whole story has been building up to.
- The climax is not always at the end of the story. Most writers take some time to reflect on how things have turned out.
- Endings quite often refer back to openings, giving a sense of how things have changed.

Key Point

When analysing a literary text, always consider the 'narrative voice' and your reaction to it.

Narrative Perspectives

- Many stories are told in the first person singular ('I'), so that we see the story through the eyes of one of the characters, usually the **protagonist**, for example, Jane in *Jane Eyre* or Harri in *Pigeon English*. This encourages us to empathise with them.
- Sometimes the **narrator** is another character, acting more as an observer and putting some distance between the reader and the protagonist. Dr Watson in the Sherlock Holmes stories is an example of this.
- Each narrator has his or her own 'voice'. In *Pigeon English*, for example, the kind of language the narrator uses tells us about his west African heritage.
- A writer might use different several narrators so that we get different characters' experiences and points of view: Mary Shelley does this in *Frankenstein*.
- In a 'third-person **narrative**' the narrator is not involved in the story at all. If there is a sense of the narrator's 'voice', it is the voice of the author. This gives the writer the opportunity of sharing with us the thoughts, feelings and experiences of many characters.
  A narrator who can see everything in this way is called an **omniscient narrator**.
  Sometimes omniscient narrators comment on characters and action using the first person. If so they are called **intrusive**. Dickens uses this technique in *A Christmas Carol*.

Key Words

exposition
inciting incident
turning point
climax
protagonist
narrator
narrative
omniscient narrator
intrusive narrator

Quick Test

1. Does the exposition come at the beginning or end?
2. When the narrator is part of the action is it a first-person or third-person narrative?
3. Which comes first: the climax or the inciting incident?
4. What is an omniscient narrator?

Creative Reading 2

You must be able to:

- Read and understand a range of literature
- Critically evaluate texts.

Character

- We learn about **characters** in different ways.
- The narrator can directly describe a character. In this example (from *The Strange Case of Dr Jekyll and Mr Hyde*) we can infer something about the man's character from his appearance.

> …the lawyer was a man of a rugged countenance, that was never lighted by a smile.

Key Point

Descriptions of people make the characters seem more real and can tell us a lot about them.

- We can learn about characters from what they say and how they say it, as well as from what other characters say about and to them. In this quotation from *Pride and Prejudice* Mr Bennet gives his opinion of his daughters:

> 'They are all silly and ignorant like other girls; but Lizzy has something more of quickness than her sisters.'

We can infer from this that Lizzy is the only daughter that Mr Bennet is interested in and that he can be quite blunt and dismissive. However, we might get a slightly different impression if we know that he is talking to his wife. It could be that he is trying to provoke her and/or that his remark about the girls being 'silly and ignorant' is intended as a joke. Always consider context when analysing text.

- Most importantly, you should consider how characters behave and how others react to them. Dickens leaves us in no doubt about Scrooge's character:

> Even the blindmen's dogs appeared to know him; and when they saw him coming on, would tug their owners into doorways and up courts.

This comes at the beginning of *A Christmas Carol* and gives us a strong first impression, which is built on by descriptions of his treatment of his clerk, his nephew and the men who come collecting for charity.

Description

- This description (from *The Withered Arm* by Thomas Hardy) is fairly simple:

> …it was not a main road; and the long white riband of gravel that stretched before them was empty, save for one moving speck.

This tells us that the story is set in a remote place and sets up the encounter between the people in the carriage and the boy, whom they first see as a 'moving speck'.

- In the first chapter of *Great Expectations*, Dickens describes the **setting** in a way that gives us information about the landscape while creating an **atmosphere** that prepares us for the frightening event that is about to happen:

> …and that the dark flat wilderness beyond the churchyard, intersected with dykes and mounds and gates, with scattered cattle feeding on it, was the marshes; and that the low leaden line beyond, was the river; and that the distant savage lair from which the wind was rushing, was the sea…

Dickens uses adjectives like 'dark', 'low' and 'leaden' to give us a sense of an unattractive, featureless landscape, but adds words like 'wilderness' and 'savage' to make it seem dangerous and threatening.

- The description above uses **literal imagery** to create **mood** and atmosphere, the lonely, rather frightening place reflecting the feelings of the protagonist Pip.
- **Figurative imagery**, too, is often used in descriptive writing. In *The Withered Arm* Hardy uses a simile to describe one of his characters:

> Her face too was fresh in colour, but it was of a totally different quality – soft and evanescent, like the light under a heap of rose-petals.

The imagery helps us to picture her complexion and gives us a sense of her beauty and fragility.

Key Point

Writers describe places to root their stories in a time and place, and to create mood and atmosphere.

Quick Test

Identify what kind of imagery is being used in these sentences:
1. The lake shone like a silver mirror.
2. Angry crags surrounded us.
3. A veil of snow hid it from view.
4. There was a cluster of jagged black rocks.

Key Words

character
setting
atmosphere
literal imagery
mood
figurative imagery

Narrative Writing

You must be able to:

- Write clear and imaginative narratives.

Narrative

- A **narrative** is an account of events – a story, whether real or imagined.
- One of the writing tasks in Paper 1 will ask you to write a story or part of a story. This gives you the opportunity to use your imagination and be creative.
- You may be asked to write for a particular audience. If so, it is most likely to be for people of your own age.
- You will be given a 'stimulus' for your story. This could be a picture or just a brief instruction:
  - Write the opening of a story suggested by the picture above.
  - Write a story about someone whose life changes suddenly.

  These instructions are deliberately vague so you can develop your own ideas in your own style.

Planning

- Before you start to write, spend a few minutes planning, making decisions about the main elements of your story.

Character and Voice

- Decide whether you are going to write in the first or third person. If you opt for the first person, is the narrator the **protagonist** or an observer?

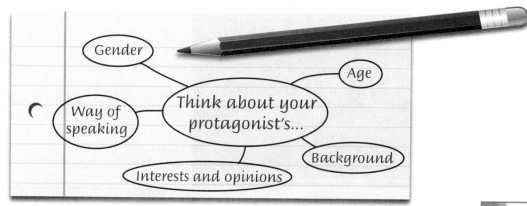

Gender · Age · Way of speaking · Think about your protagonist's... · Background · Interests and opinions

- The protagonist could be a version of you, but it can be much more interesting to write about someone who is completely different.
- There may also be an **antagonist**, someone who stands in the way of or opposes the protagonist.
- Think about other, minor characters – but beware of inventing too many. You don't want to make things too complicated.

> **Key Point**
>
> You can tell a story in your own voice or you can invent a character (persona) to tell the story.

Structure

- The same applies to the plot. If you are writing a complete story, keep it fairly simple.
  - You need an inciting incident, a climax and at least one turning point, but not too many.
  - You need to establish your 'world,' but don't spend too much time on exposition.
  - You might end with a shock or surprise. It has been said that writers should give their readers what they want but not in the way they expect.
- If you are only writing the opening, make sure something interesting or dramatic happens that would make a reader want to know what happens in the rest of the story. You should know how the story would develop and end.
- It is less likely that you would be asked to write the end of a story, but if you are asked to do this, you need to know what happened before the point at which you start your story.
- Stories are normally written mainly in chronological order but you might want to use 'flashbacks'.

Language and Style

- Normally you would write in Standard English but if you use a first-person narrator, you should write in that person's **voice**. Think about its tone – formal or chatty? – as well as whether to use dialect or slang.
- Stories are usually written in the past tense. Using the present tense can make the action seem more immediate and vivid, though. You can use either, but stick to one.
- **Direct speech** can help to move on the story and tell us about character, but use it sparingly. Think about whether it adds anything – and make sure you set it out properly. Sometimes **indirect** (or **reported**) **speech** can be more effective.
- Write in paragraphs. These should usually be linked by discourse markers, particularly ones that relate to time:
  - After they left, he sank to his knees.
- Use a variety of sentence structures, for example using complex sentences for descriptions and simple or even minor sentences for dramatic impact:
  - It was her.
  - A gun beneath the leaves.
- Use a range of punctuation but avoid using a lot of exclamation marks.

Key Point

Be careful not to just tell the 'bare bones' of the story. You also need to describe people and places.

Key Words

narrative
protagonist
antagonist
voice
direct speech
indirect speech
reported speech

Quick Test

What is meant by the following?
1. The protagonist.
2. The antagonist.
3. The inciting incident.
4. A turning point.

Descriptive Writing

You must be able to:

- Write clear and imaginative descriptions.

Description

- One of the tasks in Paper 1 will be to write a description, possibly based on a picture. If there is a picture, you are not limited to describing what is actually in the picture. It is there to stimulate your imagination.
- When writing a description you can draw on your memories of real people, places or things.
- You might also be inspired by something you've read.
- Think about different aspects of your subject – and not just positive ones. This is especially important when describing a person – there is only so much you can write about how lovely someone is.
- Think about all five senses: sight, hearing, smell, taste and touch. When you have decided what you want to describe, it is a good idea to jot down what you experience through each sense. If you were describing a beach you might put:

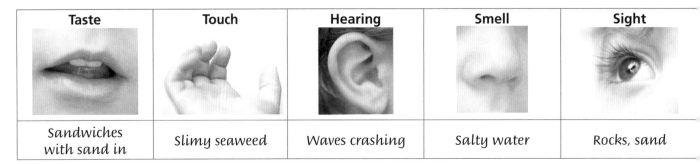

Taste	Touch	Hearing	Smell	Sight
Sandwiches with sand in	Slimy seaweed	Waves crashing	Salty water	Rocks, sand

- Another useful way of approaching description is 'big to small', starting with what something is like from a distance and moving in like a camera:

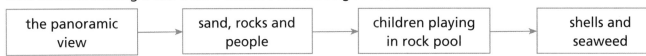

| the panoramic view | → | sand, rocks and people | → | children playing in rock pool | → | shells and seaweed |

Language and Style

- Consider whether to use the first or third person – you may or may not want to describe personal feelings:

  I feel a huge sense of regret as the train leaves.

- Decide whether to write in the present or past tense: they can be equally effective but you should stick to one.
- Use **imagery** and figurative language, including metaphors and similes:

  The train roared like an angry lion.

> **Key Point**
>
> When you describe something, remember that you can use all five senses.

- Use adjectives and adverbs:

  - *The deep mysterious sea*
  - *The engine spluttered fitfully.*

- Be adventurous in your choice of vocabulary. Use words that have precise, rather than general, meanings. Does the man walk across the road? Or does he amble, trot, stride or even swagger?

- Use techniques such as alliteration, assonance and onomatopoeia:

  - *sparkling, shining sea*
  - *gloomy blue rooms*
  - *the fizz and pop of the fireworks*

- Use both active and passive voices:

  - *A dark forest surrounded the cottage.*
  - *The cottage is surrounded by a dark forest.*

- Write in paragraphs. Vary their length and link them with a variety of discourse markers:

  - *Beyond this lies a flat, wide bog.*
  - *But these sights were as nothing to what lay beyond.*

> **Key Point**
>
> If the task is to write a description, do not write a story.

- Vary your sentence lengths and use techniques such as **parallel phrasing**. This is the use of phrases constructed in the same way and arranged in pairs or sequences:

  - *Tiny rivulets run down the lane; a massive lake covers the fields.*

Example

- This description of a person uses some of the techniques described above.

> George lived alone. Gnarled and weather-beaten, he looked older than his sixty years: his skin was sun-baked and blemished; his forehead grooved with deep furrows; his few remaining teeth black and crooked, like ancient gravestones. His teeth were rarely seen, for he had few reasons to smile. His one companion was his terrier Barney, whom he loved. In return Barney offered unquestioning love, loyalty and apparent affection.

It is written in the past tense and the third person.

It describes George's appearance but also gives us some background.

The imagery is mainly literal but figurative imagery is also used.

Both active and passive voices are used.

There is a variety of sentence structures.

> **Quick Test**
>
> Look at the example above. Find examples of:
> 1. A simple sentence.
> 2. A simile.
> 3. Alliteration.
> 4. The passive voice.

> **Key Words**
>
> imagery
> parallel phrasing

1 Read the passage below (Source A), in which Charlotte Brontë describes how she and her sisters, Anne and Emily, went about publishing their poems.

From Charlotte Brontë's *Biographical Notice of Ellis and Acton Bell*

We agreed to arrange a small selection of our poems, and, if possible, get them printed. Averse to personal publicity, we veiled our own names under those of Currer, Ellis, and Acton Bell; the ambiguous choice being dictated by a sort of conscientious scruple at assuming Christian names positively masculine, while we did not like to declare ourselves women, because – without at that time suspecting that our mode of writing and thinking was not what is called 'feminine' – we had a vague impression that authoresses are liable to be looked on with prejudice […]

The bringing out of our little book was hard work. As was to be expected, neither we nor our poems were at all wanted; but for this we had been prepared at the outset; though inexperienced ourselves, we had read the experience of others. The great puzzle lay in the difficulty of getting answers of any kind from the publishers to whom we applied. Being greatly harassed by this obstacle I ventured to apply to the Messrs. Chambers, of Edinburgh, for a word of advice; they may have forgotten the circumstance, but I have not, for from them I received a brief and business-like, but civil and sensible reply, on which we acted, and at last made a way.

The book was printed; it is scarcely known, and all of it that merits to be known are the poems of Ellis Bell. The fixed conviction I held, and hold of the worth of these poems has not indeed received the confirmation of much favourable criticism; but I must retain it notwithstanding.

Which of the following statements are TRUE? Tick the correct boxes.

a) All three sisters contributed poems to the book. ☐

b) They wrote under their own names. ☐

c) They felt that critics were prejudiced against female authors. ☐

d) They were not keen on publicity. ☐

e) They had lots of replies from publishers. ☐

f) Charlotte Brontë found the advice of Chambers sensible and useful. ☐

g) The book was a great success. ☐

h) Emily's (Ellis's) poems were the worst thing about the book. ☐

i) Bringing out the book was simple, easy work. ☐

j) The sisters were all very experienced at working with publishers. ☐ [4]

2 Now read this article (Source B) and write a summary of the differences between Brontë's and Fordyce's experience.

How I Made My Own Luck

by Misha Fordyce

People often ask me for advice about writing, which really means they want me to give them the magic key that opens the door to publication, fame and fortune. I can't promise any of that. All I can do is say how it was for me, and that what worked for me won't work for everyone. There are two essential ingredients: hard work and luck. Some people say you make your own luck. If that's true, this is the luck I made:

1. I started reading out my poetry in public. It wasn't that hard for me. I'm one of life's show-offs. I was welcomed with enthusiasm, especially because I'm a woman. 'We don't get enough women' was a cry I heard again and again.

2. I sent my poems to every poetry magazine going, whether they pay or not (mostly they don't) and very soon I was seeing my work in print.

3. I entered almost every competition I could find.

And finally, I won a competition, which led to my first book, which did very well – and here I am: a hardworking and very lucky poet.

_____

_____

_____

_____

_____

_____

_____

_____

_____

_____ [8]

3 Look again at Source B. How does Fordyce use language to convey her feelings about becoming a poet? You could include her choice of:

- words and phrases
- language features and techniques
- sentence forms.

Write your answer on a separate piece of paper. [12]

Reading

Read the passage below, which is the opening of *The Withered Arm* by Thomas Hardy, and then answer the questions.

It was an eighty-cow dairy, and the troop of milkers, regular and supernumerary, were all at work; [...] The hour was about six in the evening, and three-fourths of the large, red, rectangular animals having been finished off, there was opportunity for a little conversation.

'He do bring home his bride tomorrow, I hear. They've come as far as Anglebury today.'

The voice seemed to proceed from the belly of the cow called Cherry, but the speaker was a milking-woman, whose face was buried in the flank of that motionless beast.

'Hav' anybody seen her?' said another.

There was a negative response from the first. 'Though they say she's a rosy-cheeked, tisty-tosty little body enough,' she added; and as the milkmaid spoke she turned her face so that she could glance past her cow's tail to the other side of the barton,[1] where a thin fading woman of thirty milked somewhat apart from the rest.

'Years younger than he, they say,' continued the second, with also a glance of reflectiveness in the same direction.

'How old do you call him, then?'

'Thirty or so.'

'More like forty,' broke in an old milkman [...]

The discussion waxed so warm that the purr of the milk streams became jerky, till a voice from another cow's belly cried with authority, 'Now then, what the Turk do it matter to us about Farmer Lodge's age, or Farmer Lodge's new mis'ess? [...] Get on with your work, or 'twill be dark afore we have done. The evening is pinking in a'ready.' This speaker was the dairyman himself, by whom the milkmaids and men were employed.

Nothing more was said publicly about Farmer Lodge's wedding, but the first woman murmured under her cow to her next neighbour.[1] ''Tis hard for she,' signifying the thin worn milkmaid aforesaid.

'O no,' said the second. 'He ha'n't spoke to Rhoda Brook for years.'

When the milking was done they washed their pails and hung them on a many-forked stand made as usual of the peeled limb of an oak-tree, set upright in the earth, and resembling a colossal antlered horn. The majority then dispersed in various directions homeward. The thin woman who had not spoken was joined by a boy of twelve or thereabout, and the twain[2] went away up the field also.

Their course lay apart from that of the others, to a lonely spot high above the water-meads, and not far from the border of Egdon Heath, whose dark countenance was visible in the distance as they drew nigh to their home.

'They've just been saying down in barton that your father brings his young wife home from Anglebury tomorrow,' the woman observed. 'I shall want to send you for a few things to market, and you'll be pretty sure to meet 'em.'

'Yes, Mother,' said the boy. 'Is Father married then?'

'Yes...You can give her a look, and tell me what she's like, if you do see her.'

[1] *barton* – cowshed

[2] *twain* – two

1   This text is the opening of a short story. How has the writer structured the text to interest you?

You could write about:
- what the writer focuses on at the beginning
- how and why the writer changes this focus as the extract develops
- any other structural features that interest you.   [8]

_____

_____

_____

_____

_____

2   Halfway through this extract the writer introduces Rhoda Brook. What impression do you get of her?

In your response you could:
- write about the attitude of the other characters to her
- evaluate the ways in which the writer describes her
- support your answer with quotations from the text.   [20]

_____

_____

_____

_____

_____

_____

_____

_____

_____

Writing

3   Write the opening of a story about a mother and her son. Write on a separate piece of paper.

[24 marks for content and organisation; 16 marks for technical accuracy; total 40]

Reading Non-fiction 1

You must be able to:

- Read and understand a range of non-fiction texts
- Compare writers' ideas and perspectives.

Viewpoints and Perspectives

- Paper 2 of the English Language exam requires you to compare two non-fiction texts.
- The exam is called 'Writers' Viewpoints and Perspectives'. In order to understand **viewpoints** and **perspectives** you are expected to consider writers' opinions, ideas and feelings.

Form, Purpose and Audience

- Your texts could come from a number of **non-fiction forms** and **genres**. The most likely are discussed below.
- Think about the writer's purpose. It could be to describe, to inform and explain, to argue, to persuade or to advise. Remember that a text can have more than one purpose.
- Think about the intended audience. It might be aimed at people of a certain age (children, teenagers, older people). It could be intended for people in a particular job or with particular interests: for example, doctors, gardeners, cyclists. It might, however, be written for a general audience or with no audience in mind.

>
> ### Key Point
> Non-fiction is any writing that is not made up by the writer. It is not necessarily fact but it is what the writer believes to be true.

Diaries

- Diaries and **journals** are very personal. They are written by people who want to keep a record of what they have done and to express their opinions and feelings about what is happening around them.
- They can seem very immediate and spontaneous. We expect to get a genuine, uncensored and sincere point of view.
- They also give us an insight into what people really did and thought in the past.
- However, many diaries have been edited. We can still learn what the writer thought at the time of writing but it may not be exactly what he or she wrote.
- Some diaries may have been written with publication in mind by writers conscious of giving their 'version' of events.
- Diaries can vary a lot in style. Some use chatty, **informal language**. Others are quite formal.
- Some **diarists** jot down impressions and thoughts in a quite disorganised way. Other diaries are considered and crafted.

Letters

- Letters can give us an insight into people's everyday lives. Their style and tone depend a lot on their purpose.
- Letters give news and opinions, discuss ideas and express feelings. Letters might also be asking for something (like a job), complaining about something, or thanking someone for something.
- Unlike diarists, letter writers are always conscious of their audience. A letter to a close friend would be different in tone, style and content from a letter to a grandmother. It would be very different from a letter to a newspaper about current events, or to a prospective employer.
- The tone of a letter – friendly, angry, ironic, cold – will tell you a lot about the relationship between the writer and the **recipient** at the time of writing.

Autobiography and Biography

Biography means writing about life. **Autobiography** means writing about one's own life.

An autobiography can be reflective, even 'confessional', as the writer considers his or her past actions. It may also be self-justifying, naive or untrue. Autobiographies written by current celebrities (or their 'ghostwriters') are often written with the purpose of promoting the subject's career.

Biographies range from what are known as 'hatchet jobs', designed to ruin their subjects' reputations, to 'hagiographies' (originally written about saints), which have nothing but good to say. Most are something in between.

A biographer's point of view may come from his or her own relationship with the subject. On the other hand, it might be based on a careful consideration of the evidence.

Key Point

An autobiography is written by someone looking back on events, and so has the benefit of hindsight.

Key Words

viewpoint
perspective
non-fiction
form
genre
journal
informal language
diarist
recipient
biography
autobiography

Quick Test

Where are you most likely to find the following?
1. An account of someone's whole life.
2. Thanks for a present.
3. The writer's secret feelings.
4. How the writer became a megastar.

Reading Non-fiction 2

You must be able to:

- Read and understand a range of non-fiction texts
- Compare writers' ideas and perspectives.

Travel Writing

- Travel writing includes newspaper and magazine **articles** about places to visit, which give readers opinions and advice about a place. These are similar to reviews.
- You are more likely to be given **autobiographical** accounts of more adventurous trips – a journey down the Amazon or climbing a mountain in the Himalayas. These contain information about the places described but are more concerned with the personal experience of challenge and adventure. Texts like this are very popular with examiners and there is a good chance that one will be used in your exam.
- Some writers might seem awestruck and/or delighted by everything they encounter. Others are more critical, especially when writing about people and their way of life. They might even give opinions on political or other controversial issues, although extracts containing controversial or unfashionable views tend to be avoided by examiners.
- Some writers use the techniques of fiction writers to build suspense and involve readers. Others go in for colourful, even poetic description. Some write wittily about their reactions to new experiences.
- Some writers are experts, perhaps using a lot of unfamiliar terminology, for example, about mountaineering. Others see themselves as naive travellers – 'innocents abroad' – who tell jokes at their own expense.

> **Key Point**
>
> Many non-fiction texts use 'literary' techniques associated with fiction.

Journalism

- **Journalism** is anything that is published in a newspaper or magazine.
- Newspaper **reports** give the news and are mainly factual. **Features** – in both newspapers and magazines – look at issues in more depth. Sometimes they are balanced discussions. They can, however, strongly argue for a point of view.
- Articles can be serious or amusing. Most newspapers have regular feature writers. Some of them write about themselves and their families in a way that encourages readers to empathise with them. Others focus on more controversial issues. Examiners, however, usually avoid extreme or controversial views, preferring more personal features.
- Most magazines are aimed at particular readerships – for example, women, men, teenagers, older people.
- Newspapers are aimed at a general, adult audience. However, different newspapers have different readerships, often associated with particular political views. Examiners usually avoid politics.

Reviews

- A **review** is an article that gives a point of view about, for example, a film, book, concert, game or restaurant.

- Reviews give information, such as venue, date, time and price. Their main purpose, however, is to give the writer's point of view.
- Some reviews are quite balanced, giving positive and negative views, though they usually do arrive at a judgement. Others express their views very strongly, sometimes in a witty way.

Comparing Points of View

The two **sources** you are given will be about similar subjects but written from different points of view. Question 4 on Paper 2 asks you to compare these viewpoints:

- Compare how the writers convey different attitudes to the environment. You should discuss what these attitudes are:

Smith feels that we need to save rural areas, whereas Jones is happy for towns to expand.

The attitudes shown in the sources might be directly stated or implied:

While Williams is shocked at the idea of women doing 'men's work', Roberts seems not to share the view as she does not comment on the fact that the engineer is a woman.

Think about the impression you get of the writer:

Jones is clearly an expert on the subject, while Smith writes as a confused voter.

Consider the general tone:

Williams uses humour to make his point, but Roberts writes seriously about her emotions.

And remember to comment on structure and language:

Jones's use of subheadings breaks the article into clear 'points', making it more accessible.

Smith uses slang, trying to appeal to young readers, whereas Jones uses formal, quite technical language.

> **Key Point**
>
> Remember that you are being asked to compare the writers' views, not to give your own.

> **Quick Test**
>
> In which of the following are you least likely to find the writer's point of view?
> 1. A review.
> 2. A news report.
> 3. A feature.
> 4. Travel writing.

> **Key Words**
>
> article
> autobiographical
> journalism
> report
> feature
> review
> source

Writing Non-fiction 1

You must be able to:

- Communicate clearly, effectively and imaginatively
- Adapt your writing for different forms, purposes and audiences.

Quick Recall Quiz

The Task

- Paper 2 of the English Language exam includes one writing task. According to the syllabus you could be writing to inform, explain, instruct, or argue. However, in practice, the question will almost certainly require you to express your views on a theme explored in the reading section of the exam.
- You will be given a statement or scenario, and instructions which include details of purpose, form and audience:

> School holidays create problems for parents and damage children's education.
>
> Write an article for a student website in which you argue for or against this view.

Audience

- Sometimes the task specifies an audience:

> Write a letter to your head teacher.

- Sometimes the audience is implied by the form:

> – Write an article for your school website.

- Your intended audience determines what sort of language you use. Think about whether a formal or informal tone is called for.
- You would write informally for people you know well, using the sort of language that you use when chatting with them. However, you should avoid using 'text language' (abbreviations, emoticons etc.) in the exam.
- It can be appropriate to write informally for people you don't know, for example, in a magazine article aimed at teenagers.
- For almost everything else use a formal tone and write in Standard English (see pages 14–15).
- Be aware of your audience's interests and points of view. For example, if you were writing for a local audience you would focus on known local concerns:

> Here in Bingley, we have always been proud of our green spaces.

- – You would expect school governors to be concerned about the school's reputation:

> I know that you are just as concerned as I am about recent complaints of unsocial behaviour.

Key Point

You are free to agree or disagree with the stimulus you are given. The important thing is to try to convince the reader of your view.

- And a little flattery can go a long way:

I have always been impressed by your commitment to our community.

Purpose

- The purpose of your writing is usually to express your point of view. The wording of the task might give a slightly different emphasis. For example, 'argue' sounds more passionate than 'explain' or 'inform', while 'persuade' suggests more emphasis on the audience.

Constructing Your Argument

- In constructing your **argument**, start with a powerful opening paragraph, which grabs your audience and makes your point clear.
- Make sure you offer a number of points in support of your argument, starting a new paragraph for each.
  Acknowledge other points of view but then give your **counter-arguments**, pointing out why you think they are wrong:

Some people argue that school uniforms stifle individuality. However,...

Structure your argument in a logical order, using **discourse markers** to 'signpost' the development of your argument:

Another point I would like to make is...

Back up your points with evidence if you can. You can use the sources for the reading question to help you with this.
Give appropriate examples, including **anecdotes**:

Only last week, I encountered such behaviour...

Address your audience directly (**direct address**), using 'you', and show your own involvement by using 'I' and 'we'.
Use a full range of **rhetorical devices**, including lists of three, repetition and **hyperbole** (see pages 28–29).
Use humour if you think it is appropriate.
Use a variety of sentence structures, and use the passive as well as the active voice.
Finish with a strong conclusion, summing up the main points and stating your opinion.

Key Point

Spend a few minutes (but only a few!) planning your answer, using whatever method works best for you.

Key Words

audience
abbreviation
argument
counter-argument
discourse marker
anecdote
direct address
rhetorical device
hyperbole

Quick Test

Your head teacher has banned packed lunches. You want to write to the governors giving your reaction. What would be the:
1. purpose?
2. audience?
3. form?

Writing Non-fiction 2

You must be able to:

- Communicate clearly, effectively and imaginatively
- Adapt your writing for different forms, purposes and audiences.

Form: Articles

- You could be asked to write an article for a newspaper, magazine or website.
- If it is a newspaper, the task might specify whether it is a **broadsheet**, **tabloid** or local newspaper.
- Broadsheets are 'serious' newspapers, which look at news in more detail and depth, such as the *Daily Telegraph* and *The Guardian*.
- Tabloids, like *The Sun* and the *Daily Mirror*, cover news in less depth and devote more space to things like celebrity gossip.
- Tabloids use short paragraphs and sentences, and simple vocabulary. Broadsheets use longer paragraphs and sentences, and more sophisticated vocabulary. Because of this you are more likely to be asked to write an article for a broadsheet.
- Do not try to make your answer look like a newspaper or magazine. There are no marks for design. Do not include:
  - a masthead (the newspaper's title)
  - columns
  - illustrations
- You can, however, include organisational devices such as:
  - a **headline** – perhaps using alliteration ('Ban this Beastly Business'), a **pun** or a play on words ('A Tale of Two Kitties'). But don't put it in huge coloured letters!
  - a **strapline**, under the headline, expanding on or explaining the headline ('Why We Should Boycott Cosmetics')
  - **subheadings** – to guide the reader through the text.
- You must write in paragraphs.
- Magazine and website articles are similar to newspaper articles in form.

> **Key Point**
>
> You are not likely to be asked to write a tabloid article: it would not give you enough scope to demonstrate your skills.

Form: Letters

- There are a number of 'rules' or conventions that are used in letter-writing. These are often not used in informal letters.
- If you are asked to write a letter in the exam, it will probably be quite formal.

Example of How to Open a Letter

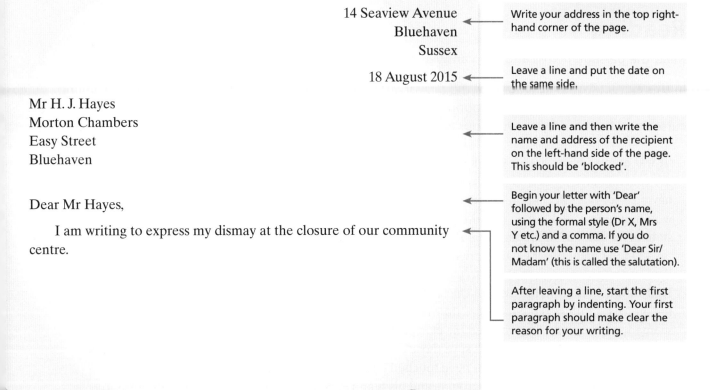

14 Seaview Avenue
Bluehaven
Sussex

18 August 2015

Write your address in the top right-hand corner of the page.

Leave a line and put the date on the same side.

Mr H. J. Hayes
Morton Chambers
Easy Street
Bluehaven

Leave a line and then write the name and address of the recipient on the left-hand side of the page. This should be 'blocked'.

Dear Mr Hayes,

I am writing to express my dismay at the closure of our community centre.

Begin your letter with 'Dear' followed by the person's name, using the formal style (Dr X, Mrs Y etc.) and a comma. If you do not know the name use 'Dear Sir/Madam' (this is called the salutation).

After leaving a line, start the first paragraph by indenting. Your first paragraph should make clear the reason for your writing.

- Continue with paragraphs that make further relevant points before ending with one that tells the reader what you would like to happen next.
- Connect your paragraphs with discourse markers.
- If you have addressed the reader by name, sign off with 'Yours sincerely'. If you haven't, use 'Yours faithfully'.
- Remember the 'five Cs'. Letters should be:
  - Clear – Say what you mean in good English.
  - Complete – Include everything necessary, giving enough detail and explaining your points properly.
  - Concise – Don't 'ramble'. Do not include irrelevant information or ideas.
  - Correct – Say what you believe to be true.
  - Courteous – Be polite. Consider the recipient and his or her possible reaction to your letter.

> **Key Point**
>
> Unless you are writing informally for young people, avoid slang or dialect words, contractions and abbreviations.

> **Quick Test**
>
> How should you end a letter beginning with the following salutations?
> 1. Dear Mr Mahmood
> 2. Dear Principal
> 3. Dear Madam
> 4. Dear Sir Arthur

> **Key Words**
>
> **broadsheet**
> **tabloid**
> **headline**
> **pun**
> **strapline**
> **subheading**

Reading

Read the passage below and then answer the questions.

In this extract from *The Hound of the Baskervilles* by Sir Arthur Conan Doyle, Dr Mortimer is telling Sherlock Holmes and Dr Watson about the death of Sir Charles Baskerville, who believed his family was cursed and haunted by a mysterious beast.

'It was at my advice that Sir Charles was about to go to London. His heart was, I knew, affected, and the constant anxiety in which he lived, however chimerical[1] the cause of it might be, was evidently having a serious effect upon his health. I thought that a few months among the distractions of town would send him back a new man. Mr Stapleton, a mutual friend who was much concerned at his state of health, was of the same opinion. At the last instant came this terrible catastrophe.

'On the night of Sir Charles's death Barrymore, the butler who made the discovery, sent Perkins the groom on horseback to me, and as I was sitting up late I was able to reach Baskerville Hall within an hour of the event. I checked and corroborated all the facts which were mentioned at the inquest. I followed the footsteps down the yew alley, I saw the spot at the moor-gate where he seemed to have waited, I remarked the change in the shape of the prints after that point, I noted that there were no other footsteps save those of Barrymore on the soft gravel, and finally I carefully examined the body, which had not been touched until my arrival. Sir Charles lay on his face, his arms out, his fingers dug into the ground, and his features convulsed with some strong emotion to such an extent that I could hardly have sworn to his identity. There was certainly no physical injury of any kind. But one false statement was made by Barrymore at the inquest. He said that there were no traces upon the ground round the body. He did not observe any. But I did – some little distance off, but fresh and clear.'

'Footprints?'

'Footprints.'

'A man's or a woman's?'

Dr Mortimer looked strangely at us for an instant, and his voice sank almost to a whisper as he answered:

'Mr Holmes, they were the footprints of a gigantic hound!'

[1] *chimerical* – fanciful or imagined

1 This extract comes from the end of the second chapter of *The Hound of the Baskervilles*, a detective story featuring Sherlock Holmes.

How has the writer structured the text to interest you as a reader?

You could write about:

- how Dr Mortimer builds up to the discovery of the body
- how the information about the footprints is revealed
- any other structural features that interest you.

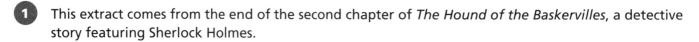

_____

_____

_____

_____ [8]

2 Look at the whole text.

What impression do you get of the narrator and his story?

* Write about your impressions of Dr Mortimer and his story.
* Evaluate how the writer has created these impressions.
* Support your opinions with quotations from the text.

Write your answer on a separate piece of paper. [20]

Writing

3 You have been asked to write a creative piece for your school magazine or website.

Either

Write a description suggested by this picture.

Or

Write the opening of a story set in a wild, isolated place. Write on a separate piece of paper.

[24 marks for content and organisation; 16 marks for technical accuracy; total 40]

Reading

Source A

Source A is an article from *The Times* newspaper, 15 May 1914.

The Cult of Little Dogs: An Irresistible Appeal **by Our Correspondent**

There is a certain melancholy attaching to shows of toy dogs. Not that toy dogs are themselves melancholy – indeed it is their sprightly unconsciousness of their degeneracy that most confounds the moralist – but that they suggest melancholy reflections. The Englishman, perhaps alone among the peoples of the world, understands fully the great soul of the dog; he feels his own kinship with it – as he did in former days with that of the fighting cock; and he has accepted with pride the bull-dog as the type of his national qualities. It is not, then, without misgiving that he watches the process of minimising the dog, or a large proportion of him, in an eager competition to crib, cabin, and confine the great soul in the smallest possible body, until, in place of the dignified friend and ally of man, there will be left nothing but, at worst, a pampered toy; at best, a pathetic creature, all eyes and nerves, whose insurgent soul frets the puny body to decay.

Where will the process end? Already we have held up to the admiration of the world a Pomeranian puppy which, at the age of three months, can be comfortably bestowed in a tumbler, over the edge of which his picture shows him looking, with shy eyes and apprehensively, at the disproportionate scheme of things. Presently, maybe, we shall have a childhood's dream realised and really see the little dog of the fairy-story who was hidden in a walnut and, when the shell was cracked, leapt forth barking and wagging his tail to the delight of all the noble company.

Source B

Source B is a letter to a newspaper

14 Raglan Terrace
Tillingbourne

12 July 2015

Dear Editor,

I was saddened to read yet more negative coverage of so-called 'purse pets' in your paper. What is it about celebrities who own small dogs that inspires such vitriol?

I know some people think celebrities use their pets as fashion accessories – and this is questionable. But it is not, as you suggest, cruel. We like to think of our four-legged friends as free and independent spirits – equal companions on life's journey – but they're not. Dogs depend on us for food, shelter and love.

This is the case whether they are tiny little chihuahuas that can fit in a Versace handbag or massive Afghans – or even breeds like pit bulls. Now, I don't want to be accused of the kind of prejudice I'm criticising others for, but let's just reflect for a moment. Which is crueller? Pampering your pet with little treats or training her to fight and kill other dogs?

Of course, I'm not saying that all Staffie owners do this. But you should not imply that everyone who owns a little dog is cruel. Taking dogs shopping for little doggy clothes is a bit silly, but it does not damage their health or well-being. On the contrary, it shows that the owners care about their pets. In fact, many celebrity dog owners go further to show they care. Actress Kristin Chenoweth has even founded a charity, named after her tiny Maltese, to help homeless pets.

These dogs are beautiful, loyal and lovable. I know. I've got one. I don't keep her in my handbag or take her to canine boutiques, but I love and cherish her – and I wouldn't be without her. I don't think you'd write an article castigating me for those feelings, so why aim your vitriol at Paris Hilton and Mariah Carey, whose only crime is to love their pets?

Yours faithfully

Joanna P. Hanlon

1   Refer only to Source A. How does the writer use language to express his feelings about small dogs?

_____

_____

_____

_____

_____

_____

_____

_____

_____ [12]

2   Refer to both Source A and Source B.

Compare how the two writers convey different attitudes to small dogs.

In your answer you should:
*   compare their attitudes
*   compare the methods they use to convey their attitudes
*   support your ideas with quotations from both texts.

Write your answer on a separate piece of paper. [16]

Writing

3   'A dog is for life, not just for Christmas.'

Write an article for a magazine aimed at people your own age, inspired by this quotation, in which you give your views about dogs, dog owners, or both.

Write on a separate piece of paper.

[24 marks for content and organisation, 16 marks for technical accuracy. Total 40]

Context

You must be able to:

- Understand the social, historical and cultural context of a Shakespeare play
- Use this understanding to evaluate the play.

History

- The historical **context** in which Shakespeare lived was very different from ours.
- He lived from 1564 to 1616 and started writing during the reign of Queen Elizabeth I, a time of great prosperity for England, when explorers were discovering and colonising new lands across the world. Such adventures inspired *The Tempest*.
- There was also a great flowering of literature and theatre, inspired by the Renaissance in Italy.
- In 1603 Elizabeth I was succeeded by King James I, who was already King of Scotland. He became patron of Shakespeare's theatre company and *Macbeth* was written in his honour.

Religion

- England was an overwhelmingly Christian country. The official church was the Church of England, but many people were still Roman Catholics, while others (like Puritans) had stricter Protestant beliefs.
- Most people believed that after death God would judge them and decide whether they should spend eternity in Heaven or Hell. The idea of Hell is ever-present in *Macbeth*.
- The general attitude to non-Christians is reflected in the way other characters treat Shylock in *The Merchant of Venice*, although some would say that Shakespeare's writing causes the audience to question their assumptions.
- Many people also believed in astrology. The tension between the popular belief that everything is mapped out in the stars and the Christian belief in free will is present in many plays. We see this in *Romeo and Juliet*. Astrology is also prominent in *Julius Caesar*.

> **Key Point**
>
> Elizabethans and Jacobeans would have recognised the many biblical references found in Shakespeare.

Morality

- Society's moral and ethical standards were rooted in Christian teaching and the Ten Commandments.
- Most people shared similar ideas about sexual **morality**. Chastity, especially among women, was much more highly prized than in today's society and marriage was for life. This idea is central to *Much Ado About Nothing* and *Romeo and Juliet*.

Social Order

- Many people believed that the **social order**, with the King or Queen at the top, was derived from God and should not be tampered with.
- King James believed in 'the **divine right** of kings'.
  - This is a major theme in *Macbeth*.
  - The rights and wrongs of opposing rulers are also a theme of *Julius Caesar* and *The Tempest*.
- The **authority** of parents over children might also be seen as sacred, although this authority is challenged in *Romeo and Juliet*.

Society

- Although there was a parliament, England was not democratic in the modern sense.
- Political power centred on the **court**, around the Queen or King. Here, aristocrats competed for the monarch's favour.
- There was a growing middle class. Shakespeare was the son of a well-off glover from Stratford-upon-Avon. He benefited from a good education at the local grammar school. In these schools boys studied ancient history and Latin literature, the source of *Julius Caesar*.
- Most people, however, were illiterate. Many worked on the land, although cities were expanding. London's thriving port attracted merchants and travellers from all over the world.
- Women were usually dependent on their husbands or fathers, so making the right marriage was important. However, there were examples of rich and powerful women.
  - Portia in *The Merchant of Venice* has inherited her wealth from her father but she still cannot choose her own husband.
- Many of Shakespeare's female characters, like Beatrice in *Much Ado About Nothing*, show themselves to be equal to men. However, both Portia, in disguising herself as a man, and Lady Macbeth, in her desire to be 'unsexed', are conscious of taking on a 'man's role'.

> **Key Point**
>
> It is important to understand the differences between Shakespeare's society and ours.

> **Quick Test**
>
> True or False?
> 1. *Macbeth* was written for Queen Elizabeth.
> 2. Astrology is a Christian belief.
> 3. Divorce was common in Shakespeare's time.
> 4. James I believed that his authority came from God.

> **Key Words**
>
> context
> morality
> social order
> divine right
> authority
> court

Themes

You must be able to:

- Identify themes in a Shakespeare play
- Write about how Shakespeare presents themes.

Themes and Ideas

- A **theme** is part of the subject matter of a text – a concern that runs through the play.
- Shakespeare's plays are full of ideas about relationships, morality and society.
- Your exam question could focus on themes and ideas:
  - Write about how Shakespeare presents ideas about kingship in *Macbeth.*
  - Write about how Shakespeare explores ideas about love in *Romeo and Juliet.*

Identifying Themes

- Throughout his career, Shakespeare would return to the same themes. Here are some themes that occur frequently in his plays:

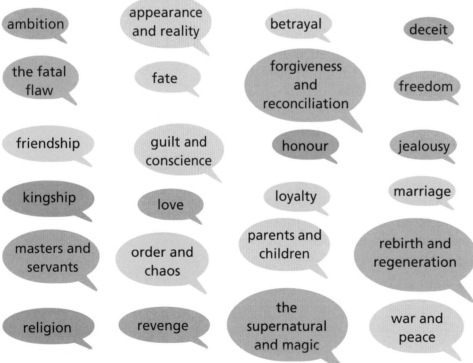

ambition

appearance and reality

betrayal

deceit

the fatal flaw

fate

forgiveness and reconciliation

freedom

friendship

guilt and conscience

honour

jealousy

kingship

love

loyalty

marriage

masters and servants

order and chaos

parents and children

rebirth and regeneration

religion

revenge

the supernatural and magic

war and peace

> **Key Point**
>
> Shakespeare uses his characters and plots to explore issues that mattered to people at the time he wrote. Most of them still matter.

- You may think of more themes. In over 30 plays Shakespeare looked at almost every aspect of human life.
- Write down some themes that occur in the play you have studied. Try to find at least five. Here are some to get you started:
  - *Macbeth* – marriage…
  - *Much Ado About Nothing* – misunderstandings…

- *The Merchant of Venice* – the outsider...
- *The Tempest* – forgiveness...
- *Romeo and Juliet* – betrayal...
- *Julius Caesar* – ambition...

- Now write a sentence or two about each theme:

> *Ambition is an important theme in 'Julius Caesar' because Caesar is killed when he achieves his ambition to rule Rome alone. The conspirators are also ambitious and their ambitions also destroy them.*
>
> *Forgiveness and reconciliation are central to 'The Tempest'. Prospero has his enemies at his mercy but chooses not to have his revenge on them.*

How Themes are Presented

- Shakespeare's plays have been interpreted in many different ways over the past 400 years. You must come to your own conclusions about his themes by considering the evidence.
- Think about the **plot** – what happens in the play:
  - Macbeth's murder of Duncan brings together the themes of ambition and kingship.
  - The theme of friendship comes to the fore in *Much Ado About Nothing* when Beatrice asks Benedick to kill his friend Claudio because of how he has treated Hero.
- Theatre is a visual medium. Shakespeare presents powerful **images**:
  - The appearance of Banquo's ghost in *Macbeth* speaks volumes about betrayal and guilt.
  - Juliet's appearance on a balcony above Romeo demonstrates the kind of love that he has for her.
- **Dialogue** can give us insight into themes by presenting more than one point of view:
  - The trial scene in *The Merchant of Venice* gives us both Shylock's and Antonio's views about business ethics.
  - In *Julius Caesar* idealist Brutus and pragmatist Cassius debate the rights and wrongs of their actions. We might side with one or the other, or feel that there is a middle way.
- Characters can raise themes and **issues** when they speak directly to the audience in a soliloquy or aside. When they do this they reveal what they really think:
  - Macbeth shares his doubts about killing Duncan. His soliloquies draw us into a consideration of the themes of kingship, loyalty and ambition.
  - In *The Tempest* Prospero tells us he intends to give up his 'rough magic', making us think about power and old age.

Key Point

Shakespeare does not tell us what he thinks or what we should think. There are more questions than answers.

Quick Test

Give a single word defined by the following:
1. A speech made to the audience.
2. Speech between two or more people.
3. What happens in the play.
4. A concern that runs through the play.

Key Words

theme
plot
image
dialogue
issue

Characters

You must be able to:

- Write about how Shakespeare presents characters.

Quick Recall Quiz

Characters

- Shakespeare is known for his huge range of characters and his understanding of human psychology.
- Your exam question might focus on a character, for example:
  - Write about how Shakespeare presents Brutus as an idealist.
  - Write about how far you think Shakespeare presents Shylock as a victim.
- You will get an extract from the play as a starting point. Look at what this reveals about the character before considering what else you know about him/her and how s/he develops in the rest of the play.
- When revising, think about each character's:
  - background
  - personality
  - relationships
  - **motivation**
  - function in the plot.
- Identify the main characters in your play and draw up a chart like the (partially completed) one below:

> **Key Point**
>
> When looking at characters, consider their historical and social context.

Character	Background	Personality	Relationships	Motivation	Function
Romeo	The son of the Montagues			Wants to be with Juliet whatever the cost	
Juliet		Innocent but very determined			
Capulet			Loves his family but expects obedience		
Nurse		Chatty, bawdy, devoted, pragmatic			Juliet's confidante – but advises her to forget Romeo

- The main characters all find themselves in different situations by the end of the play. How did they get there and how did their experiences change them?
- Try tracing your characters' development through events that have influenced them. Here is an example for Macbeth.

What happens?	What effect does it have?
He meets the witches.	He starts to think about his future and possibly becoming king.

He kills Duncan.	He becomes king. He has power but fears losing it and turns against Banquo.
He sees Banquo's ghost.	He feels guilty and acts strangely.
He visits the witches.	He fears losing his crown, which makes him more ruthless.
Malcolm invades Scotland.	Thinking he is invincible, he becomes defiant and brave.

How Characters are Presented

What They Say

A **soliloquy** is a speech to the audience, usually with no other characters on stage. Soliloquies let us into characters' thought processes, revealing a lot about their character and motivation:

- Juliet shows her excitement and impatience when waiting for the Nurse to return from seeing Romeo.

Sometimes characters comment briefly on what others are saying and doing in an **aside**. We can assume they mean what they say.

Characters do not always tell the truth. All Shakespeare plays include people who lie to others.

We do not, however, have to guess who is lying. It is clear when someone cannot be trusted:

- Lady Macbeth tells Macbeth to 'look like the innocent flower / But be the serpent under't'.

What Others Say

We learn about characters through what others say to and about them. Sometimes we get a consensus of opinion:

- Macbeth changes from being universally praised for his bravery and loyalty to being hated and feared as a 'devil' and 'fiend'.

A difference of opinion can give us something to think about:

- The violent Tybalt in *Romeo and Juliet* is a favourite of both Lady Capulet and the Nurse. This tells us about both his character and theirs.

Always be aware of who the speaker is:

- Antony's description of Brutus, in *Julius Caesar*, as 'the noblest Roman of them all' carries more weight because of their enmity.

How They Act and React

We learn about characters by their actions:

- When Bassanio chooses the lead casket in *The Merchant of Venice* we know he is genuine.

Their reactions also reveal a lot:

- Benedick's reaction to Beatrice's command to 'kill Claudio' reveals his growing feelings for her, and tells us about his sense of honour.

> ### Key Point
> When Shakespeare wants us to know what characters are really thinking and feeling, they speak to the audience.

Quick Test

True or False?
1. Everyone tells the truth.
2. Characters never address the audience.
3. Characters can change.
4. We can get differing views of a character.

> ### Key Words
> motivation
> soliloquy
> aside

Language and Structure

You must be able to:

- Analyse Shakespeare's use of language and structure
- Use relevant terminology.

Verse and Prose

- Shakespeare wrote in a mixture of **verse** and **prose**. Most of his verse is in **iambic pentameter**. 'Pentameter' means there are five stressed syllables on every line. 'Iambic' refers to the stress falling on every second syllable:

  O, **she** doth **teach** the **torch**es **to** shine **bright**.

- It is often said that the iambic pentameter follows the natural rhythms of speech and that it resembles a heartbeat.
- Sometimes Shakespeare varies the **metre** to emphasise certain words: for example, stressing the first syllable in a line or adding an extra syllable. He might create a pause (known as a **caesura**) in the middle of the line.
- **Rhyming couplets** might end a scene or emphasise an important thought.
- Other metres are occasionally used in Shakespeare, for example in songs.
- Verse tends to be used for higher-status characters when discussing serious things. However, much of the banter in *Much Ado About Nothing* is in prose. Characters such as servants usually speak in prose, but there are exceptions, as in Caliban's description of the island.

Structure

- Shakespeare's plays are divided into five acts. The first introduces the characters and their concerns. Then something happens that changes the characters' lives. In the third act things become more complicated. The fourth act tends to be about the complications being sorted out. The final act brings a resolution and the play ends with the restoration of order.
- When focusing on an extract think about which part of the play it comes from and how it fits into the play as a whole.
- Think about how Shakespeare uses contrasting scenes. He sometimes uses comic scenes to release tension before building to a tragic climax: for example, the 'porter scene' in *Macbeth*.

Key Point

You can tell verse from prose just by looking at it. Verse has definite line endings and a rhythm, often in a regular pattern or metre.

Imagery

- Shakespeare's imagery tells us about characters, creates mood and underlines key themes. His techniques include simile, metaphor and personification.

- Sometimes characters use **extended metaphors** or **conceits**. Romeo and Juliet use the **sonnet** form to develop the idea of Romeo being a pilgrim and Juliet a saint.
- Look for patterns of imagery in your play. Animal imagery, much of it connected to the Bible, runs through *The Merchant of Venice*:

> Why he hath made the ewe bleat for the lamb.

Rhetorical Language

- Rhetorical questions are common when characters are wondering what to do:

> I have railed so long against marriage, but doth not the appetite alter?

- Repetition emphasises important ideas or feelings:

> Tomorrow and tomorrow and tomorrow.

- The 'rule of three' is used by characters trying to convince others:

> Friends, Romans, countrymen, lend me your ears.

- Shakespeare uses rhetorical techniques in situations where they might be used in life, for example in the trial scene in *The Merchant of Venice*.

Playing with Words

- Elizabethans loved experimenting with words. Shakespeare shows this in characters like Romeo, who uses **oxymoron** to express his confusion:

> Feather of lead, bright smoke, cold fire, sick health.

Romeo also uses puns (double meanings), as do Beatrice and Benedick when they pit their wits against each other.
Double meanings are often used to make sexual innuendoes.
Shakespeare also uses techniques such as alliteration and assonance to create feelings and mood:

> Full fathom five thy father lies.

Key Point

Whatever the focus of the question, you must write about Shakespeare's language in your answer.

Key Words

verse
prose
iambic pentameter
metre
caesura
rhyming couplet
extended metaphor
conceit
sonnet
oxymoron

Quick Test

Of what are the following examples?
1. What, must I hold a candle to my shames?
2. Pure impiety and impious purity.
3. O mighty Caesar! Dost thou lie so low?
4. Hence will I to my ghostly sire's close cell,
   His help to crave and my dear hap to tell.

Reading

Source A

An Extract from the Journal of Dorothy Wordsworth

Thursday 15 April 1802

It was a threatening, misty morning, but mild. We set off after dinner from Eusemere. Mrs Clarkson went a short way with us, but turned back. The wind was furious and we thought we must have returned. We first rested in the large boat-house, then under a furze bush opposite Mr Clarkson's. Saw the plough going into the field. The wind seized our breath. The lake was rough. There was a boat by itself floating in the middle of the bay below Water Millock. We rested again in the Water Millock Lane. The hawthornes are black and green, the birches here and there greenish, but there is yet more of purple to be seen on the twigs. We got over into a field to avoid some cows – people working. A few primroses by the roadside – woodsorrel flower, the anemone, scentless violets, strawberries, and that starry yellow flower which Mrs C. calls pile wort. When we were in the woods beyond Gowbarrow Park we saw a few daffodils close to the water-side. We fancied that the lake had floated the seeds ashore, and that the little colony had so sprung up. But as we went along there were more and yet more; and at last, under the boughs of the trees, we saw that there was a long belt of them along the shore, about the breadth of a country turnpike road. I never saw daffodils so beautiful. They grew among the mossy stones about and about them; some rested their heads upon those stones as on a pillow for weariness; and the rest tossed and reeled and danced, and seemed as if they verily laughed with the wind that blew upon them over the lake; they looked so gay, ever glancing, ever changing.

Source B

Blog Entry

Bisma's Blog, 2nd June

Yesterday was a complete washout. First, it was a two-hour trip in the rickety school minibus squashed in with rucksacks, suitcases and sweaty bodies.

We made it – just – and were decanted from ancient minibus into even more ancient, more rickety and smellier youth hostel. Six in a room! It's like the workhouse in Dickens. We were barely given time to unpack – although time enough to notice that Anoushka O'Reilly had brought six pairs of high-heeled shoes and eight towels – before the Camp Commandant, alias Miss Frobisher, marched in with her whistle round her neck.

'Right, girls! Gentle walk round the lake before lunch!' Gentle! It was like one of those forced marches they do in boot camps. Hours of wading through mud and getting soaked to our skins. As for the wonderful scenery we were promised. What scenery? We could barely see six inches in front of our faces through the driving rain.

Thankfully, today's been a huge improvement – they took us to an assault course thing, swinging on ropes and stuff, which is a lot better than boring walking. And there was actually a shop and a café – so I was able to replace my lost energy with a massive dose of CAKE. So now I'm feeling maybe the country's not so bad – as long as we don't have to stay much longer.

1 Refer only to Source A.

How does the writer use language to express the feelings inspired by her walk? [12]

_____

_____

_____

_____

_____

_____

_____

_____

_____

_____

_____

_____

_____

2 Refer to both Source A and Source B.

Compare how the two writers convey different attitudes to the countryside.

In your answer you should:
- compare their attitudes
- compare the methods they use to convey their attitudes
- support your ideas with quotations from both texts.

Write your answer on a separate piece of paper. [16]

Writing

3 'School trips are a waste of time and money.'

Write an article for a magazine aimed at people your own age giving your views on this statement.

Write your answer on a separate piece of paper.

[24 marks for content and organisation, 16 marks for technical accuracy; total 40]

Answer the question on the play you have studied.

Write your answer on a separate piece of paper.

1 *Romeo and Juliet* – Read the extract specified and answer the question below.

In this extract, Juliet is waiting for the Nurse to return.

Act 2 Scene 5

From

JULIET   The clock struck nine when I did send the nurse;

To

             She would be as swift in motion as a ball.

How does Shakespeare present Romeo and Juliet's love in this speech?

Write about:

- the feelings that Juliet expresses in this speech
- how Shakespeare uses language to describe Juliet's feelings.   [30

2 *Macbeth* – Read the extract specified and answer the question below.

In this extract, Macbeth has just been told by the witches that he will be king.

Act 1 Scene 3

From

MACBETH   Two truths are told
             As happy prologues to the swelling act
             Of the imperial theme.

To

             My thought, whose murder yet is but fantastical,
             Shakes so my single state of man that function
             Is smothered in surmise, and nothing is
             But what is not.

How does Shakespeare present Macbeth's feelings about power and ambition in this speech?

Write about:

- Macbeth's feelings about power and ambition
- how Shakespeare uses language to convey Macbeth's feelings.   [30

3 *The Tempest* – Read the extract specified and answer the question below.

In this extract, Ariel has just reported to Prospero that he has carried out his orders and caused the shipwreck.

Act 1 Scene 2

From

ARIEL   Is there more toil?

To

PROSPERO   Dost thou forget

          From what a torment I did free thee?

Write about how Shakespeare presents Ariel and Prospero's relationship in this extract.

Write about:
- the relationship Ariel has with Prospero
- how Shakespeare uses language to present this relationship.   [30]

4 *The Merchant of Venice*

Explore how Shakespeare presents Shylock's relationship with Jessica. Refer to the whole of the play. Write about:

- the sort of relationship they have
- the methods Shakespeare uses to present their relationship.   [30]

5 *Julius Caesar*

Explore how Shakespeare presents the attitudes of Brutus and Cassius to Caesar. Refer to the whole of the play. Write about:

- the attitudes Brutus and Cassius have towards Caesar
- the methods Shakespeare uses to present their attitudes.   [30]

6 *Much Ado About Nothing*

To what extent does Shakespeare present Beatrice as an independent woman? Refer to the whole of the play. Write about:

- how far and in what ways you think Beatrice can be described as 'independent'
- the methods Shakespeare uses to present Beatrice.   [30]

Context

Quick Recall Quiz

You must be able to:

- Understand the social, historical and cultural context of a 19th-century novel
- Use this understanding to evaluate the text.

Religion and Morality

- In the nineteenth century, Britain was a Christian country, with many more churchgoers than now; religion was part of the fabric of most people's lives. Ministers of religion feature in *Jane Eyre* and *Pride and Prejudice.*
- People tended to share similar ideas about what was acceptable, particularly sexually. Deviations from the norm, like Lydia eloping with Wickham in *Pride and Prejudice*, are shocking.
- Many novels are concerned with right and wrong. Dr Jekyll wants to separate his 'evil' and 'good' sides. In *A Christmas Carol*, Dickens asks his readers to think about what Christmas and Christianity really mean.

Society

- Britain was a very wealthy country with a worldwide empire. Some people made huge fortunes, giving them as much power as the old aristocrats.
- There was a growing middle class of people who had comfortable homes and money to spend – including on novels.
- However, there was also great poverty, especially in towns and cities. With no welfare state and low wages, many people lived in terrible conditions.
- Social reformers fought against inequality. Dickens's work made people think about social issues.

Gender

- Women did not have a vote (although neither did most men) and their career options were limited. *Pride and Prejudice* is based on the need of middle-class women to find husbands. Jane Eyre has to earn her living as a governess.
- Many writers and thinkers supported women's rights. Mary Shelley's mother, Mary Wollstonecraft, was an early feminist.

Race

- It is unusual to find characters who are not white. Some modern readers are shocked by the attitudes shown to ethnic minorities. They are often seen as wild or savage, like Tonga in *The Sign of Four*, or as exotic and mysterious.

> **Key Point**
>
> The nineteenth century was a time of great change in Britain. Literature reflected this.

Science

- There were many scientific discoveries and advances. Shelley in *Frankenstein* and Stevenson in *The Strange Case of Dr Jekyll and Mr Hyde* use science as a starting point to consider 'what if', as science fiction writers do today. Frankenstein harnesses the power of electricity to create his monster, while Dr Jekyll mixes chemicals to find his formula.
- Sherlock Holmes uses a range of methods to solve his cases. Some of his **deductions** might seem fanciful but Conan Doyle was knowledgeable about forensics and Holmes is ahead of his time in using this new science.
- Many writers took an interest in new ideas about **psychology**. Shelley's work reflects current discussion of 'nature and nurture'. Stevenson explores ideas about behaviour and responsibility.

Literature: Movements and Genre

- Novelists were influenced by the Romantic movement, led by poets like Wordsworth. This movement rejected the eighteenth-century taste for order and rationality in favour of an emphasis on personal feelings and nature.
- While Jane Austen belongs more to the eighteenth-century tradition, her characters do reflect the fashion for **sentiment** and poetry.
- Mary Shelley was the wife of the Romantic poet Percy Bysshe Shelley, and her work can be described as Romantic. However, *Frankenstein* is more often described as Gothic, a genre related to Romanticism but more sensational, thrilling its readers with horror and the **supernatural**.
- Brontë, Dickens and Stevenson use elements of the Gothic. *A Christmas Carol* and *The Strange Case of Dr Jekyll and Mr Hyde* both cashed in on the popular taste for ghost stories. *The Strange Case of Dr Jekyll and Mr Hyde* also owes something to the increasingly popular detective story, of which Sir Arthur Conan Doyle was the best-known exponent.

> **Key Point**
>
> Whatever aspect of a text you are looking at, consider its context.

> **Quick Test**
>
> True or False?
> 1. All men had the vote.
> 2. Nobody cared about social injustice.
> 3. Romantic poets thought feelings mattered.
> 4. Britain changed a lot during the nineteenth century.

> **Key Words**
>
> deduction
> psychology
> sentiment
> supernatural

Themes

You must be able to:

- Identify themes in a 19th-century novel
- Write about how themes are presented.

Identifying Themes

- Here are some themes you will find in the set books.
- Look at the themes of the books you have not studied and think about whether they are also present in your novel.
- *Pride and Prejudice*
  - Marriage: marrying well is vital for the women. They want to marry for love but they also think in practical terms.
  - Class: the class system seems rigid and there is a lot of snobbery but Elizabeth breaks through it.
- *Frankenstein*
  - The pursuit of knowledge: Frankenstein's intellectual curiosity has terrible results.
  - Nature and nurture: the monster's potential for good is destroyed because of the way he is treated.
- *A Christmas Carol*
  - The spirit of Christmas: the 'spirit of Christmas' is the true message of Christianity.
  - Ignorance and Want: the monstrous children are a warning of what will happen if society does not tackle poverty and improve education.
- *Jane Eyre*
  - Women's roles: Jane does not accept an inferior role. She is independent, determined and outspoken.
  - Integrity: Jane remains honest and true to herself, and is rewarded by true love.
- *Great Expectations*
  - Money and ambition: Pip's money creates more problems than it solves.
  - Friendship: affection and loyalty are not always valued, but true friendship wins through.
- *The Strange Case of Dr Jekyll and Mr Hyde*
  - Good and evil: Jekyll's attempts to separate the good and evil parts of himself are doomed to failure.
  - Secrets: Victorian London is not as respectable as it seems, but is full of dark secrets.
- *The Sign of Four*
  - Crime: what makes people commit crimes?
  - Truth: detective stories are about finding the truth, thus making the world safer and better.

> **Key Point**
>
> Novels often focus on issues of personal morality, but they are also concerned with society as a whole.

How Themes are Presented

- Consider events in the novel:
  - In *Great Expectations* Pip suddenly acquires great wealth. The rest of the novel is about how it changes him.
  - The creation of the monster in *Frankenstein* raises questions about science and people trying to 'play God'.
- Narrators might discuss themes:
  - In *A Christmas Carol* Dickens uses his **authorial voice** to give us his views on social problems.
  - The opening lines of *Pride and Prejudice* tell us straightaway that the novel will be about courtship and marriage.
- Characters can embody themes:
  - Edward Hyde is evil personified.
  - The character of Bertha Rochester in *Jane Eyre* brings together themes of madness and duty.
- Characters discuss themes and **issues**:
  - Elizabeth in *Pride and Prejudice* discusses money, class, love and marriage with her sister Jane, and with Darcy, who has a quite different **perspective** on life.
  - Dr Watson disagrees with Sherlock Holmes about women, Watson being shocked at his friend's misogyny.
- It can be helpful to look for **motifs** in a novel. A motif is an image, idea or situation that recurs through a work, suggesting a theme:
  - Characters in *Frankenstein* find comfort and healing in natural beauty.
  - Fire is a recurring motif in *Jane Eyre*, symbolising passion as well as moving on the story.
- **Settings** can encapsulate themes:
  - Satis House in *Great Expectations* could symbolise the emptiness of wealth and the gloom of lovelessness.
  - The London of *The Strange Case of Dr Jekyll and Mr Hyde* gives us a sense of the dark side of life.

> ### Key Point
>
> A novel's themes emerge in many ways. Think about the themes of your novel. How do you know they are there?

Quick Test

1. Can a novel have more than one theme?
2. What is a motif?
3. Can a narrator discuss themes and ideas?
4. Can a writer give us differing perspectives on a theme?

> ### Key Words
>
> authorial voice
> issue
> perspective
> motif
> setting

Characters

Quick Recall Quiz

You must be able to:

- Write about how characters are presented in a 19th-century novel.

Characters

- Your exam question might focus on a character.
- It could be about a character's personality:
  - How does Austen present Elizabeth as a strong-minded woman?
- Or attitudes and feelings:
  - Explore how Stevenson conveys Jekyll's feelings about good and evil.
- Or relationships:
  - Write about how Conan Doyle presents Watson and Holmes's relationship.

Protagonists

- When the protagonist is also the narrator, we are invited to share the character's thoughts and feelings.
- Jane Eyre, and Pip in *Great Expectations*, speak to the readers as if they are looking back over their past, sharing feelings and thoughts as well as experiences.
- Pip can be seen as a **naive narrator**, as he does not understand what is going on. Jane Eyre is more perceptive, even though she does not fully understand everything she experiences.
- Both these novels are accounts of growing up. This sort of novel is known by the German word **Bildungsroman**.
- Victor Frankenstein relates most of his own story, but we do get other perspectives. Part of *The Strange Case of Dr Jekyll and Mr Hyde* is narrated by Jekyll, giving us some insight into his mind and a degree of empathy for him.
- Sherlock Holmes is seen through the eyes of Dr Watson. Conan Doyle keeps him distant, to be admired by the readers as he is by Watson.
- Although Elizabeth in *Pride and Prejudice* and Scrooge in *A Christmas Carol* do not tell their own stories, the writers give us access to their thoughts and feelings. However, the third-person narrative allows authors to stand aside and comment on their characters.

> ### Key Point
>
> Questions on character are most likely to be about the protagonists, but you should not neglect other characters.

Other Characters

- You could be asked to focus on other characters as individuals or as a group.
- Look at these in terms of:
  - their relationship to the protagonist: for example, Elizabeth Bennet's relationship with her sisters
  - their **function** in the novel, perhaps as a way of looking at

themes: for example, Shelley's use of the monster to present ideas about nature and nurture.

- their **significance** in terms of plot: for example, Miss Havisham's influence on Pip's life.

How Characters are Presented

What They Say

- Characters who are also narrators have plenty to say about their ideas and feelings.
- Those who are not main narrators sometimes express themselves in letters.
- Characters reveal themselves in conversation with other characters. Sometimes this is by giving an opinion or expressing feelings, as when the monster confronts Frankenstein. Sometimes it is by the way they talk. Mr Collins, in *Pride and Prejudice*, reveals his snobbery by constantly referring to Lady Catherine de Burgh.

What the Narrator Says

Narrators describe characters' personalities as well as their appearance. In *Great Expectations* Pip, as narrator, describes Estella as 'beautiful and self-possessed'. We see her through his eyes.

In a third-person narrative, however, we can take comments on characters as being trustworthy and neutral, as when Stevenson describes Mr Utterson as having 'an approved tolerance for others'. A narrator might go further and describe a character's thoughts and feelings. Jane Austen often takes us into her characters' heads.

> **Key Point**
>
> Look for what one character says about another and think about what this tells you about both.

How They Act and React

As in life, character is best seen through actions. In *Pride and Prejudice* Wickham charms everyone, including Elizabeth and the reader, but when he runs away with Lydia, we can all see him for what he is. Reactions are just as important. Darcy's reaction to the elopement of Lydia and Wickham makes Elizabeth and the reader see his true character.

> **Quick Test**
>
> 1. Without looking at your novel or your notes, write down the names of as many characters as you can in 10 minutes.

> **Key Words**
>
> naive narrator
> Bildungsroman
> function
> significance

Language and Structure

Quick Recall Quiz

You must be able to:

- Analyse the use of language and structure in a 19th-century novel
- Use relevant terminology.

Structure

- *Jane Eyre* starts near the beginning of the protagonist's life and tells her story in chronological order. The novel starts at Gateshead (her aunt's house), moves to Lowood school, then Thornfield Hall, on to Moor House and back again to Thornfield. These places represent five stages in Jane's development.
- Dickens divides Pip's 'expectations' into three stages, coinciding with the three volumes in which it was published: his childhood in Kent, his life in London as a young man, and his 'growing up' from the return of Magwitch to the end.
- In *A Christmas Carol* each chapter (Stave) is devoted to a different spirit. Dickens uses the power of his spirits to introduce 'flashbacks' to Scrooge's past life and 'flash forwards' to show how things might turn out.
- *Pride and Prejudice* uses letters as a form of flashback, filling in details about events in London, for example, which have previously been kept from the reader.
- *Frankenstein* starts with a series of letters from Walton, which lead us to Frankenstein's narrative, which in turn includes the creature's narrative. At the end we return to Walton's letters to bring the story up to date. This use of multiple narratives is quite common in the Gothic tradition and 'distances' the story, making it seem almost mythical.
- This technique is also used in *The Strange Case of Dr Jekyll and Mr Hyde*. The third-person narrative focuses on Mr Utterson, the reader knowing only what he knows, until the events leading up to Jekyll's death are revealed in his own and Dr Lanyon's narratives.
- The story told by Jonathan Small in *The Sign of Four* performs a similar function, fully explaining the mystery to the reader as well as to the narrator, Dr Watson.

> **Key Point**
>
> Although all stories follow more or less the same structure (see page 36), novelists arrange their narratives in very different ways.

The Narrative Voice

- Narrators in nineteenth-century novels always use Standard English. However, narratives can be very different in **tone**. In a first-person narrative this can reflect the character of the protagonist. In other novels, we can still detect a distinctive authorial voice.
- Is your narrator's tone:
  - friendly?
  - colloquial?
  - formal?
  - ironic?
  - authoritative?
- As you are reading, do you feel the narrator is talking to you personally?
- In *A Christmas Carol* Dickens tells the story as if we were in a room with him.
- Jane Austen's authorial voice is more detached – amused and ironic.

Speech

- Different characters can use language in different ways, adding to our understanding of them.
- They might:
  - use dialect or slang
  - use language in a comic way
  - have oddities or peculiarities of speech
  - use over-formal language
  - use language others might not understand.
- Magwitch's language, in *Great Expectations*, tells us a lot about him instantly. His pronunciation 'pint', 'wittles' places him in a different social class from Pip, and his cursing scares Pip.
- Sherlock Holmes uses technical terms to dazzle his listeners.

Descriptive Language

- Novelists use techniques in the same way as poets do to create mood and atmosphere. You might find that your novelist uses:
  - detail
  - varied sentence structures
  - alliteration, assonance and onomatopoeia
  - imagery
  - symbolism.
- Stevenson uses detail to build a vivid picture of Soho, where Hyde lives.
- In *Jane Eyre*, Brontë's description of the chestnut tree is **symbolic**.

Revise

> **Key Point**
>
> The question in the exam will include a short extract from your novel. You should analyse the language used in it in detail.

> **Key Words**
>
> tone
> colloquial
> formal
> ironic
> authoritative
> symbolic

> **Quick Test**
>
> What is meant by the following terms?
> 1. Dialect
> 2. Colloquial
> 3. Symbol
> 4. Flashback

Answer the question on the play you have studied.

Write your answer on a separate piece of paper.

1 *Julius Caesar* – Read the extract specified and answer the question below.

In this extract, Cassius is trying to persuade Brutus to join him in conspiring against Caesar.

Act 1 Scene 2

From

CASSIUS	Ye gods, it doth amaze me
	A man of such a feeble temper should
	So get the start of the majestic world
	And bear the palm alone.

To

| | Brutus and Caesar: what should be in that 'Caesar'? |
| | Why should that name be sounded more than yours? |

Explore how Shakespeare presents the attitude of Cassius to Caesar in this extract.

Write about:

- the attitudes and feelings shown in this extract
- how Shakespeare uses language to present them.

[30]

2 *Much Ado About Nothing* – Read the extract specified and answer the question below.

In this extract, the marriage between Hero and Claudio has just been arranged.

Act 2 Scene 1

From

| BEATRICE | Good Lord, for alliance! Thus goes everyone to the world but I, and I am sunburnt. I may sit in a corner and cry, 'Heigh-ho for a husband!' |

To

| BEATRICE | No, sure, my lord, my mother cried. But then there was a star danced, and under that was I born. |

How does Shakespeare present Beatrice in this extract?

Write about:

- the ideas and feelings expressed by Beatrice
- how Shakespeare uses language to present her in this extract.

[30]

3 *The Merchant of Venice* – Read the extract specified and answer the question below.

In this extract, Tubal has brought Shylock news about his daughter, who has eloped with Lorenzo.

Act 3 Scene 1

From

TUBAL   Your daughter spent in Genoa, as I heard, one night fourscore ducats.

To

SHYLOCK   Out upon her! Thou torturest me, Tubal. It was my turquoise; I had it of Leah when I was a bachelor. I would not have given it for a wilderness of monkeys.

Explore how Shakespeare presents Shylock's relationship with Jessica in this extract.

Write about:

- the nature of the relationship presented in this extract
- how he uses language to present the relationship.   [30]

4 *Romeo and Juliet*

Explore how Shakespeare presents the growing love of Romeo and Juliet. Write about the whole of the play. Write about:

- how their love develops during the play.
- the methods Shakespeare uses to present their love.   [30]

5 *Macbeth*

How does Shakespeare present Macbeth's feelings about power and ambition? Write about the whole of the play. Write about:

- Macbeth's feelings about power and ambition
- the methods Shakespeare uses to present Macbeth's feelings about power and ambition.   [30]

6 *The Tempest*

Write about how Shakespeare presents Ariel as a spirit and a slave. Write about the whole of the play. Write about:

- Ariel's relationship with Prospero and his position as a spirit and a slave
- the methods Shakespeare uses to present him as a spirit and a slave.   [30]

Answer the question on the novel you have studied.

1 Robert Louis Stevenson: *The Strange Case of Dr Jekyll and Mr Hyde*

> **Read Chapter 4**
>
> *From*
>
> When they had come within speech (which was just under the maid's eyes) the older man bowed and accosted the other with a very pretty manner of politeness.
>
> *To*
>
> And next moment, with ape-like fury, he was trampling his victim under foot and hailing down a storm of blows, under which the bones were audibly shattered and the body jumped upon the roadway.

In this extract, the murder of Sir Danvers Carew has been witnessed by a maid.

In this extract, how does Stevenson convey a sense of horror?

Write about:

- the sense of horror conveyed in the extract
- how he uses language, structure and form to convey a sense of horror in the extract.

[30]

2 Charles Dickens: *A Christmas Carol*

> **Read Stave (Chapter) 1**
>
> *From*
>
> 'Are there no prisons?' asked Scrooge.
>
> *To*
>
> 'It's not my business', Scrooge returned. 'It's enough for a man to understand his own business, and not to interfere with other people's. Mine occupies me constantly. Good afternoon, gentlemen!'

In this extract, two gentlemen have just asked Scrooge to make a contribution to charity to help the poor.

In this extract how does Dickens present Scrooge's attitude to other people? Write about:

- Scrooge's attitude in the extract
- how Dickens uses language, structure and form to present Scrooge's attitude in the extract.

[3

3 Jane Austen: *Pride and Prejudice*

> **Read Chapter 3**
>
> *From*
>
> Elizabeth Bennet had been obliged, by the scarcity of gentlemen, to sit down for two dances; and during part of that time, Mr Darcy had been standing near enough for her to overhear a conversation between him and Mr Bingley, who came from the dance for a few minutes to press his friend to join it.
>
> *To*
>
> 'You had better return to your partner and enjoy her smiles, for you are wasting your time with me'.

In this extract, Mr Darcy and his friend Mr Bingley are attending a ball at Meryton, where they meet the Bennet family.

In this extract, how does Austen present Mr Darcy's 'pride'?

Write about:

- the impression we get of Mr Darcy in the extract
- how Austen uses language, form and structure to present his pride in the extract.   **[30]**

4 Charles Dickens: *Great Expectations*

> **Read Chapter 21**
>
> *From*
>
>   'So you were never in London before?' said Mr Wemmick to me.
>
> *To*
>
>   We had got to the top of Holborn Hill before I knew that it was merely a mechanical appearance, and that he was not smiling at all.

In this extract, Pip has just arrived in London.

In this extract, how does Dickens present Pip's arrival in London?

Write about:

- the impressions we get of London and Pip's feelings about it in the extract
- how Dickens uses language, form and structure to present Pip's arrival in London in the extract.   **[30]**

5 Mary Shelley: *Frankenstein*

How does Shelley present Frankenstein's feelings about his creation?

Write about the whole novel. Write about:

- Frankenstein's feelings about the monster
- the methods Shelley uses to present Frankenstein's feelings about the monster.   **[30]**

6 Sir Arthur Conan Doyle: *The Sign of Four*

Write about how Conan Doyle presents Sherlock Holmes as a great detective.

Write about the whole novel. Write about:

- what makes Holmes a great detective
- the methods Conan Doyle uses to present Holmes in the novel as a whole.   **[30]**

7 Charlotte Brontë: *Jane Eyre*

Write about how Brontë presents Jane's feelings for Mr Rochester.

Write about the whole novel. Write about:

- Jane's changing feelings about Rochester
- the methods Brontë uses to convey Jane's feelings towards him.   **[30]**

Context

You must be able to:

- Understand the social, historical and cultural context of a modern text
- Use this understanding to evaluate the text.

Context

- You need to consider the social and historical context of your text. Think about the kind of society presented in the text.
- Think about 'cultural context', including genre and intended audience.

Time

- British society has changed a lot over the last 100 years. The set texts were written over a period of more than 60 years. They reflect increasing ethnic and cultural diversity.
- The Britain portrayed in them ranges from the hypocritical, class-conscious world of 1912 shown in *An Inspector Calls* to the violent, morally confused twenty-first-century world shown in *Pigeon English* and *DNA*.
- Taken together, the stories in *Telling Tales* paint a picture of a changing, diverse country.
- *An Inspector Calls*, written in 1945, looks back on an earlier **period**. This is 1912 seen from the perspective of a country that had experienced two world wars and in which many were looking forward a new, fairer society. Someone writing in 1912 would have seen things differently.
- Other texts set in earlier periods include:
  - *Blood Brothers* (written 1983, set 1950s–1970s)
  - *The History Boys* (written 2004, set 1980s)
  - *Anita and Me* (written 1996, set 1960/1970s).
  If you have studied one of these texts, think about why the writer has chosen the period and how his or her view of it is coloured by the events, ideas and attitudes of later years.
- *Animal Farm* (1945) and *Lord of the Flies* (1954) are not set at a particular time but they are the product of their time. *Animal Farm* is based on the Russian Revolution of 1917 and written at a time of great concern about totalitarianism. *Lord of the Flies* picks up on post-war concerns about what is meant by civilisation.
- Other texts – from *A Taste of Honey* (1956) to *Pigeon English* (2011) – reflect the world at the time they were written.

> ### Key Point
>
> Think about how your text reflects the concerns, attitudes and assumptions of the time and how these might differ from those of today.

Place

- The place where a text is set can help to give it a distinctive tone and atmosphere.
- Regional differences come out most strongly in the way characters speak:
  - Meera Syal presents the way people from a Black Country village speak by writing their speech phonetically, imitating the way they pronounce words.

- Helen in *A Taste of Honey* uses dialect expressions, such as 'I'd sooner be put on't street', reflecting the play's Lancashire setting.
- Some texts establish a sense of place by referring to specific **locations**:
  - *Blood Brothers* refers to places in and around Liverpool. The family's move from the city to a 'new town' marks the end of Act 1.
- Factors such as whether the setting is urban or rural, in the inner city or the suburbs, can be more important than the exact location:
  - *An Inspector Calls* takes place in a 'large suburban house' in a fictional industrial city.
- Some texts are set within a particular community or communities:
  - *Anita and Me* is about two very different communities co-existing: the village of Tollington and Meena's 'family' of Indians, who visit her house.

Cultural Context

- If you are studying a play, think about where and for whom it was/is performed.
  - *Blood Brothers* is a musical. In **musical theatre** characters use songs to express emotion and to move the story on.
  - *DNA* was written to be performed by and for young people.
- With prose, too, genre can be important:
  - *Never Let Me Go* is sometimes categorised as science fiction. It is about what could happen as a result of science.
  - Golding has called *Lord of the Flies* a **fable**, and *Animal Farm* is subtitled 'A fairy story'. What are the implications of these descriptions?

> **Key Point**
>
> Think about whether the place where your text is set makes a difference and, if so, how.

> **Quick Test**
>
> True or False?
> 1. A text's setting can determine how characters speak.
> 2. Characters in musicals express emotion by singing.
> 3. Science fiction is about things that have really happened.
> 4. Some texts are set in imaginary places.

> **Key Words**
>
> period
> location
> musical theatre
> fable

Themes

You must be able to:

- Identify themes in a modern text
- Write about how themes are presented.

Quick Recall Quiz

Identifying Themes

- Think about:
    - what the writer is saying
    - what the text makes you think about.
- Try answering, in one sentence, the question, 'What is the text about?'

  Lord of the Flies is about a group of boys stranded on an island.

- Ask yourself why the writer might want us to read about this situation and what it makes us think about. You are now moving from the situation to the themes.
- Try to come up with some new answers to the question. 'What is the text about?' You could make a spider diagram or a list:

- Some themes crop up again and again in the set texts. Here are some questions that might get you thinking about themes and ideas in your text:

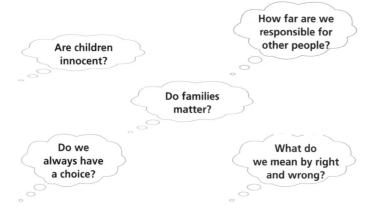

- Write down as many questions as you can that might come out of your text. Then try to find more than one answer to each, backing up your answer with evidence from the text.

Key Point

Themes in modern texts reflect current concerns, as well as issues that have always interested writers.

How Themes are Presented in Novels and Short Stories

Modern **prose** presents themes:

- through events:
  - In *Animal Farm*, a pig walks on its hind legs, showing that the pigs have become like the humans they replaced.
- through the narrator:
  - In *Anita and Me*, Meena draws lessons from her experiences about culture, friendship and growing up.
- through characters:
  - Steve in 'My Polish Teacher's Tie' represents identity and new possibilities to Carla.
- through what characters say:
  - In *Lord of the Flies*, the boys discuss issues like responsibility and survival.
- through motifs and symbols:
  - In 'The Odour of Chrysanthemums', the symbolism of the chrysanthemums is **ambiguous**. They represent unhappiness and death to Elizabeth, but she also associates them with happy memories.

How Themes are Presented in Plays

- The stage is a visual **medium**. It is about showing, not telling. Look in the stage directions for striking **images** which encapsulate themes:
  - The image of Mickey and Edward lying dead at the end of *Blood Brothers* brings together many of the play's themes.
  Remember, though, that play **scripts** can be interpreted differently by different **directors**, designers and actors. The images of one production may not be the same as those of another.
- Characters sometimes speak directly to the audience, bringing our attention to themes and issues:
  - In *The History Boys*, Scripps occasionally steps out of the action to reflect on the meaning of the boys' experiences.
- Mostly, we encounter themes and ideas through dialogue. There can be as many different points of view about an issue as there are characters on stage:
  - In *DNA* different ideas about guilt and honesty emerge as the characters discuss their actions.
- Some writers present us with several viewpoints and leave us to make up our own minds. Others give their preferred point of view to a character who is presented as being wiser or more trustworthy than others:
  - Inspector Goole in *An Inspector Calls* stands apart from the action, and his **interpretation** of what has happened can be seen as that of the writer.

> ### Key Point
>
> Our interpretation of themes and ideas can depend as much on our background and opinions as on those of the writer.

> ### Key Words
>
> diagram
> prose
> ambiguous
> medium
> image
> script
> director
> interpretation

> ### Quick Test
>
> In the theatre, which of the following influence how themes are presented?
> 1. The writer.
> 2. The director.
> 3. The actors.
> 4. The designer.

Characters

You must be able to:

- Write about how characters are presented in a modern text.

Prose: First-Person Narratives

- *Never Let Me Go*, *Anita and Me* and *Pigeon English* are first-person narratives, as are most of the stories in *Telling Tales*.
- Kathy in *Never Let Me Go* and Meena in *Anita and Me* write as adults looking back on their past. Harrison in *Pigeon English* tells us the story as it happens, like a diary.
- We might expect the adult narrators to have a greater understanding of their stories. Kathy (like the narrator in 'A Family Supper') seems quite detached and thoughtful. She writes as if she is trying to work out the meaning of the things she remembers.
- We can get an idea of what other characters think of the narrators, but this is always filtered through the narrator's perspective:
  - In *Never Let Me Go* Kathy does not always understand how others are responding to her, but the reader can make inferences from what she reports.
- Readers might draw conclusions about narrators which the narrators (and possibly writers) do not foresee:
  - Some readers might think Meena in *Anita and Me* comes across as a snob who looks down on her old friends.
- We might draw our own conclusions, different from those of the narrator, about other characters:
  - The narrator in 'Chemistry' is **naive** and his naivety makes him **unreliable**. At the end his assessment of other characters is called into question.

Prose: Third-Person Narratives

- Although it is a third-person narrative, the action in 'The Darkness Out There' is seen through the eyes of Sandra, so we learn about her thoughts and feelings. Similarly, in 'The Odour of Chrysanthemums' we share Elizabeth's thoughts.
- Golding is an **omniscient** narrator in *Lord of the Flies*. The character we are given most insight into is the protagonist, Ralph, but he also takes us into the minds of other characters.
- In *Lord of the Flies* there is a strong antagonist in Jack. Other characters, like Piggy and Simon, are important because of what they do in the story and because of what they represent.
- The characters in *Animal Farm* are different from conventional characters. Most of them are animals, which fits with the novel being called a 'fairy tale' or 'fable'. Some of them can be identified with real

> ### Key Point
>
> Modern novelists tell us about characters in the same ways as nineteenth-century novelists did.

historical figures, such as Lenin and Trotsky, but they can also be seen as 'types': for example, the honest worker, the spy, the tyrant.

Drama

- Sometimes **playwrights** tell us about characters in stage directions:
  - Arthur Birling in *An Inspector Calls* is described as 'a heavy-looking, rather portentous man in his middle fifties, with fairly easy manners but rather provincial in his speech'.
- Characters can reveal themselves, either directly to the audience or to other characters. Judy in *The Curious Incident of the Dog in the Night-Time* gives her side of things through letters:

> And your father is really patient, but I'm not. I get cross, even though I don't mean to […] and I felt really lonely.

- We learn about characters through dialogue. When Dakin and Scripps converse in *The History Boys* we hear their differing points of view, and we see that they are both intellectually, if not emotionally, mature as they can express themselves well, using sophisticated diction:

> No more the bike's melancholy long withdrawing roar as he dropped you off at the corner, your honour still intact.

- What really matters is what characters do:
  - Mrs Johnstone in *Blood Brothers* gives away one of her children. Why? And what are the consequences?

Key Point

Always remember when writing about a play, that it is a script to be performed. Actors can interpret characters in different ways.

Quick Test

Rearrange the letters to find a useful term:
1. TSGNROAPTOI
2. RRRTNAOA
3. GIDOULEA
4. GATES TIRODENIC

Key Words

naive narrator
unreliable narrator
omniscient narrator
playwright

Language and Structure

You must be able to:

- Analyse the use of language and structure in a modern text
- Use relevant terminology.

Prose

The Narrative Voice

- In *Pigeon English* the narrator appears to be speaking to the reader. Because of his age and background, he does not use Standard English. His use of dialect and slang ('donkey hours', 'hutious') gives a sense of where he lives and where he comes from.
- Some narrators, like Kathy in *Never Let Me Go*, adopt a colloquial tone while using Standard English, as if explaining things to a friend:

  I suppose that might sound odd.

- Others, like the boy in 'Chemistry', write about their lives in a more detached, adult way, also using Standard English.

Speech

- The language characters use adds to our understanding of them and the world they inhabit.
- Most of the boys in *Lord of the Flies* speak in Standard English, but in the rather clipped manner of public schoolboys in the 1950s:

  'Give him a fourpenny one!'

Piggy is shown to be from a different class:

  'I got the conch, ain't I Ralph?'

- In *Anita and Me*, the local people use dialect and their **accent** is shown phonetically:

  'Ay up, Mr K! Havin a bit of a do then?'

The Indian characters use Standard English except when speaking Punjabi.

Structure

- Most of the set texts are written in chronological order, although some of them (*Anita and Me*, *Never Let Me Go*) jump backwards and forwards as one event reminds the narrator of another.
- Think about how the text is divided. Why does the writer decide to start a new chapter at a certain point?

> **Key Point**
>
> In first-person narratives, the language of the narration can reflect the background of the narrator.

- Look for anything different or odd about your text's structure:
  - Some sections of *Pigeon English* start with the pigeon narrating, distinguished from the rest of the text by being in italics.

Drama

Language

- **Dialogue** can reflect where the play is set and also tell us about the characters
- The class divisions of *Blood Brothers* are shown in the contrast between the way the Johnstone and Lyons families speak:

> EDWARD: Do you…Do you really? Goodness, that's fantastic.

> MICKEY: Come on, bunk under y'fence, y'Ma won't see y'.

- Christopher in *The Curious Incident of the Dog in the Night-Time* speaks in a deliberate, rather impersonal way:

> I remember 20 July 2006. I was 9 years old. It was a Saturday.

Structure

- Most plays are in two **acts**, with an **interval** between them. Because of this, writers usually build up to a **turning point** at the end of Act 1, leaving the audience wanting to know what happens next.
- When *An Inspector Calls* was written, most plays had a three-act structure, so both Act 1 and Act 2 end with turning points.
- *An Inspector Calls* and *A Taste of Honey* have clear act and **scene** divisions. Within each section, action is continuous and happens in one place.
- In other, more recent plays the action flows from one short scene to another, time and place changing frequently.
- Look for anything unusual about your play's structure, for example:
  - At the end of *An Inspector Calls*, it looks as though the play is about to start all over again.
  - In *The History Boys* characters seem to jump out of the 'past' to speak to us and then return seamlessly.

> ### Key Point
>
> When we discuss language in a play we are discussing the language the characters use.

> ### Key Words
>
> accent
> dialogue
> act
> interval
> turning point
> scene

Quick Test

1. Can a narrator use a colloquial tone and Standard English?
2. In the same play, which is longer, a scene or an act?
3. What would the use of dialect tell us about a character?
4. Are the events in a play or novel always in chronological order?

Answer the question on the novel you have studied.

1 Mary Shelley: *Frankenstein*

> **Read Chapter 5**
>
> *From*
>> It was on a dreary night of November that I beheld the accomplishment of my toils.
>
> *To*
>> His yellow skin scarcely covered the work of muscles and arteries beneath; his hair was of a lustrous black, and flowing; his teeth of a pearly whiteness; but these luxuriances only formed a more horrid contrast with his watery eyes, that seemed almost of the same colour as the dun white sockets in which they were set, his shrivelled complexion and straight black lips.

In this extract, Victor Frankenstein describes seeing the monster he has created.

In this extract, how does Shelley present Frankenstein's feelings about his creation?
Write about:

- Frankenstein's reaction to the monster in this extract
- how Shelley uses language, form and structure to convey Frankenstein's feelings about the monster in this extract.

[30]

2 Sir Arthur Conan Doyle: *The Sign of Four*

> **Read Chapter 6**
>
> *From*
>> He held down the lamp to the floor, and as he did so I saw for the second time that night a startled, surprised look come over his face.
>
> *To*
>> 'What then?' I asked.
>>
>> 'Why, we have got him, that's all', said he.

In this extract, Holmes and Watson are searching Pondicherry House for clues about the murder of Bartholomew Sholto.

In this extract, how does Conan Doyle present Sherlock Holmes as a great detective?
Write about:

- what Sherlock Holmes does and says in this extract
- how Conan Doyle uses language, form and structure to present Holmes as a great detective in this extract.

[30]

3 Charlotte Brontë: *Jane Eyre*

> **Read Chapter 12**
>
> *From*
>> I was in the mood for being useful, or at least officious, I think, for I now drew near him again.
>
> *To*
>> He looked at me when I said this; he had hardly turned his eyes in my direction before.

In this extract, Jane meets Mr Rochester for the first time.

In this extract, how does Brontë present Jane's feelings about Mr Rochester?
Write about:
* how Jane describes and reacts to Rochester in this extract
* how Brontë uses language, structure and form to convey Jane's feelings towards Rochester in this extract. [30]

4 Robert Louis Stevenson: *The Strange Case of Dr Jekyll and Mr Hyde*

How does Stevenson convey an atmosphere of mystery and horror?
Write about the whole novel. Write about:

* the atmosphere of mystery and horror in the novel
* the methods Stevenson uses to convey an atmosphere of mystery and horror. [30]

5 Charles Dickens: *A Christmas Carol*

How does Dickens present Scrooge's attitude to other people?
Write about the whole novel. Write about:

* Scrooge's attitude to other people
* how Dickens presents Scrooge's attitude. [30]

6 Jane Austen: *Pride and Prejudice*

How does Austen present Mr Darcy's 'pride'?
Write about the whole novel. Write about:

* to what extent and in what ways Darcy is proud
* the methods Austen uses to present his 'pride'. [30]

7 Charles Dickens: *Great Expectations*

Write about how Dickens presents Pip's journey into adulthood.
Write about the whole novel. Write about:

* the stages in Pip's journey into adulthood
* the methods Dickens uses to present Pip's journey into adulthood. [30]

Answer the question on the text you have studied.

Your answer should be in note form, using bullet points.

1. J. B. Priestley: *An Inspector Calls*

   Make notes on the character and significance of Inspector Goole in *An Inspector Calls*.

   Write down five statements about the character and give evidence from the text in support of each one. [10]

2. Willy Russell: *Blood Brothers*

   Make notes on the character and significance of Mrs Lyons in *Blood Brothers*.

   Write down five statements about the character and give evidence from the text in support of each one. [10]

3. Alan Bennett: *The History Boys*

   Make notes on the character and significance of Dakin in *The History Boys*.

   Write down five statements about the character and give evidence from the text in support of each one. [10]

4. Dennis Kelly: *DNA*

   Make notes on the character and significance of Leah in *DNA*.

   Write down five statements about the character and give evidence from the text in support of each one. [10]

5. Simon Stephens: *The Curious Incident of the Dog in the Night-Time*

   Make notes on the character and significance of Christopher in *The Curious Incident of the Dog in the Night-Time*.

   Write down five statements about the character and give evidence from the text in support of each one. [10]

6. Shelagh Delaney: *A Taste of Honey*

   Make notes on the character and significance of Jo in *A Taste of Honey*.

   Write down five statements about the character and give evidence from the text in support of each one. [10]

7. William Golding: *Lord of the Flies*

   Make notes on the character and significance of Simon in *Lord of the Flies*.

   Write down five statements about the character and give evidence from the text in support of each one. [10]

8 AQA Anthology: *Telling Tales*

Make notes on the character and significance of Carla in 'My Polish Teacher's Tie'.

Write down five statements about the character and give evidence from the text in support of each one. [10]

9 George Orwell: *Animal Farm*

Make notes on the character and significance of Boxer in *Animal Farm*.

Write down five statements about the character and give evidence from the text in support of each one. [10]

10 Kazuo Ishiguro: *Never Let Me Go*

Make notes on the character and significance of Tommy in *Never Let Me Go*.

Write down five statements about the character and give evidence from the text in support of each one. [10]

11 Meera Syal: *Anita and Me*

Make notes on the character and significance of Anita in *Anita and Me.*

Write down five statements about the character and give evidence from the text in support of each one. [10]

12 Stephen Kelman: *Pigeon English*

Make notes on the character and significance of Harrison in *Pigeon English*.

Write down five statements about the character and give evidence from the text in support of each one. [10]

Context

Quick Recall Quiz

You must be able to:

- Understand the social, historical and cultural context of poetry
- Use this understanding in your evaluation of texts.

Time and Place

- Many of the 'Love and Relationships' poems focus on personal memories, and the poets evoke a sense of the time and place they are remembering:
  - Carol Ann Duffy's memories of her mother in 'Before You Were Mine' include specific references that 'place' her mother in terms of time (Marilyn), place (Portobello) and even religion (Mass).
  - Charles Causley freezes his parents in time, with references to their clothes and their picnic (Thermos, HP Sauce bottle), although he ends by teasing the reader with his assertion that the place is made up.
- Some 'Power and Conflict' poems, such as 'Poppies', can also be seen in a personal context, but more often they are about historical events, and some knowledge and understanding of these events can be helpful:
  - 'Exposure' is both personal and historical as it is based around Owen's own experiences in the First World War. His reactions are personal and immediate.
  - 'Remains' is inspired by the memories of a soldier who fought in the recent war in Iraq.
- The attitudes of the poets to their subjects should be seen in the context of their own time:
  - 'The Charge of the Light Brigade', inspired by a newspaper article, reflects popular sentiment at the time by criticising the orders given to the Brigade but glorifying the soldiers themselves.
- When a poet writes about something in the past, consider both the time when it was written and the time it was written about.
  - Browning's **dramatic monologues** use historical settings to present characters that must have been shocking as well as fascinating to his huge Victorian readership, reflecting an interest in psychology.
  - 'Kamikaze' presents the attitudes of Japanese people in the Second World War to a modern audience.

Key Point

When comparing poems from the anthology, you must think about similarities and differences between their contexts.

The Romantic Movement

- Blake, Byron, Shelley and Wordsworth were all part of the Romantic **movement** in literature. An understanding of Romanticism will inform your reading of their poetry.
- In the eighteenth century most English poets admired and imitated Greek and Latin poetry. Intellectuals valued logic and reason above feelings.

- The Romantics rebelled against this. They used more traditional forms of poetry, such as the **ballad**, using simpler rhythms and rhyme schemes and more everyday language. They sometimes wrote about ordinary people.
- Most of their poetry, whether **lyric** poetry (short poems about feelings) like 'Love's Philosophy' or the lengthy autobiographical 'Prelude', focuses on emotions, which they often associated with nature.
- They could also be political, inspired by events like the French Revolution to write anti-establishment poems like 'London'.
- Later poets continued to be influenced by the Romantics. You can see this in Hardy and Mew, and modern poets like Sheers and Hughes.

Social Issues

Gender is important in several of the poems:

- The relationship between the farmer and his bride in Charlotte Mew's poem seems to have more to do with power than love. The traditional roles the man and woman are given create misery for both.
- To the Duke in 'My Last Duchess', his wife is just a possession.

Ideas about cultural identity are central to 'Checking Out Me History'. The poet is angry about being given a 'white' version of history when growing up in the British Empire.

'London' is concerned with the poverty, disease and inequality of its time.

> **Key Point**
>
> 'Context' refers to literary traditions and movements as well as to social and historical influences.

 **Quick Test**

True or False?
1. Romantic poets were not political.
2. When a poem is set does not matter.
3. Wordsworth is a Romantic poet.
4. Lyric poetry is about feelings.

> **Key Words**
>
> dramatic monologue
> movement
> ballad
> lyric

Themes

You must be able to:

- Identify themes in poetry
- Compare how themes are presented.

Themes and Ideas in the Anthology

- The poems in the anthology have been grouped together under two broad themes, 'Love and Relationships' and 'Power and Conflict'. You will have studied one of these 'clusters'.
- Consider what aspect of the main theme the poet is writing about.
- Look for other themes, ideas and issues that might be present.
- Consider the poet's **attitudes** to these themes.
- Think about how the poets' backgrounds may have influenced their attitudes to the themes.
- Connect the poems through their treatment of themes, looking for both similarities and differences.

How Themes are Presented in Poetry

- Because most poems are quite short, they tend not to explore themes and ideas in great depth or detail.
- Poems often focus on an incident or moment in life, perhaps an anecdote or a snapshot of someone's feelings at a certain time.
- Poems that tell a story include 'My Last Duchess', 'The Charge of the Light Brigade' (Power and Conflict), 'Porphyria's Lover' and 'The Farmer's Bride' (Love and Relationships).
- Some poems, like 'The Charge of the Light Brigade', tell a story and then reflect on its meaning. Others, like 'Porphyria's Lover', do not include the poet's thoughts, leaving readers to infer meaning.
- Many poems have no story but tell us directly about the poet's thoughts and feelings. Some poets express strong views and feelings, as in 'Checking Out Me History' and Sonnet 29 'I think of thee!'.
- Others, like 'Neutral Tones', present us with images and experiences, leaving us to infer the poet's attitudes and feelings.
- At times it is impossible to 'work out' what the poet's feelings are, as the poem is **ambiguous**. The poet might not have the answer or might want readers to come up with their own answers.

Key Point

The same poem can mean different things to different people. Your response and interpretation is as valid as anyone else's – and it is your response that the examiner wants to read.

Connections

- In the exam you are required to compare two poems (one named) from the cluster you have studied. Here are some questions you could ask when comparing poems during revision.

Love and Relationships

- What sort of relationship is it?

Lovers

Husband and wife

Parents and children

Other family relationships

Friends

- What else is the poem about?

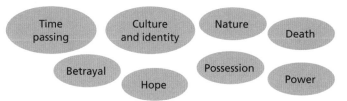

Time passing • Culture and identity • Nature • Death • Betrayal • Hope • Possession • Power

- What feelings does the **voice** or **persona** in the poem have about the subject of the poem?

Love • Jealousy • Indifference • Disgust • Gratitude • Obsession • Admiration • Anger

What are the feelings of the subject?

Power and Conflict

- What kind of conflict is it?

A battle • An argument • A war • A psychological conflict

- What kind of power is it?

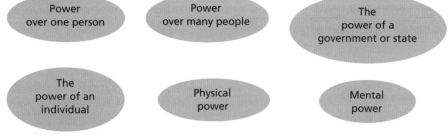

Power over one person • Power over many people • The power of a government or state • The power of an individual • Physical power • Mental power

Or is it about lack of power?
What else is the poem about?

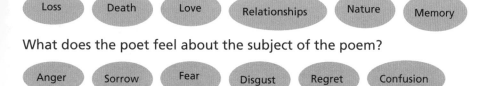

Loss • Death • Love • Relationships • Nature • Memory

What does the poet feel about the subject of the poem?

Anger • Sorrow • Fear • Disgust • Regret • Confusion

If there are other people in the poem, how do they feel?
How does it make you feel?

Key Point

You will also need to think about and comment on themes and ideas when writing about unseen poetry.

Quick Test

1. Can a poem be about conflict and relationships?
2. Can the title of the cluster help you think about themes?
3. Should you write about your response to the poems?
4. Will you always know what the poet's feelings are?

Key Words

attitude
ambiguous
voice
persona

Language

You must be able to:

- Analyse poets' use of language, using appropriate terminology
- Compare how poets use language.

Sound

- Look at the ways poets use sound. Read the poems out loud or listen to someone else reading them.
- The most obvious way in which sound reflects meaning is through **onomatopoeia**:
  - Elizabeth Barrett Browning uses the phrase 'rustle thy boughs' to convey the sound of the wind in the trees (Sonnet 29).
- **Alliteration** can convey different moods, according to the sound used:
  - In 'Kamikaze' Beatrice Garland uses 's' sounds (also known as sibilance) to reflect the peaceful mood, as she describes fish 'flashing silver as their bellies swivelled toward the sun'.
  - She adds 'sh' within words as well as at the beginning of them ('shoals of fishes flashing'), adding to the mood.
- Browning uses plosive sounds to sinister effect, almost as if he were spitting, in 'Porphyria's Lover':

> Blushed bright beneath my burning kiss.

- **Assonance** is the use of a series of similar vowel sounds to create patterns and atmosphere:

> but as we moved on through the afternoon light ('Winter Swans')

- Poets often repeat not just sounds, but whole words and phrases, emphasising their importance, as in Blake's 'London':

> In every cry of every Man

Or reflecting the repetition of an action and its impact, as in 'The Charge of the Light Brigade':

> Cannon to the right of them.
> Cannon to the left of them.

- A phrase which is repeated at the end of each stanza is often called a **refrain**.

> ### Key Point
>
> The poet Coleridge defined poetry as 'the best words in the best order'. Poets choose their words carefully.

Diction

- When poets use a **persona**, their choice of words helps to create the character. Browning, in 'My Last Duchess', uses colloquial language to make it seem as if the persona is having a conversation:

> A heart – how shall I say? – too soon made glad

- In 'Singh Song!' Daljit Nagra changes the spelling of words to reflect his persona's accent:

> But ven nobody in, I do di lock.

- In 'Checking Out Me History', John Agard speaks as himself but he uses the dialect of his childhood to convey both character and situation:

> Dem tell me bout de man who discover de balloon

Key Point

Think about the 'voice' in the poem. Is the poet writing as him/herself or as a character – a 'persona'?

- Other poets use specialised or technical vocabulary to give us a sense of a character, as Seamus Heaney does in 'Follower':

> He would set the wing
> And fit the bright steel-pointed sock.

- You might see self-consciously 'poetic' or even archaic (outdated) words used for effect, as in Barrett Browning's use of 'thee' rather than 'you'.

Imagery

- Imagery is central to our understanding of how poets create meaning. When a poet compares something to something else, think about why that comparison has been made.
- In 'The Farmer's Bride' Charlotte Mew's persona uses a series of similes to describe his bride:

> Straight and slight as a young larch tree,
> Sweet as the first wild violets, she.

He compares her to things that he, as a farmer, would be familiar with, and he describes her as a wild thing, part of nature.

- In 'Winter Swans' Owen Sheers uses the metaphor of 'porcelain' to convey the fragility and beauty of the swans.
- In 'Love's Philosophy' Shelley uses pathetic fallacy, personifying nature:

> See the mountains kiss high heaven.

- In 'Ozymandias' his description of the statue can be read as a symbol of the futility of power and the passing of time.

Key Words

onomatopoeia
alliteration
assonance
refrain
persona
archaic
simile
metaphor
symbol

Quick Test

Give the correct term for:
1. The use of a word that sounds like what it describes.
2. Writing about a thing or idea as if it were a person.
3. Starting a series of words with the same sound.
4. A character in a poem who speaks in the first person.

Poetry

Form and Structure

Quick Recall Quiz

You must be able to:

- Analyse poets' use of form and structure, using appropriate terminology
- Compare how poets use form and structure.

Stanzas

- Look at how many **stanzas** there are and whether they are equal in length.
- Hardy's 'Neutral Tones' is divided into four stanzas of four lines each. This is the traditional form of the ballad, a poem that tells a story. It is about strong feelings, so you might expect the poet to lose control. Instead he imposes order on his emotions. What effect does the tension between form and content have on the reader?
- Other poets, like Tennyson in 'The Charge of the Light Brigade', vary the length of their stanzas. If this is the case, think about what is happening in the poem when a poet adds an extra line or includes a very short stanza.
- Think about when the poet starts a new stanza. Is there a new idea being introduced? Or is there a change in place or time?
- Where a poem is not divided into stanzas, think about why this might be. Browning's 'Porphyria's Lover' is a dramatic monologue, in which the poet gives the impression that the persona is speaking to us spontaneously. Perhaps he does not stop to think.
- Single-stanza poems can have their own internal structure. Sonnets, such as Sonnet 29, follow strict rules, in this case those of the **Petrarchan sonnet**. These consist of an **octave** (8 lines) followed by a **sestet** (6 lines). Traditionally the change from the octave to the sestet reflects a turn (called the **volta**) or change in the argument or mood. You may also come across **Shakespearean sonnets**, which consist of three **quatrains** followed by a rhyming couplet.
- If a line ends with a punctuation mark, it is called **end-stopping**. If a poet continues across lines or even stanzas without a pause, it is called **enjambment**. Think about why the poet would choose one or the other.

> **Key Point**
>
> 'Stanza' is Italian for 'room', so if a poem is a house the stanzas are its rooms.

Rhyme

- **Rhyme** is easy to spot but can be difficult to comment on. It can be used to make us laugh, to emphasise something, or to give a sense of order.
- The simplest form of rhyme is the **rhyming couplet**, rhyming one line with the next. This is an almost childish use of rhyme, so when it is used in a poem like 'The Farmer's Bride' it could be telling us something about the persona.
- Rhyming couplets are also used to underline important points.

The traditional rhyme scheme of the ballad is *abab.* This is used in 'London'. Although 'Neutral Tones' has the shape of a ballad, the rhyme scheme is different.

Some poets use more complex rhyme schemes, while others use rhyme occasionally for effect, sometimes within lines (internal rhyme). You might come across sight or eye rhymes, where the words look as if they should rhyme but do not, for example, 'rough' and 'bough'. Many poets use 'half rhyme' (also known as 'slant rhyme' and 'pararhyme'), where the final consonants agree but the vowel sounds do not match, softening the effect of the rhyme. Heaney rhymes 'pluck' and 'sock' in 'Follower'.

Rhythm

A poem's **rhythm** comes from its pattern of **stressed** and unstressed **syllables**. You can get a sense of this by reading a poem aloud. Some poems have a very strong rhythm. 'The Charge of the Light Brigade' is written in dactyls (a stressed syllable followed by two unstressed syllables), giving a sense of the pounding of horses' hooves and cannons:

> **Half** a league **half** a league

One of the most commonly used **metres** is the iambic pentameter. This is quite a gentle rhythm, often compared to a heartbeat. Wordsworth uses it in 'The Prelude':

> And **as** I **rose** up**on** the **stroke**, my **boat**

Contemporary poets are less likely to use strong rhythmical patterns, though there are exceptions like 'Checking Out Me History'. However, if you listen carefully you should still hear a rhythm.

If you hear a rhythm, think about how the poet uses it to create the mood and tone of the poem.

Poetry that has a regular metre but no rhyme is called **blank verse**. Poetry that has no regular pattern, either of rhyme or metre, is called **free verse**.

 Key Point

When looking at rhyme and metre, look for patterns and variations in patterns.

 Key Words

stanza
Petrarchan sonnet
octave
sestet
volta
Shakespearean sonnet
quatrain
end-stopping
enjambment
rhyme
rhyming couplet
rhythm
stress
syllable
metre
blank verse
free verse

Quick Test

Give the correct term for:
1. A set of two lines that rhyme.
2. A rhyme within a line.
3. A poem that tells a story in four-line stanzas.
4. Poetry that has no regular pattern.

Unseen Poetry

Quick Recall Qui

You must be able to:

- Respond to and analyse a poem you have not seen before
- Compare two unseen poems.

Approaching an Unseen Poem

- In Section C of Paper 2 you will be given two poems you have never seen before. You will have to answer a question about one of them, before comparing them.
- Start by reading the poem to gain a general sense of its themes, mood and atmosphere. Then use your knowledge of poetry to 'interrogate' the text. Here are some questions you could ask yourself when reading an unseen poem.

Title	What does it make you think about?
	Does it tell you what the poem is about or is it ambiguous?
Speaker	Is the voice in the poem that of the poet or a persona?
	Who, if anyone, is being addressed?
Setting	Where and when is it set?
	Does the place change?
	Does the time change?
Form and structure	How is it arranged?
	When and why does the poet start a new stanza?
	Is there a strong regular rhythm? If so, what effect does it have?
	Does it rhyme? If so, is there a regular rhyme scheme? What is the effect of the rhyme?
Language	How does the poet use sound?
	What kind of vocabulary/register does the poet use?
	What sort of imagery does the poet use?
	Is there anything else interesting about the language?
Themes and ideas	Is there a story? If so, what is it?
	What do you think the poem is really about?
	Is more than one theme touched on?
	What do you think is the poet's attitude / point of view?
Personal response	What does the poem make you think about?
	How does it make you feel?

Key Point

To answer the questions, you will need all the skills you have learned studying poems from the anthology.

Comparing Unseen Poems

- You will be asked to compare a poem which you have already written about with another poem on a similar theme.
- Be careful not to repeat everything you have already said about the first poem. Focus on the second poem but make sure that every point you make refers back to the first one.
- You could go through the new poem line by line, linking it to the first poem as you go.
- Or you could take different aspects of the poem in turn, starting a new paragraph for each.
- Whichever way you approach the comparison, consider:

<table>
<tr><td>Structure and form</td><td>Brown's structure is regular, the four stanzas of four lines giving a sense of order and logic, whereas Smith's stanzas vary in length, as if her memories are random and disordered.</td></tr>
<tr><td>Language</td><td>Brown's use of harsh-sounding words such as 'rough' and 'dour' contrast with the softness of Smith's 'silken voice' and 'shuffling step'.</td></tr>
<tr><td>Imagery</td><td>Both poets use imagery connected with nature but in very different ways...</td></tr>
<tr><td>How the poets approach the theme</td><td>Both poems focus on the child's relationship with her father.</td></tr>
<tr><td>The poets' feelings and attitude</td><td>Unlike Brown, Smith remembers her father with affection.</td></tr>
<tr><td>Your response to the poems</td><td>Brown conveys a sense of regret and anger, whereas the way Smith describes her feelings, although sad, is somehow comforting.</td></tr>
</table>

Back up every point you make with short quotations from both poems. Try to use correct **terminology** but remember that you do not get marks just for 'spotting' things like alliteration and metaphors. You must show that you understand how they are used and their effect on the reader.

Key Point

Remember to comment on both similarities and differences.

Quick Test

Would you use the following connectives to express a similarity or a difference?
1. Both...and
2. whereas...
3. On the other hand...
4. Neither...nor

Key Word

terminology

Answer the question on the text you have studied.

Your answer should be in note form, using bullet points.

1 J. B. Priestley: *An Inspector Calls*

How does Priestley write about attitudes to women in *An Inspector Calls*?

Write down five statements and give evidence from the text to support each statement. [10

2 Willy Russell: *Blood Brothers*

How does Russell write about fate in *Blood Brothers*?

Write down five statements and give evidence from the text to support each statement. [10

3 Alan Bennett: *The History Boys*

How does Bennett write about history in *The History Boys*?

Write down five statements and give evidence from the text to support each statement. [10

4 Dennis Kelly: *DNA*

How does Kelly write about guilt and responsibility in *DNA*?

Write down five statements and give evidence from the text to support each statement. [10

5 Simon Stephens: *The Curious Incident of the Dog in the Night-Time*

How does Stephens explore ideas about families in *The Curious Incident of the Dog in the Night-Time*?

Write down five statements and give evidence from the text to support each statement. [10

6 Shelagh Delaney: *A Taste of Honey*

How does Delaney present ideas about love in *A Taste of Honey*?

Write down five statements and give evidence from the text to support each statement. [10

7 William Golding: *Lord of the Flies*

How does Golding explore ideas about civilisation in *Lord of the Flies*?

Write down five statements and give evidence from the text to support each statement. [10

8 AQA Anthology: *Telling Tales*

How does Lawrence write about death in 'The Odour of Chrysanthemums'?

Write down five statements and give evidence from the text to support each statement. [10

9. George Orwell: *Animal Farm*

   How does Orwell present ideas about oppression in *Animal Farm*?

   Write down five statements and give evidence from the text to support each statement. [10]

10. Kazuo Ishiguro: *Never Let Me Go*

    How does Ishiguro write about friendship in *Never Let Me Go*?

    Write down five statements and give evidence from the text to support each statement. [10]

11. Meera Syal: *Anita and Me*

    How does Syal write about living in two cultures in *Anita and Me*?

    Write down five statements and give evidence from the text to support each statement. [10]

12. Stephen Kelman: *Pigeon English*

    How does Kelman present ideas about violence in *Pigeon English*?

    Write down five statements and give evidence from the text to support each statement. [10]

Answer the question on the cluster you have studied. You will need your copy of the Anthology.

Either

1 Look at how Owen describes conflict in 'Exposure' and answer the following questions.

    a) What person is it written in? _____

    b) What tense is used? _____

    c) What effect do the person and tense have? _____

    _____

    d) Briefly describe where and when it is set. _____

    e) How is it organised? _____

    f) What is the effect of having four equal lines followed by a shorter line in each stanza?

    _____

    g) Look at the last line of each stanza and explain how and why the refrain changes.

    _____

    h) Find two examples of personification / pathetic fallacy in the first three stanzas. Explain their effect.

    _____

    _____

    i) Find an example of onomatopoeia and explain its effect. _____

    _____

    j) What is the significance of the scene Owen describes in stanza 6, beginning 'Slowly our ghosts drag home'?

    _____ [20

Or

2 Look at the way Hardy presents a relationship in 'Neutral Tones' and answer the following questions.

    a) What person is it written in? _____

    b) What tense is used? _____

    c) What effect do the person and tense have? _____

    _____

    d) Briefly describe where and when it is set. _____

    e) How is it organised? _____

    f) Describe the rhyme scheme and explain its effect.

    _____

    g) Identify the simile in the second stanza. What does it tell us about how the woman feels about the speaker? _____

    _____

h) What is the effect of the ellipsis at the end of the third stanza? _____

_____

i) Find an example of alliteration and explain its effect. _____

_____

j) What does the description of the scene in the first stanza tell us about the relationship?

_____

_____ [20]

3 Read the poem below and answer the questions that follow.

The Song of the Old Mother by W. B. Yeats

I rise in the dawn, and I kneel and blow
Till the seed of the fire flicker and glow;
And then I must scrub and bake and sweep
Till stars are beginning to blink and peep;
And the young lie long and dream in their bed
Of the matching ribbons for bosom and head,
And their day goes over in idleness,
And they sing if the wind but lift a tress:
While I must work because I am old,
And the seed of the fire gets feeble and cold.

a) Is the voice in the poem that of the poet or a persona? What sort of person is speaking?

_____

b) Where and when is it set? _____

c) Is there a strong, regular rhythm? If so, what effect does it have? _____

_____

d) Does it rhyme? If so, is there a regular rhyme scheme? What is the effect of the rhyme?

_____

e) What sort of imagery does the poet use? _____

f) Is there a story? If so, what is it? _____

g) What is the significance of the line 'And the seed of the fire gets feeble and cold'?

_____

h) What do you think the poem is really about? _____

i) What do you think is the poet's attitude / point of view? _____

_____

j) How does the poem make you feel? _____

_____ [20]

1 Answer the question on the cluster you have studied.

Write your answer on a separate piece of paper.

Either

a) Compare the way poets present the effect of war on people in 'Kamikaze' and one other poem from 'Power and Conflict'. [30]

Or

b) Compare the way poets present ideas about love in 'Love's Philosophy' and one other poem from 'Love and Relationships'. [30]

2 Read the two poems below and answer both questions.

Sonnet

by John Clare

I love to see the summer beaming forth

And white wool sack clouds sailing to the north

I love to see the wild flowers come again

And Mare drops stain with gold the meadow drain

And water lilies whiten on the floods

Where reed clumps rustle like a wind shook wood

Where from her hiding place the Moor Hen pushes

And seeks her flag nest floating in bull rushes

I like the willow leaning half way o'er

The clear deep lake to stand upon its shore

I love the hay grass when the flower head swings

To summer winds and insects happy wings

That sport about the meadow the bright day

And see bright beetles in the clear lake play.

The Eagle

by Alfred Tennyson

He clasps the crag with crooked hands,
Close to the sun in lonely lands,
Ring'd with the azure world he stands.

The wrinkled sea beneath him crawls;
He watches from his mountain walls,
And like a thunderbolt he falls.

a) How does Clare present his feelings about nature in 'Sonnet'?
Write your answer on a separate piece of paper. [24]

b) Both 'Sonnet' and 'The Eagle' describe aspects of nature. What are the similarities and differences between the way the poets present feelings about the natural world?

_____

_____

_____

_____

_____

_____

_____

_____

_____

_____

_____

_____

_____

[8]

English Language

Read the passage below and answer the questions that follow.

In this extract from 'Tickets, Please', D. H. Lawrence describes the trams of an English mining area, and the people who work on them, during the First World War.

To ride on these cars is always an adventure. Since we are in war-time, the drivers are men unfit for active service: cripples and hunchbacks. So they have the spirit of the devil in them. The ride becomes a steeple-chase.[1] Hurray! We have leapt in a clear jump over the canal bridges – now for the four-lane corner. With a shriek and a trail of sparks we are clear again. To be sure, a tram often leaps the rails – but what matter! It sits in a ditch till other trams come to haul it out. It is quite common for a car, packed with one solid mass of living people, to come to a dead halt in the midst of unbroken blackness, the heart of nowhere on a dark night, and for the driver and the girl conductor[2] to call, 'All get off – car's on fire!' Instead, however, of rushing out in a panic, the passengers stolidly reply: 'Get on – get on! We're not coming out. We're stopping where we are. Push on, George.' So till flames actually appear.

The reason for this reluctance to dismount is that the nights are howlingly cold, black, and windswept, and a car is a haven of refuge. From village to village the miners travel, for a change of cinema, of girl, of pub. The trams are desperately packed. Who is going to risk himself in the black gulf outside, to wait perhaps an hour for another tram, then to see the forlorn notice 'Depot Only', because there is something wrong! Or to greet a unit of three bright cars all so tight with people that they sail past with a howl of derision. Trams that pass in the night.

This, the most dangerous tram-service in England, as the authorities themselves declare, with pride, is entirely conducted by girls, and driven by rash young men, a little crippled, or by delicate young men, who creep forward in terror. The girls are fearless young hussies.[3] In their ugly blue uniform, skirts up to their knees, shapeless old peaked caps on their heads, they have all the *sang-froid*[4] of an old non-commissioned officer. With a tram packed with howling colliers, roaring hymns downstairs and a sort of antiphony[5] of obscenities upstairs, the lasses are perfectly at their ease. They pounce on the youths who try to evade their ticket-machine. They push off the men at the end of their distance. They are not going to be done in the eye – not they. They fear nobody – and everybody fears them.

'Hello, Annie!'

'Hello, Ted!'

'Oh, mind my corn, Miss Stone. It's my belief you've got a heart of stone, for you've trod on it again.'

'You should keep it in your pocket,' replies Miss Stone, and she goes sturdily upstairs in her high boots.

'Tickets, please.'

---

[1] *steeple-chase* – a horse race over fences

[2] *conductor* – someone who sells tickets on a tram, bus or train

[3] *hussies* – cheeky or immoral girls

[4] *sang-froid* – coolness

[5] *antiphony* – singing in responses (usually in hymns)

1 According to the passage, which of the following statements are TRUE?
Tick the correct answers.

a) The trams are driven by women. ☐

b) Trams often come off the rails. ☐

c) Passengers are reluctant to leave the trams when told there's a fire. ☐

d) The girls are easily shocked. ☐

e) People are afraid of the girl conductors. ☐

f) Riding on the trams is a very boring experience. ☐

g) Not many people use the trams. ☐

h) The kind of people who work on the trams has changed because of the war. ☐ [4 marks]

2 Look in detail at the first paragraph. How does the writer use language here to describe the atmosphere on the trams?

You could include the writer's choice of:
*   words and phrases
*   language features and techniques
*   sentence forms.

Write your answer on a separate piece of paper. [8 marks]

3 Now think about the whole text.

This extract comes near the beginning of a short story.

How has the writer structured the text to interest you as a reader?

You could write about:
*   what the writer focuses on at the beginning
*   how and why he changes this focus
*   any other structural features that interest you.

Write your answer on a separate piece of paper. [8 marks]

4 Think about the whole text.

What impression do you get of the people who work on the trams and who use them?
*   Write about your own impressions of the people.
*   Evaluate how the writer has created these impressions.
*   Support your opinions with quotations from the text.

Write your answer on a separate piece of paper. [20 marks]

5 You are going to enter a creative writing competition.

Either

Write a description suggested by this picture.

Or

Write the story of a bus, tram or train journey.

[24 marks for content and organisation and 16 marks for technical accuracy; total 40 marks]

Read the sources below and answer the questions that follow.

Source A

In the extract below, taken from *Pictures from Italy*, Charles Dickens describes his visit to Florence in the 1840s.

But, how much beauty of another kind is here, when, on a fair clear morning, we look, from the summit of a hill, on Florence! See where it lies before us in a sun-lighted valley, bright with the winding Arno, and shut in by swelling hills; its domes, and towers, and palaces, rising from the rich country in a glittering heap, and shining in the sun like gold!

Magnificently stern and sombre are the streets of beautiful Florence; and the strong old piles of building make such heaps of shadow, on the ground and in the river, that there is another and a different city of rich forms and fancies, always lying at our feet. Prodigious palaces, constructed for defence, with small distrustful windows heavily barred, and walls of great thickness formed of huge masses of rough stone, frown, in their old sulky state, on every street. In the midst of the city – in the Piazza of the Grand Duke, adorned with beautiful statues and the Fountain of Neptune – rises the Palazzo Vecchio, with its enormous overhanging battlements, and the Great Tower that watches over the whole town. In its courtyard – worthy of the Castle of Otranto[1] in its ponderous gloom – is a massive staircase that the heaviest waggon and the stoutest team of horses might be driven up. Within it, is a Great Saloon, faded and tarnished in its stately decorations, and mouldering by grains, but recording yet, in pictures on its walls, the triumphs of the Medici and the wars of the old Florentine people. The prison is hard by, in an adjacent court-yard of the building – a foul and dismal place, where some men are shut up close, in small cells like ovens; and where others look through bars and beg; where some are playing draughts, and some are talking to their friends, who smoke, the while, to purify the air; and some are buying wine and fruit of women-vendors; and all are squalid, dirty, and vile to look at. 'They are merry enough, Signore,' says the jailer. 'They are all blood-stained here,' he adds, indicating, with his hand, three-fourths of the whole building. Before the hour is out, an old man, eighty years of age, quarrelling over a bargain with a young girl of seventeen, stabs her dead, in the market-place full of bright flowers; and is brought in prisoner, to swell the number.

---

[1] *Castle of Otranto* – the setting of a popular Gothic horror story of the same name

Source B

In this article for *The Times* (13 October 1982) Joyce Rackham discusses the problems caused by tourism in the Italian city of Florence.

FLORENCE: A city of dilemma

by Joyce Rackham

The bust of Benvenuto Cellini looks down sternly on the tourists littering the Ponte Vecchio. The younger ones loll – even sleep beneath him. Graffiti, although rarer than in the past, still scar some walls, and there is a very ugly souvenir stall. Yet the bridge is lined with fine shops, including jewellers whose best work follows Cellini's tradition of superb craftsmanship.

This scene reflects the dilemma of contemporary Florence – a matchless medieval city which has to stand up to the pressures, dirt and overcrowding of life in the 1980s.

Dr Silvio Abboni, a heart specialist who is also cultural assessor of the municipality, told me: 'We are victims of our big tourist boom. Florence was built as a fortress to withstand invaders. Now we must defend ourselves against too much mass tourism and potential speculators.'

Among his solutions are promoting itineraries off the beaten track, which will be published for visitors, as well as out of season attractions, both artistic and musical. He said that traffic jams could be intolerable in Florence and pointed to a new map showing plans to restrict car and bus parking and extend pedestrian precincts 'to allow city life to unfold in an orderly and pleasant manner'.

Dr Giorgio Chiarelli, Director of the Florence Tourist Board, said: 'We are a Renaissance city with about half a million inhabitants and an annual influx of around two million tourists.' He admitted that traffic pollution, litter and policing had been neglected, but said that this was changing.

Off-season tourism, with special art weekends from November to March, as well as extended shop and museum hours and more accommodation for young tourists, are intended to help ease pressures. The great Uffizi Gallery, the first public museum in the world, built by the Medici, celebrates its 400th anniversary this year. Professor Luciano Berti, its director since 1969, is also superintendent of the artistic and historic patrimony of Florence. 'Restoration is a continuous necessity and costs a great deal of money, and we don't have enough', he told me. 'We are most anxious that people see far more than the Uffizi. We cannot cope with a further growth of crowds. Since 1975 their volume has doubled.' He explained that dust from clothes and tramping feet, humidity from breath and wet clothes all have an adverse effect on paintings, many of which are now protected by glass. Crowd control measures are helping, as are the extended hours. Since August the Uffizi and most important museums, which used to close at 2pm, have been open until 7pm.

6 Read again the first five paragraphs of Source B (from 'The bust' to 'changing').

According to the article, which four of the following statements are TRUE?

- Shade the boxes of the ones you think are true.
- Choose a maximum of four statements.

a) The souvenir stall at the Ponte Vecchio is very attractive. ☐

b) There are shops on the bridge. ☐

c) There is no pollution in Florence. ☐

d) Dr Abboni believes the increase in tourists has been bad for Florence. ☐

e) Florence is a modern city. ☐

f) The jewellers produce some very good work. ☐

g) The authorities in Florence are encouraging tourists to go to less well-known parts of the city. ☐

h) Dr Abboni wants to ban tourists from Florence. ☐ [4 marks]

7 You need to refer to Source A and Source B for this question.

Use details from both sources.

Write a summary of the differences between the two descriptions of Florence. [8 marks]

8 You need only to refer to Source A for this question.

How does Dickens use language to convey his impressions of Florence? [12 marks]

9 For this question you need to refer to the whole of Source A together with the whole of Source B.

Compare how the two writers convey their different reactions to the city of Florence.

In your answer you should:
- compare their different reactions
- compare the methods they use to convey their reactions
- support your ideas with quotations from both texts. [16 marks]

10 'Travel might broaden the mind, but tourism is destroying some of the world's most beautiful places. It is time we put the good of the planet before our own pleasure.'

Write an article for a broadsheet newspaper in which you explain your point of view on this statement.

[24 marks for content and organisation; 16 marks for technical accuracy; total 40]

English Literature: Shakespeare

- **Answer the question on the play you have studied.**

11 *Julius Caesar*

Read the extract specified and answer the question below.

Here, Antony addresses the Roman people after the death of Caesar.

> ## Act 3 Scene 2
>
> *From*
>
> ANTONY   Friends, Romans, countrymen, lend me your ears.
>
> *To*
>
>   Come I to speak in Caesar's funeral.

Starting with this speech, explore how Shakespeare presents Antony as a politician.
Write about:

- how Shakespeare presents Antony as a politician in this speech
- how Shakespeare presents Antony as a politician in the play as a whole. [30 marks + AO4 4 mark

12 *Much Ado About Nothing*

Read the extract specified and answer the question below.

Here, Benedick approaches Beatrice after Hero has been rejected by Claudio.

> ## Act 4 Scene 1
>
> *From*
>
> BENEDICK   Lady Beatrice, have you wept all this while?
>
> *To*
>
> BEATRICE   It is a man's office but not yours.

Starting with this conversation, write about how Shakespeare presents ideas about honour.
Write about:

- how Shakespeare presents ideas about honour in this dialogue
- how Shakespeare presents ideas about honour in the play as a whole.   [30 marks + AO4 4 mark

13 *Macbeth*

Read the extract specified and answer the question below.

Here, Macbeth has murdered Duncan, and has returned with the blood-stained daggers

Act 2 Scene 2

From

LADY MACBETH   Infirm of purpose!

To

LADY MACBETH   I hear a knocking

At the south entry. Retire we to our chamber.

A little water clears us of this deed.

Starting with this dialogue, write about how Shakespeare presents the relationship of Macbeth and Lady Macbeth.
Write about:

- how Shakespeare presents their relationship in this dialogue
- how Shakespeare presents their relationship in the play as a whole.   [30 marks + AO4 4 marks]

14 *Romeo and Juliet*

Read the extract specified and answer the question below.

Here, Romeo has just seen Juliet for the first time.

Act 1 Scene 5

From

ROMEO   O, she doth teach the torches to burn bright.

To

Did my heart love till now? Forswear it sight.

For I ne'er saw true beauty till this night.

Starting with this speech explore how Shakespeare presents Romeo's love for Juliet.
Write about:

- how Shakespeare presents Romeo's feelings in this speech
- how Shakespeare presents Romeo's feelings in the play as a whole.   [30 marks + AO4 4 marks]

15 *The Tempest*

Read the extract specified and answer the question below.

Here, Prospero has just discovered Miranda talking to Ferdinand and has cast a spell on him.

Act 1 Scene 2

From

MIRANDA	Beseech you, father!

To

MIRANDA   My affections

Are then most humble. I have no ambition

To see a godlier man.

Starting with this extract, how does Shakespeare present Prospero as a father?
Write about:

- how Shakespeare presents Prospero as a father in the extract
- how he presents him as a father in the whole of the play.   [30 marks + AO4 4 marks]

16 *The Merchant of Venice*

Read the extract specified and answer the question below.

Here, Portia, disguised as a man, pleads with Shylock to be merciful.

Act 4 Scene 1

From

PORTIA   The quality of mercy is not strained.

To

And earthly power doth then show likest God's

When mercy seasons justice.

Starting with this speech, explore how Shakespeare presents ideas about justice and mercy.
Write about:

- how Shakespeare writes about justice and mercy in this speech
- how Shakespeare writes about justice and mercy in the play as a whole. [30 marks + AO4 4 marks

English Literature: The 19th-Century novel

- **Answer one question from this section on your chosen text.**

17 Mary Shelley: *Frankenstein*

- **Answer both parts of the question.**

In this extract, Victor Frankenstein has been confronted by the creature in the mountains.

> **Re-read Chapter 10**
>
> *From*
>
> 'Abhorred monster! Fiend that thou art! The tortures of hell are too mild a vengeance for thy crimes. Wretched devil! You reproach me with your creation; come on, then, that I may extinguish the spark which I so negligently bestowed.'
>
> *To*
>
> 'Begone! I will not hear you. There can be no community between you and me; we are enemies. Begone, or let us try our strength in a fight, in which one must fall.'

Starting with this extract, explore to what extent and how Shelley makes the monster sympathetic. Write about:
- whether and how Shelley presents the monster sympathetically in this extract
- whether and how she presents the monster sympathetically in the novel as a whole.   [30 marks]

18 Sir Arthur Conan Doyle: *The Sign of Four*

- **Answer both parts of the question.**

In this extract, Miss Morstan has come to Sherlock Holmes for help.

> **Re-read Chapter 2**
>
> *From*
>
> Miss Morstan entered the room with a firm step and an outward composure of manner.
>
> *To*
>
> I relapsed into my chair.

Starting with this extract, write about how Conan Doyle presents Miss Morstan and about her role in the novel.
Write about:
- how he presents Miss Morstan in this extract
- how he presents Miss Morstan in the novel as a whole.   [30 marks]

19 **Charlotte Brontë:** *Jane Eyre*

- **Answer both parts of the question.**

In this extract, Jane has been locked in the Red Room by her aunt.

> **Re-read Chapter 2**
>
> *From*
>
> 'Unjust! – unjust!' said my reason, forced by the agonising stimulus into precocious though transitory power: and Resolve, equally wrought up, instigated some strange expedient to achieve escape from insupportable oppression – as running away, or, if that could not be effected, never eating or drinking more, and letting myself die.
>
> *To*
>
> It must have been most irksome to find herself bound by a hard-wrung pledge to stand in the stead of a parent to a strange child she could not love, and to see an uncongenial alien permanently intruded on her own family group.

Starting with this extract, explore how Brontë presents Jane as an outsider.
Write about:
- how Brontë presents Jane in this extract
- how she presents Jane as an outsider in the novel as a whole.   [30 marks

20 **Jane Austen:** *Pride and Prejudice*

- **Answer both parts of the question.**

In this extract, Austen describes Elizabeth's visit to Pemberley.

> **Re-read Chapter 43 (Volume 3, Chapter 1)**
>
> *From*
>
> The housekeeper came; a respectable-looking, elderly woman, much less fine, and more civil, than she had any notion of finding her.
>
> *To*
>
> 'Perhaps we might be deceived.'
>
> 'That is not very likely; our authority was too good.'

Starting with this extract, explore how Austen describes Elizabeth's changing feelings towards Darcy.
Write about:
- how she writes about Elizabeth's feelings in this extract
- how she writes about Elizabeth's changing feelings in the novel as a whole.   [30 marks

21 Charles Dickens: *Great Expectations*

- **Answer both parts of the question.**

In this extract, Pip is visiting Miss Havisham for the first time. She has asked him to call for Estella.

Re-read Chapter 8

From

'Call Estella,' she repeated, flashing a look at me. 'You can do that. Call Estella. At the door.'

To

'You shall go soon,' said Miss Havisham, aloud. 'Play the game, out.'

Starting with this extract, write about how Dickens portrays Pip's relationship with Estella.

Write about:
- how he writes about their relationship in this extract
- how he writes about their relationship in the novel as a whole.　　　　　　　**[30 marks]**

22 Robert Louis Stevenson: *The Strange Case of Dr Jekyll and Mr Hyde*

- **Answer both parts of the question.**

In this extract, Stevenson describes one of Mr Utterson's Sunday walks with his cousin, Mr Enfield.

Re-read Chapter 1 ('The Story of the Door')

From

No doubt the feat was easy to Mr Utterson; for he was undemonstrative at the best, and even his friendship seemed to be founded in a similar catholicity of good-nature.

To

'Indeed?' said Mr Utterson, with a slight change of voice, 'and what was that?'

Starting with this extract, write about how Stevenson uses Utterson to explore 'the strange case'.
Write about:
- how he writes about Utterson and his walk in this extract
- how he writes about and uses Utterson in the novel as a whole.　　　　　　　**[30 marks]**

23 Charles Dickens: *A Christmas Carol*

- **Answer both parts of the question.**

In this extract, the Ghost of Christmas Present has taken Scrooge to observe the Cratchits' Christmas.

Re-read Stave 3 (Chapter 3) ('The Second of the Three Spirits')

From

'And how did little Tim behave?' asked Mrs Cratchit, when she had rallied Bob on his credulity and Bob had hugged his daughter to his heart's content.

To

'I see a vacant seat,' replied the Ghost, 'in the poor chimney-corner, and a crutch without an owner, carefully preserved. If these shadows remain unaltered by the Future, the child will die.'

Starting with this extract, explore how Dickens writes about the 'spirit of Christmas'.

Write about:
- how he writes about the spirit of Christmas in this extract
- how he writes about the spirit of Christmas in the novel as a whole.　　　　　　　**[30 marks]**

Mixed Exam-Style Questions

English Literature: Modern Prose or Drama

- **Answer the question on the text you have studied.**
  (In your exam you will have a choice of two questions on your text.)

24 **J. B. Priestley: *An Inspector Calls***

How does Priestley present the character of Mr Birling in *An Inspector Calls*?
Write about:
- the character of Mr Birling
- how Priestley presents the character of Mr Birling.   [30 marks + AO4 4 marks]

25 **Willy Russell: *Blood Brothers***

How does Russell use the narrator in *Blood Brothers*?
Write about:
- what the narrator does and says
- the purpose and significance of the narrator.   [30 marks + AO4 4 marks]

26 **Alan Bennett: *The History Boys***

How does Bennett present Irwin as a teacher in *The History Boys*?
Write about:
- what Irwin does and says
- how Bennett presents Irwin in the play.   [30 marks + AO4 4 marks]

27 **Dennis Kelly: *DNA***

How does Kelly present ideas about friendship in *DNA*?
Write about:
- what characters say and do
- how Kelly presents friendship in the play.   [30 marks + AO4 4 marks]

28 **Simon Stephens: *The Curious Incident of the Dog in the Night-Time***

How does Stephens present the character of Siobhan in *The Curious Incident of the Dog in the Night-Time*?
Write about:
- what Siobhan does and says
- how Stephens presents Siobhan.   [30 marks + AO4 4 marks]

29 **Shelagh Delaney: *A Taste of Honey***

How does Delaney present attitudes to sex in *A Taste of Honey*?
Write about:
- the different attitudes presented in the play
- how Delaney presents these attitudes.   [30 marks + AO4 4 marks]

30 **William Golding:** *Lord of the Flies*

How does Golding use symbols in *Lord of the Flies*?
Write about:
- symbols used in *Lord of the Flies*
- how Golding uses symbols to explore ideas and themes.   [30 marks + AO4 4 marks]

31 **AQA Anthology:** *Telling Tales*

How do writers explore relationships between men and women in 'Chemistry' and one other story from *Telling Tales*?
Write about:
- relationships between men and women in the two stories
- how the writers present relationships between men and women.   [30 marks + AO4 4 marks]

32 **George Orwell:** *Animal Farm*

Explore how the pigs change in *Animal Farm*.
Write about:
- the ways in which the pigs change
- how Orwell presents the ways in which the pigs change.   [30 marks + AO4 4 marks]

33 **Kazuo Ishiguro:** *Never Let Me Go*

How does Ishiguro present the character of Tommy in *Never Let Me Go*?
Write about:
- what Tommy does and says
- how others react to Tommy.   [30 marks + AO4 4 marks]

34 **Meera Syal:** *Anita and Me*

How does Syal write about Meena's relationship with her parents in *Anita and Me*?
Write about:
- Meena's relationship with both parents
- how Syal presents these relationships.   [30 marks + AO4 4 marks]

35 **Stephen Kelman:** *Pigeon English*

How does Kelman present gang culture in *Pigeon English*?
Write about:
- how gangs and gang members behave in *Pigeon English*
- how Kelman presents gangs and gang members.   [30 marks + AO4 4 marks]

Mixed Exam-Style Questions

English Literature: Poetry

36 Answer the question on the Anthology cluster you have studied.

Either

a) Compare the way poets present danger in 'The Charge of the Light Brigade' and one other poem from 'Power and Conflict'.

Or

b) Compare the way poets present parting in 'When We Two Parted' and one other poem from 'Love and Relationships'. [30 marks]

37 Read the two poems below and answer both questions.

The Man He Killed

by Thomas Hardy

    'Had he and I but met

    By some old ancient inn

We should have sat us down to wet

    Right many a nipperkin!

    'But ranged as infantry

    And staring face to face,

I shot at him as he at me,

    And killed him in his place.

    'I shot him dead because –

    Because he was my foe,

Just so: my foe of course he was;

    That's clear enough; although

    'He thought he'd 'list, perhaps,

    Off-hand like – just as I –

Was out of work – had sold his traps –

    No other reason why.

    'Yes; quaint and curious war is!

    You shoot a fellow down

You'd treat if met where any bar is,

    Or help to half-a-crown.'

The Soldier

by Rupert Brooke

If I should die, think only this of me:

That there's some corner of a foreign field

That is for ever England. There shall be

In that rich earth a richer dust concealed;

A dust whom England bore, shaped, made aware,

Gave, once, her flowers to love, her ways to roam,

A body of England's, breathing English air,

Washed by the rivers, blest by suns of home.

And think, this heart, all evil shed away,

A pulse the eternal mind, no less

Gives somewhere back the thoughts by England given;

Her sights and sounds; dreams happy as her day;

And laughter, learnt of friends; and gentleness,

In hearts at peace, under an English heaven.

a) How does Hardy present the speaker's feelings about being a soldier in 'The Man He Killed'? [24 marks]

b) Both 'The Man He Killed' and 'The Soldier' are about being a soldier and going to war. What are the similarities and differences between the way the poets present feelings about war? [8 marks]

Answers

GCSE Grades

Please note that we cannot give GCSE grade equivalents for numerical marks, as these are determined by the exam board after the exam has been taken.

1. Beth [1]; she is described as speaking 'contentedly'. The other girls 'grumbled', 'sighed' or sniffed. [2]
2. He is away in the army. [1]
3. a) That he might get killed. [1]
   b) They might not want to upset each other (or any reasonable answer). [1]
4. a) Giving up small things for a reason. [1]
   b) Someone who likes reading. [1]
5. They have very little money and even if they gave it to the government it would not make a lot of difference. [2]
6. Beth is saying what she wanted to spend her money on before they were told there were to be no presents, [1] implying she is not now going to spend it. [1] Amy tells us what she is planning to spend her money on. [1]
7. Suggested content:
   - They are poor so will not get any Christmas presents.
   - There are four sisters. They live with their mother, and their father seems to be in the army, fighting in a war.
   - Jo likes reading, Beth music and Amy drawing. Meg just seems to like 'pretty things'.
   - It is Meg who expresses their problem, but it is Jo who argues logically that they should still buy presents.
   - Beth is the most placid of the girls, Amy might be seen as selfish as she is so quick to take up Jo's idea and says she 'shall' get the pencils, but she could just be more decisive.
   [5 marks – 1 for one or two of these or similar points, 3 for about half of them, 5 for most of them and perhaps some original points]
   Possible ideas for your letter:
   Thank your grandfather for the money. Describe what you have spent it on / what you will spend it on. Explain why you decided to buy it. Say what your family/friends think about it. Mention that it will remind you of him. Tell him what you have been doing in school / after school / during the holidays. Say something about your family. Mention things that he might remember. Ask about his life and send your best wishes to other family members.
   An excellent answer (17–20 marks) will:
   - Show a full awareness of purpose (thanks), audience (grandfather) and form (informal letter).
   - Engage the reader's interest throughout, perhaps using humour and/or emotive language.
   - Include a full range of techniques, such as correct use of first and second

person, modal verbs, conditionals, questions.
   - Present a variety of ideas, using a sophisticated range of vocabulary and sentence structure.
   - Use paragraphs and connectives effectively.
   - Achieve a high level of accuracy in punctuation and grammar.
   - Achieve a high level of accuracy in spelling.

Page 7 Quick Test
1. no, where 2. It's. 3. whether, to.
4. practice.
Page 9 Quick Test
1. 'Where's my hamster?' Leo cried.
2. He had gone. There was no doubt about it.
3. Maureen, who lived next door, searched her bins.
4. Maureen's son found Hammy in the kitchen.
Page 11 Quick Test
1. d   2. a   3. b   4. c
Page 13 Quick Test
1. First – to give order.
2. On the other hand – to introduce a contrasting idea or point of view.
3. Before – to express passing time.
4. Therefore – to express cause and effect.
Page 15 Quick Test
1. Jay and I were put on detention.
2. I saw you on Saturday.
3. You were the best player we had.
4. After we had sung the first number, we did a dance.

1. were, weather, pouring, excited, wait, metres, There, which, coming, definitely.
   [1 mark for each correct spelling – maximum 10]
2. a) Peter Kowalski, who was the tallest boy in the class, easily won the high jump.
   b) 'What are you doing in the sand pit?' shouted Miss O'Connor. 'Get out of there at once!'
   c) Francesca won medals for the long jump, the high jump and the relay.
   d) I wasn't entered in any of the races because I'm hopeless at running.
   e) Jonathan finished last. However, he was pleased with his time.
   [1 mark for each sentence – maximum 5]
3. a) (i) Uzma stayed off school because she had a stomach ache.
      (ii) He might be in the changing rooms or he might have already left.
   b) (i) Michael, who has a really loud voice, announced the results.
      (ii) The form with the best results won a cup, which was presented by Mr Cadogan.
   c) (i) Maria, who had won the discus competition, went home early because she was feeling sick.
   [1 mark for each – maximum 5]

4. a) Noora and I are going to town tomorrow.
   b) You can come with us if you want to.
   c) We were very pleased with what we bought.
   d) I do not (don't) know anything about what they did at school.
   e) I am not truanting again because I want to get my GCSEs.
   [1 mark for each – maximum 5]
5. (1) As well as (2) As a result of (3) also (4) Consequently (5) However [5]
6. experience [1] was [1] visited [1] stories [1] stars' [1] biographies [1] Therefore [1] she and I [1] Bingley Park [1] The [1]
   [Maximum 10]

Page 19 Quick Test
1. Openly stated. 2. Yes. 3. Yes. 4. No.
Page 21 Quick Test
1. The writer. 2. The reader. 3. No.
4. You get no marks.
Page 23 Quick Test
1. Yes. 2. Yes. 3. No. 4. No.
Page 25 Quick Test
1. Quotation and paraphrase.
2. Everything that is in the original text.
3. When it does not fit easily into the sentence.
4. Point Evidence Explanation (or exploration).
Page 27 Quick Test
1. Horse and oats. 2. Was munching.
3. Old. 4. On. 5. Thoughtfully.
Page 29 Quick Test
1. Personification. 2. Alliteration.
3. Simile. 4. Metaphor.
Page 31 Quick Test
1. b, c, d, a 2. a, d, c, b 3. c, a, b, d

1. a) except, accept   b) effect, affect
   c) allowed, aloud   d) right, write
   e) whose, who's
   [1 mark for each pair – maximum 5]
2. 'Don't you think we should wait for him?' asked Eve.
   'Not at all,' Henry replied. 'He never waits for us.'
   'Well, that's true,' Eve replied, 'but he doesn't know the way.'
   [½ mark for each correct punctuation mark – maximum 10]
3. This is a suggested answer only. There are other ways of doing it:
   Henry and Eve waited for another ten minutes but Joel did not arrive, so they left without him and walked to the bus stop. There was no-one there, suggesting they had just missed the bus. Henry was very annoyed with Joel. However, Eve told him to calm down and forget about Joel. After an uneventful journey, they got off the bus by the lake, which looked eerie in the moonlight. Having sat down on a grassy bank, they took their sandwiches and drinks out of the bag. Henry felt a hand on his shoulder. [Maximum 10 marks]

4. b, d, f, h, i **[Maximum 5 marks]**
5. **a)** pizzas **b)** latches **c)** mosquitoes
   d) sheep **e)** donkeys **f)** stadia
   g) qualities **h)** churches **i)** women
   j) hypotheses **[½ mark for each –
   maximum 5]**
6. e, c, d, a, b **[Maximum 5 marks]**

Pages 34–35 **Practice Questions**

1. • Nobody greeted him cheerfully.
   • People did not ask him to come and
     see them.

• Beggars did not beg from him.
• Children did not ask him for the time.
• Nobody asked him the way anywhere.
[Maximum 4 marks]

2.

Marks	Skills	Examples of possible content
7–8	• You have analysed the effects of the choice of language. • You have used an appropriate range of quotations. • You have used sophisticated subject terminology appropriately.	The first complex sentence seems quite light-hearted, the direct speech reflecting a polite greeting, such as people might make in the street, but the sentence starts with 'Nobody', so we know Scrooge is not like others. The next sentence builds a list of those who avoid Scrooge, starting each clause with 'no' before giving an innocuous phrase such as 'what it was o'clock'. The last sentence gives us a sense of evil, 'even the blindmen's dogs' implying that a dislike of Scrooge is natural and instinctive.
5–6	• You have clearly explained the effects of the choice of language. • You have used a range of relevant quotations. • You have used subject terminology appropriately.	In three sentences, each one longer than the last, the writer gives lists of different sorts of people, starting phrases with the repeated 'no', to give a general negative impression. When he imagines what the dogs might say he uses the adjectives 'dark' and 'evil' to show that Scrooge is feared.

[Maximum 8 marks]

3. b, c, e, f   **[Maximum 4 marks]**
4.

Marks	Skills	Examples of possible content
7–8	• You have given a perceptive interpretation of both texts. • You have synthesised evidence from texts. • You have used appropriate quotations from both texts.	Although the writers have opposite views – Weston is a 'city-hater' but Lamb never wants to 'see a mountain in my life' – they are both careful not to insult people who have the opposite view ('I could gang anywhere'; 'Sorry, Londoners'). Lamb lists things like 'crowded streets' that he likes. These are the things Weston hates, calling it 'dirty' and 'noisy'. Weston knows 'it's meant to be…exciting' and this is clearly Lamb's view.
5–6	• You have started to interpret both texts. • You have shown clear connections between texts. • You have used relevant quotations from both texts.	Lamb explains that he has always lived in London so cannot see the attraction of the countryside. Weston, on the other hand, calls the country 'home' and thinks this is why he is bored with the city. Lamb loves the shops, the theatre and even the 'wickedness', but Weston can only see how 'expensive' it is and how everyone is 'bad-tempered'.

[Maximum 8 marks]

Pages 36–43 **Revise Questions**

Page 37 Quick Test
1. The beginning. 2. First.
3. The inciting incident.
4. One who knows everything.
Page 39 Quick Test
1. Simile.

2. Personification/pathetic fallacy.
3. Metaphor. **4.** Literal imagery.
Page 41 Quick Test
1. The main character.
2. A character who opposes the protagonist.
3. Something that happens to get the story going.

4. An event that changes the direction of the story.
Page 43 Quick Test
1. George lived alone.
2. Like ancient gravestones.
3. Love loyalty/apparent affection.
4. His teeth were rarely seen.

Pages 44–45 **Review Questions**

1. a, c, d, f   **[Maximum 4 marks]**
2. See 'Skills' column of table above (for pages 34–35 Practice Questions, Q4).

Marks	Examples of possible content
7–8	It took Brontë a long time to get published. She had to work out the 'puzzle' of why no-one was interested and look for advice. Fordyce, on the other hand, was published quickly and is often asked for advice by other poets. They also had very different experiences of being a woman poet. Brontë had a 'vague impression' that her sex would be a disadvantage, but Fordyce, who was 'welcomed with enthusiasm' by other poets, feels it was a positive thing for her.
5–6	The Brontës thought they might be 'looked on with prejudice' because they were women, whereas Fordyce thinks her gender was an advantage ('we don't get enough women'). Fordyce wrote to magazines and performed her poetry live, but for Brontë the only way was to write to publishers, who did not reply.

[Maximum 8 marks]

3.

Marks	Skills	Examples of possible content
10–12	• You have analysed the effects of the choice of language. • You have used an appropriate range of quotations. • You have used sophisticated subject terminology appropriately.	Fordyce gives advice in a clear, colloquial tone, as if she is talking to a friend: 'All I can do is say'. She is also modest, using the noun 'luck' three times and the adjective 'lucky' once, though this is balanced by the repetition of references to 'hard work'. She uses short, often simple sentences – 'It wasn't that hard for me' – which helps make the process seem simple. Using the metaphor 'magic key' in the first paragraph could make readers think she is saying she can't help, but this impression is contradicted by the rest of the passage, as she does try to help.

Marks	Skills	Examples of possible content
7–9	• You have clearly explained the effects of the choice of language. • You have used a range of relevant quotations. • You have used subject terminology appropriately.	Fordyce writes in a chatty, straightforward way, getting straight to the point with 'People often ask me'. She uses a metaphor, 'magic key', to show that there is no easy answer, but her tone is helpful. She emphasises that this is her personal experience by constant use of the first person.

[Maximum 12 marks]

Marks	Skills	Examples of possible content
7–8	• You have analysed the use of structural features. • You have chosen an appropriate range of examples • You have used a range of subject terminology accurately.	The text is written to gradually reveal to the reader who the 'thin woman' is and what her situation is. It starts by setting the scene in the 'barton', giving us an idea of the kind of people the story is about, just mentioning Rhoda briefly. The direct speech of the milkers tells us (and Rhoda) about the farmer's bride. When the dairyman tells them to stop, two brief lines of dialogue bring Rhoda into focus as having an interest in the farmer. At the end the focus shifts to Rhoda and her son. Through their dialogue, the writer reveals why she has an interest in the farmer, and the last thing she says leaves us wondering why she is so keen to hear about the bride and what might be the result of her curiosity.
5–6	• You have clearly explained the effect of structural features. • You have chosen relevant examples. • You have used subject terminology accurately.	At the beginning the focus is on the milking shed and we get an idea of their daily lives. The writer uses direct speech to tell us about the farmer getting married, and the last bit of dialogue tells us it has something to do with the 'worn milkmaid'. Then the focus changes to the worn milkmaid as she meets her son after work. Their conversation reveals to us that the farmer is the boy's father.

[Maximum 8 marks]

Marks	Skills	Examples of possible content
16–20	• You have critically evaluated the text in a detailed way. • You have used examples from the text to explain your views convincingly. • You have analysed a range of the writer's methods. • You have used a range of relevant quotations to support your views.	Rhoda Brook is introduced as a 'thin fading woman'. She is a milkmaid, indicating her rural working-class background, but the writer's use of the phrase 'apart from the rest' suggests that she is somehow different. Perhaps she thinks she is better than the others or perhaps they look down on her. It may be a mixture of both, as the conversation between the milkers hints that she had a relationship with the farmer. The writer tells us she also lives 'apart' from others, emphasising her solitary nature. The personification of the heath's 'dark countenance' suggests sadness and maybe mystery. This is reflected in Rhoda's nature and situation.
11–15	• You have clearly evaluated the text. • You have used examples from the text to explain your views clearly. • You have clearly explained the effect of the writer's methods. • You have used some relevant quotations to support your views.	The writer makes us interested in Rhoda Brook by not explaining anything about her but giving us hints. She is first described as 'a thin fading woman of thirty' and she does not work with the others. Perhaps she does not get on with the others or she just prefers to be alone. Because the others look at her when talking about the farmer, we can infer that she had a relationship with him. Later we find out that she had a son by him. This is scandalous and might explain why she is 'apart'.

[Maximum 20 marks]

Content and Organisation		
22–24	**Content:**	• You have communicated convincingly and compellingly throughout. • Your tone, style and register assuredly match purpose, form and audience. • You have used an extensive and ambitious vocabulary with sustained crafting of linguistic devices.
	Organisation:	• Your writing is highly structured and developed, including a range of integrated and complex ideas. • Your paragraphs are fluently linked with integrated discourse markers. • You have used a variety of structural features in an inventive way.
19–21	**Content:**	• You have communicated convincingly. • Your tone, style and register consistently match purpose, form and audience. • You have used an extensive vocabulary with evidence of conscious crafting of linguistic devices.
	Organisation:	• Your writing is structured and developed, including a range of engaging and complex ideas. • You have used paragraphs consistently with integrated discourse markers. • You have used a variety of structural features effectively.
16–18	**Content:**	• You have communicated clearly and effectively. • Your tone, style and register match purpose, form and audience. • You have used an increasingly sophisticated vocabulary with a range of appropriate linguistic devices.
	Organisation:	• Your writing is engaging, including a range of engaging and detailed connected ideas. • You have used paragraphs coherently, with integrated discourse markers. • You have used structural features effectively.
13–15	**Content:**	• You have communicated clearly. • Your tone, style and register generally match purpose, form and audience. • You have used vocabulary for effect with a range of linguistic devices.
	Organisation:	• Your writing is engaging, including a range of connected ideas. • You have usually used paragraphs coherently, with a range of discourse markers. • You have usually used structural features effectively.

Technical	Accuracy
13–16	• You have consistently demarcated sentences accurately. • You have used a wide range of punctuation with a high level of accuracy. • You have used a full range of sentence forms for effect. • You have used Standard English consistently and accurately, with secure control of grammatical structures. • You have achieved a high level of accuracy in spelling, including ambitious vocabulary. • Your use of vocabulary is extensive and ambitious.
9–12	• You have usually demarcated sentences accurately. • You have used a range of punctuation, usually accurately. • You have used a variety of sentence forms for effect. • You have used Standard English appropriately, with control of grammatical structures. • You have spelled most words, including complex and irregular words, correctly. • Your use of vocabulary is increasingly sophisticated.

[Maximum 40 marks]

Pages 48–55 **Revise Questions**

Page 49 Quick Test
1. Biography. **2.** Letter.
3. Diary. **4.** Autobiography.

Page 51 Quick Test
2 (news report).
Page 53 Quick Test
1. To argue your point of view.
2. The governors. **3.** Letter.

Page 55 Quick Test
1. Yours sincerely.
2. Yours faithfully.
3. Yours faithfully.
4. Yours sincerely.

Pages 56–57 **Review Questions**

1. See 'Skills' column of table on p. 129 (for p. 46–47 Practice Questions, Q1).

Marks	Examples of possible content
7–8	The writer wants to create an air of mystery and to keep the reader curious. He distances the death of Sir Charles by describing it in Dr Mortimer's speech. In his first paragraph he talks about Sir Charles's health, which the reader might think explains his death, but he ends with the word 'catastrophe'. This makes us want to know what the awful thing was. The next paragraph is about his experience on the night of the death and builds up to his revelation that there was more to it than was revealed at the inquest. This adds to the mystery but he still does not reveal his information. Holmes asks him questions that might be in the reader's mind, while delaying the shock revelation.
5–6	The doctor builds up to a revelation by describing following Sir Charles's footprints. At the end he mentions that he knows something no-one else has noticed but keeps back the information until Holmes questions him. This makes the fact that 'they were the footprints of a gigantic hound' have more impact on the reader.

[Maximum 8 marks]

2. See 'Skills' column of table on p. 129 (for p. 46–47 Practice Questions, Q2).

Marks	Examples of possible content
16–20	We are not told anything about the doctor's character, but the fact that he is a professional, scientific man implies he is a reliable witness. This is confirmed by his suspicion that Sir Charles's illness was 'chimerical', suggesting he is not easily convinced of things. He describes how he 'checked and corroborated' the evidence from the inquest, implying that he is both thorough and independent-minded. The fact that he has done this, and the careful and detailed description he gives, make the reader more inclined to accept his story than if it had been told in a sensational way.
11–15	The story of finding the footprints is far-fetched but the use of Dr Mortimer to tell it makes it more believable. This is because he is a doctor and he tells the story in a calm way, remembering details: 'I noted that there were no other footsteps save those of Barrymore on the soft gravel.' When the writer says 'his voice sank almost to a whisper', the reader gets the impression that he is scared and shocked.

[Maximum 20 marks]

3. Look at the mark scheme for Question 3 on pages 46 and 47, decide which description is closest to your answer and then decide which mark to give yourself. This task is marked for content and organisation, and for technical accuracy.

Pages 58–59 **Practice Questions**

1. Look at the mark scheme below, decide which description is closest to your answer and then decide which mark to give yourself.
   See 'Skills' column of table on p. 128 (for pages 44–45 Review Questions, Q3).

Marks	Examples of possible content
10–12	The writer's tone is quite serious and authoritative. The expression 'confounds the moralist' suggests that he is dealing with a moral problem. He uses hyperbole to show he loves dogs ('the great soul'). Other rhetorical devices he uses include the rhetorical question ('Where will the process end?') and the list of three, combined with alliteration ('crib, cabin, and confine'). He uses emotive language to make us feel sorry for the small dogs: 'frets the puny body to decay'.
7–9	The writer uses Standard English and sounds as if he knows what he's talking about. He uses impressive phrases like the 'great soul' to show he loves dogs and feels sad that they are made into 'puny' animals. He uses a rhetorical question ('Where will the process end?') to make us think about the consequences of breeding these dogs.

[Maximum 12 marks]

2. Look at the mark scheme below, decide which description is closest to your answer and then decide which mark to give yourself.

Marks	Examples of possible content	
13–16	• You have compared ideas and perspectives in a perceptive way. • You have analysed methods used to convey ideas and perspectives. • You have used a range of appropriate quotations.	Both these writers are very passionate about their subject. The first writer attacks those who breed small dogs by making the dogs sound like victims ('all eyes and nerves') but also calls them 'pampered'. Hanlon picks up on this but cannot see what's wrong with pampering – she sees it as love. Her tone is chatty and personal, while his is impersonal and authoritative.

9–12	• You have compared ideas and perspectives in a clear and relevant way. • You have explained clearly methods used to convey ideas and perspectives. • You have used relevant quotations from both texts.	The writer in *The Times* uses rhetorical devices to convince his readers. He claims to love dogs but is against breeding small dogs and treating them like toys. Hanlon defends people who have small dogs, saying those who attack them are just having a go at celebrities. She too uses rhetorical questions.

[Maximum 16 marks]

Look at the mark scheme for the answer to Question 3 on pages 46 and 47, decide which description is closest to your answer and then decide which mark to give yourself. This task is marked for content and organisation, and for technical accuracy.

Pages 60–67 Revise Questions

Page 61 Quick Test
False. **2.** False.
3. False. **4.** True.

Page 63 Quick Test
1. Soliloquy. **2.** Dialogue.
3. Plot. **4.** Theme.
Page 65 Quick Test
1. False. **2.** False. **3.** True. **4.** True.

Page 67 Quick Test
1. Metaphor/Rhetorical question.
2. Oxymoron. **3.** Rhetorical question.
4. Rhyming couplet.

Pages 68–69 Review Questions

Look at the mark scheme below, decide which description is closest to your answer and then decide which mark to give yourself.
See 'Skills' column of table on p. 128 (for pages 44–45 Review Questions, Q3).

Marks	Examples of possible content
10–12	Most of the passage is a quite straightforward account of the walk, which is what you would expect from a diary entry – it is written in the first person and the past tense and just describes what she saw, often using simple sentences ('The lake was rough'), and fragments ('A few primroses by the roadside'). The effect of this is to make it seem fresh and immediate. When she describes the daffodils she uses more 'literary' language, personifying them: they 'rested their heads' and 'reeled and danced'.
7–9	She does not always used complete sentences ('Saw the plough…') which makes it seem like she's writing notes for herself. She describes nature in great detail – 'The hawthornes are black and green' – so you can picture it. The simple sentence 'I never saw daffodils so beautiful' emphasises her strong emotion.

[Maximum 12 marks]

See 'Skills' column of table on p. 130 (for pages 58–59 Review Questions, Q2).

Marks	Examples of possible content
13–16	Wordsworth seems to be writing for herself, reflecting on her day, whereas Bisma is very aware of her audience. She uses hyperbole, 'complete washout' and 'like the workhouse', for comic effect. She writes in a colloquial way, as she might talk to her friends – 'ropes and stuff'. She also describes other members of the party in a critical yet amusing way (the Camp Commandant…with her whistle round her neck'), while Wordsworth makes no comment about her companions.
9–12	While Wordsworth clearly gets a lot of pleasure from observing nature, Bisma hates walking round the lake. Bisma is quite sarcastic and exaggerates everything for humour – 'It's like the workhouse'. Wordsworth's writing is serious and descriptive, not saying much about her feelings, but Bisma only thinks about herself.

[Maximum 16 marks]

Look at the mark scheme for the answer to Question 3 on pages 46 and 47. This task is marked for content and organisation, and for technical accuracy.

Pages 70–71 Practice Questions

For all questions, look at the mark scheme below.

Marks	Skills
26–30	• You have responded to the task in an exploratory and critical way. • You have used precise, appropriate references to support your interpretation. • You have analysed the writer's methods using subject terminology appropriately. • You have explored the effects of the writer's methods. • You have explored links between text and ideas/context.
21–25	• You have responded to the task in a thoughtful, developed way. • You have used appropriate references to support your interpretation. • You have examined the writer's methods using subject terminology effectively. • You have examined the effects of the writer's methods. • You have thoughtfully considered links between text and ideas/context.

[Maximum 30 marks]

Your answers could include some of the following points.

Romeo and Juliet
• Juliet's impatience with the Nurse – references to time.
• Use of the soliloquy.
• Her thoughts jumping about – use of caesura.
• Personification of love.
• Allusions to classical mythology.

• Contrast of old and young – her belief that the old cannot understand.
• Imagery of light and dark.
• Her dependence on the Nurse, reflecting social context.

2. *Macbeth*
• He sees power as good and desirable – 'happy prologues'.
• He uses a metaphor of music to express how he sees things developing.

• He immediately has doubts because of the source of the prophecy.
• Use of soliloquy.
• Use of rhetorical questions.
• The 'horrid' image is the idea of killing the king to gain power.
• The prophecy has a physical effect on him.

3. *The Tempest*
• Ariel is a slave who has to do as he is told.

- He is loyal to Prospero and does not rebel, but wants to hold him to his bargain.
- Prospero reacts angrily to mention of Ariel's 'freedom'.
- Use of questions, exclamations and caesura to show this.
- Prospero treats Ariel like a naughty child. Father/child relationship?
- Prospero feels Ariel is indebted to him and has to be reminded of his past.

4. *The Merchant of Venice*
- She is his only daughter.
- He is protective to the point of locking her up – his main fear is that she marries a gentile.
- There is no evidence of any affection between them.
- When she elopes he seems more concerned with the money she has stolen than with her.
- Her giving of the ring for a monkey indicates how little respect she has for him.
- The audience's sympathies may change.

5. *Julius Caesar*
- They both feel he has taken too much power.
- Cassius persuades Brutus to join the conspiracy.
- Cassius seems to have a personal grudge against Caesar.
- He describes him as physically weak and tells a story to prove it.
- Brutus is more interested in principles. He wants to defend Rome rather than attack Caesar.
- Caesar is shocked by Brutus's action ('Et tu, Brute?').

6. *Much Ado About Nothing*
- She is not married and is ambivalent about being single.
- She is witty, opinionated and happy to express her opinions to men.
- She does not like being told what to do – but the less assertive Hero can trick her.
- She has a strong sense of justice and family loyalty.
- She is dependent on her uncle.
- She marries but on her own terms.

Pages 72–79 **Revise Questions**

Page 73 Quick Test
1. False. 2. False. 3. True. 4. True.
Page 75 Quick Test
1. Yes. 2. An image or idea that recurs in a text. 3. Yes. 4. Yes.
Page 77 Quick Test
No definitive answer – check your notes.
Page 79 Quick Test
1. A variation of English spoken in a particular region. 2. The language of conversation. 3. An object that represents an idea or feeling. 4. Part of the story that takes place at an earlier time.

Pages 80–81 **Review Questions**

For mark scheme, see answers above to questions on pages 70 and 71. Your answers could include some of the following points.
1. *Julius Caesar*
   - He starts with an oath ('Ye gods') to express the strength of his feelings.
   - The contrast between Cassius's attitude and that of the people of Rome is underlined by the off-stage noises, which form a background.

- He compares Caesar to one of the wonders of the ancient world, the Colossus, describing his power in terms of physical size.
- He uses words like 'petty' and 'dishonourable' to emphasise that Caesar is 'great' only because others let him be.
- He argues against the idea that we're controlled by fate and can do nothing.
- He insists that Caesar is no better than anyone else.
- He hammers home his point with two rhetorical questions.

2. *Much Ado About Nothing*
- Beatrice's tone is light-hearted and jokey, although she is talking about a serious matter.
- The extract is written is prose.
- She feels that she is different – 'Thus goes everyone to the world but I'.
- She flirts with Don Pedro, making a joke from the double meaning of 'get' to imply that she would like to marry him.
- She uses the metaphor of clothes to express the difference in status between her and Don Pedro.
- She tries to avoid a serious conversation by saying she does not take things seriously – 'born to speak all mirth and no matter'.
- The last line sums up her ambiguous attitude to life.

3. *The Merchant of Venice*
- It would seem that Shylock is anxious about Jessica as he had asked for news of her.
- However, he is more concerned about the money she has spent than her whereabouts.
- This is what the Elizabethan audience might expect from a Jew. Modern audiences might think such a stereotype was anti-Semitic.
- The dramatic exclamation (using a metaphor) 'Thou stick'st a dagger in me' suggests pain.
- His attention is soon taken by news about Antonio and he uses violent language to show his delight.
- The revelation about the ring changes our perception again. Shylock cares for his wife's memory, even if Jessica does not.

4. *Romeo and Juliet*
- Romeo's love for Juliet can be compared to his feelings for Rosaline.
- Their use of a sonnet suggests mutual love.
- Religious imagery could show the love to be sacred or could suggest it is sacrilegious.
- In spite of her age, Juliet takes control and makes conditions, wanting to be sure.
- Constant references to 'the stars' suggest their tragedy is inevitable.
- Although the audience's sympathies are with the couple, some could feel they are in the wrong when they defy their parents.

5. *Macbeth*
- Macbeth starts off loyal and happy with his status, but the meeting with the witches gives him ideas.
- His soliloquies show us he is ambitious for power but has a conscience.

- He gives all the reasons for not killing Duncan and seizing power.
- Lady Macbeth taunts him and pushes him into killing Duncan.
- When he gains power he cannot enjoy it because of his conscience and his feelings of vulnerability.
- He commits more and more terrible acts to keep power, abuses power and ruins his country.

6. *The Tempest*
- Ariel is shown doing things that humans cannot, unseen by most characters.
- When he asks for liberty, we know he is a slave.
- Prospero tells the story of how he free Ariel from Sycorax.
- Ariel is contrasted with Caliban, Prospero's other slave. They can be seen as two parts of humanity, or as two ways of being a slave.
- Ariel obeys Prospero and is rewarded with his freedom.
- An interest in discovery and colonisation is reflected in Prospero and Ariel's relationship.

Pages 82–83 **Practice Questions**

For mark scheme, see answers above to questions on pages 70 and 71. Your answers could include some of the following points.
1. *The Strange Case of Dr Jekyll and Mr Hyde*
   - The extract is in the third person but is seen through the eyes of a maid, distancing it from the narrator.
   - The old man has a 'pretty manner' and 'an innocent and old-world kindness', contrasting with the cruelty of the attacker.
   - There is some mystery about why he has 'accosted' Hyde in the street.
   - The mention of Hyde's name halfway through alerts the reader to what might happen.
   - The violence builds over a few sentences – from impatiently playing with the cane, to brandishing the cane 'like a madman', to attacking him with the cane.
   - The expression 'ape-like fury' makes him seem inhuman.

2. *A Christmas Carol*
   - The extract shows Scrooge refusing to give to charity.
   - His questions show that he thinks the poor are being taken care of and it is none of his business.
   - The gentleman mentions 'Christian cheer', reminding us that caring about others is central to Christianity.
   - His manner is abrupt and aggressive.
   - His language is quite extreme and shocking, suggesting people should die and 'decrease the surplus population'. He thinks of people as just statistics.
   - At the end he sets out his philosophy, using the double meaning of 'business' to show both that money is the most important thing for him and that he does not think people like the gentleman should be concerned with others.

3. *Pride and Prejudice*
   - The incident is seen through the eyes of Elizabeth, who overhears it, so the impression we get is the same as hers

- The conversation is a private one with his friend, so we can take it to be his true feelings.
- He is contrasted with Bingley, who is enjoying dancing and is sociable.
- The phrase 'such an assembly as this' makes him sound very snobbish and is an insult to the others there.
- Austen uses Bingley to confirm this impression, calling him 'fastidious'.
- When Bingley suggests he dance with Elizabeth, Darcy shows himself to be bad-mannered as well as snobbish. The adverb 'coldly' sums up his attitude.
- He damns Elizabeth with faint praise, calling her 'tolerable, but not handsome enough to tempt me', asserting his sense of his own superiority.

Great Expectations
- We learn straightaway that Pip knows nothing about London and it is established that Mr Wemmick has been there some time.
- Pip's question about London being 'wicked' implies an assumption made by people outside London.
- However, he says it 'for the sake of saying something', which implies that he is not concerned or nervous.
- It seems as if Wemmick is more concerned about danger than Pip is, as Pip wants to 'soften' the idea of people being wicked.
- Mr Wemmick paints a picture of an amoral city, but again he does not see London as being different from anywhere else.
- Most of the extract is in dialogue, without much comment. We know nothing about Wemmick and, like Pip, do not know whether to take notice of his opinions.

Frankenstein
- For most of the novel Frankenstein is the narrator, so his changing feelings are shared with the reader.
- The description of the monster is shocking, causing fear in Frankenstein.
- Frankenstein is concerned about his safety and that of those he loves.
- He does not see beyond the appearance of the monster when he rejects him.
- The monster's actions are horrifying and Frankenstein feels both guilt and hatred.
- The monster can be seen as representing part of Frankenstein.
- His feelings change when the monster is given his own narrative, as do the feelings of the reader.
- Finally there is a sense of a shared tragedy.

The Sign of Four
- Holmes draws conclusions from seemingly trivial evidence.
- Watson's narrative puts the reader in Watson's place. We know only what Watson knows, not what Holmes knows.
- When Holmes explains his findings they seem logical and, to him, obvious.
- Holmes always keeps something back from Watson, teasing the reader.
- Holmes displays wide and detailed knowledge of what to most people are obscure things.
- In his use of forensics he is ahead of his time and ahead of the police.

- He is set apart from other people. His distrust of women and his drug-taking suggest a mysterious past.

7. *Jane Eyre*
- Brontë builds an air of mystery about Rochester before Jane meets him.
- Their first meeting is dramatic and, while he seems strong, it is she who helps him.
- The relationship between employer and governess is odd. She is neither a servant nor a family member.
- Jane and Rochester both seem to 'earn' each other's love.
- The fire and the discovery of Bertha turn her world upside down. She has been lied to and betrayed.
- The first-person narrative allows us to share Jane's knowledge of Rochester and her feelings about him.
- Symbolism and imagery are important – fire, the chestnut tree etc.
- Rochester's blindness might signify that he can finally see the truth.
- At the end Jane is in control. It is as if she needs Rochester to be weakened in order to truly love him.

Pages 84–91 **Revise Questions**

Page 85 Quick Test
1. True. 2. True. 3. False. 4. True.
Page 87 Quick Test
All of them.
Page 89 Quick Test
1. Protagonist. 2. Narrator.
3. Dialogue. 4. Stage direction.
Page 91 Quick Test
1. Yes. 2. An act.
3. Where he/she comes from. 4. No.

Pages 92–93 **Review Questions**

For mark scheme, see answers above to questions on pages 70 and 71. Your answers could include some of the following points.
1. *Frankenstein*
   - The time – 'a dreary night of November' – sets the tone. The description could be seen as pathetic fallacy – 'the rain pattered dismally'.
   - His feelings are almost physical ('agony') and give us a feeling of dread rather than excitement.
   - He has tried to create a man but does not describe him in human terms. It is a 'creature' and a 'thing'.
   - Frankenstein is disgusted by its appearance – the skin and eyes are yellow; the complexion is shrivelled.
   - He uses a rhetorical question – 'How can I describe my emotions?' – but then describes the creature, not his emotions.
   - His feelings are implied by his description, using adjectives like 'horrid', 'shrivelled' and 'dun'.
   - The first-person narrative makes us see the experience as Frankenstein sees it.
2. *The Sign of Four*
   - The narrator, Watson, watches and listens carefully. He is in the same position as the reader, waiting for Holmes to act and speak.
   - Watson and Holmes have similar reactions to the footprints, but Holmes is less emotional.
   - Holmes sees the meaning almost immediately – 'the thing is quite natural'.

- Holmes does not share his conclusions with Watson, challenging him to 'try a little analysis' using his 'methods'. This and his 'offhand way' tell us that he has gifts which seem natural to him but extraordinary to others.
- He is described measuring and examining things, showing that his detection is based on science, not just luck or instinct.
- A simile, 'like…a trained bloodhound', is used to show his keenness and his sensitivity.
- When Watson asks questions – 'What then?' Holmes does not give full answers, keeping us wondering.
- He is confident about his conclusions – 'Why, we have got him, that's all.'

3. *Jane Eyre*
   - Jane comes to his aid. He is the master and she the servant, but due to his fall he is in a weak position.
   - Jane is the narrator, so we see what she sees and she shares her feelings.
   - She does not fall for his looks but points out that he is not handsome or young and, from the point of view of someone writing about her younger self, mocks her own 'theoretical reverence'.
   - She concentrates on what he is not rather than what he is, building an idea of an atypical hero.
   - At the same time she sees this as something they have in common, because she sees herself as unattractive.
   - It is paradoxical that his frown and roughness 'set me at my ease'.
   - Fire and lightning might be associated with passion. Does she want to avoid sexual passion?

4. *The Strange Case of Dr Jekyll and Mr Hyde*
   - Descriptions of London are central. It is a city of wealth and poverty side-by-side.
   - Most events take place in the dark or half-light.
   - The multiple narratives mean that the story is 'distanced' from us. Truth is revealed gradually.
   - The sealed letters add suspense because we know they might contain answers.
   - Many elements are typical of the Gothic tradition.
   - Lots of characters have secrets or do things that are not fully explained.
   - The narrators, Mr Utterson and Dr Lanyon, are logical, professional men, so they are sceptical. If they're afraid, it must be something awful.
   - The physical descriptions of Hyde make him seem almost animal-like.

5. *A Christmas Carol*
   - Scrooge is introduced with a description of his appearance, using imagery, and of how strangers react to him.
   - In the first chapter, he is seen as having no interest in family, through his conversation with his nephew.
   - He expresses his feelings about charity and caring for others in his

conversation with the charitable gentlemen.

- All these encounters are written in quite a comic way, with Dickens as narrator commenting on Scrooge's absurdity.
- The Ghost of Christmas Past is used to show how Scrooge became like he is, making him think about what might have been and gaining some sympathy for him.
- The Ghost of Christmas Present takes the idea of 'other people' beyond family and acquaintances, showing Scrooge that he cannot cut himself off from the world.
- The Ghost of Christmas Yet to Come shows the result of his attitudes.
- Other characters are used as a contrast with Scrooge, showing love and the 'spirit of Christmas' – his nephew, the Cratchits, Mr Fezziwig.

6. *Pride and Prejudice*
- Darcy is mostly seen through Elizabeth's eyes. If he is proud, she is prejudiced.
- His first appearance shows him to be snobbish and unsociable, in contrast with his friend Mr Bingley.
- Society is very class-conscious. Darcy and Lady Catherine de Burgh are the highest-status characters in the novel. Her attitudes are seen as being shared by him, though it turns out he is not really as snobbish.
- Some of his 'pride' could be reserve – perhaps the result of his social class or of his own nature.
- Those who know him best do not see him as proud, while those who criticise him, like Wickham, are not reliable.
- He is concerned about his reputation and that of his family, which can be seen as proud.
- His actions, especially with regard to Wickham, show his true nature.
- In his letter to Elizabeth he admits he did not want Bingley to marry Jane because of the 'connection' but claims this was not of class but because of the way other family members behaved. Is this pride?

7. *Great Expectations*
- Pip as narrator. Is he naive? Is he unreliable?
- The novel as a 'Bildungsroman'. Pip makes mistakes but learns from his experiences.
- Pip's childhood is vividly portrayed. The atmosphere of the marshes adds to his sense of isolation and a general air of mystery.
- The journey is sometimes literal, as he goes from Kent to London and back again.
- His 'expectations' change him and he is seduced by money and false friends.
- Things change again when Magwitch reappears and he begins to unravel the past.
- His changing relationship with Joe shows how much he is changing, for the worse and then for the better.
- Dickens uses the excitement of the Magwitch story to show Pip taking control and acting as an adult.
- His changing emotions towards Estella reflect a growing maturity.

Give yourself 2 marks for each valid point supported by appropriate evidence. The points below are just suggestions. There are many other valid points to be made.

1. *An Inspector Calls*
- He comes from the 'future' so has the benefit of hindsight.
- He acts like a real detective, trying to solve a crime.
- However, he seems more interested in the other characters' attitudes to Eva – and is it really a crime that would be investigated?
- He is the mouthpiece for the writer, with his speech about the 'future'.
- He is an outsider.
- He sometimes shows his impatience with the responses he gets.

2. *Blood Brothers*
- She is middle-class and well-off.
- Despite her money, she is unhappy because she cannot have a baby, and it's her idea to take one of the babies.
- She seems to be aware that it will end tragically once Edward meets Mickey.
- Her wanting to get away from Mickey looks like snobbery but she is frightened of the secret getting out.
- She has mental health problems, maybe as a result of the secret.
- Her actions precipitate the tragic outcome.

3. *The History Boys*
- He could be seen as the leader of the group – others look up to him.
- He is sexually active and has an amoral attitude to sex.
- He is aware of his own attraction and quite vain – he uses it to bestow favours.
- His language can be very crude but he can also be eloquent.
- He does not understand why he is attracted to Irwin – although he himself sees everything in sexual terms, it is probably something else.
- He can adapt easily from one teacher's ways to another's.
- He realises that he enjoys having power and using it.

4. *DNA*
- She talks constantly, unlike most of the other characters, in a 'stream of consciousness' style, giving access to her thoughts.
- Her speeches punctuate the action, giving context to the play.
- She comments on what's been going on 'off-stage', giving us an insight into developments.
- She gives her views on all sorts of subjects, some of them quite eccentric.
- She is discovering a lot of things for the first time and finds the world full of wonder.
- What is the meaning of her revelation that she killed her pet?
- What is the point of her relationship/ non relationship with Phil?

5. *The Curious Incident of the Dog in the Night-Time*
- He is the protagonist. It is the story of him growing up.
- He is 'different'. Many people would call him 'autistic' but this is not specifically mentioned.

- He takes things literally and speaks mostly of facts. He does not describe or speculate.
- The audience knows only what he knows so we discover things with him.
- He proves to himself and others that he can cope, but in his own way.
- Is he the victim or the cause of his family's problems?

6. *A Taste of Honey*
- Her relationship with her mother is central – there is an element of role-reversal in it.
- In some ways she is mature for her age and in others naive.
- She might be seen as typical of a girl of her age and class at the time, but her circumstances are unusual.
- She is witty and honest, and shows signs of creativity.
- She is motivated by not wanting to be like her mother.
- Through her eyes we see a world that is quite prejudiced and repressive, but she is not part of it.

7. *Lord of the Flies*
- Simon is inherently good, the opposite of Jack.
- He is gentle, and kind to the little 'uns.
- He has the same sort of background as the other boys but, in his case, morality and civilisation are not superficial.
- He sees what the 'beast' means.
- His hallucinations are almost mystical.
- His murder represents the ultimate triumph of evil and savagery.
- He can be seen as a sacrificial victim, perhaps like Jesus.

8. *Telling Tales*
- Carla is the narrator, so we see things through her eyes.
- She is the 'tea lady' in a staffroom, a person people do not really notice, so she can observe things without being part of them.
- She tells her story in a straightforward way, as if telling it to a friend.
- She is conscious of her status – not being a teacher – and keeps it from Steve.
- She is half-Polish and her friendship with Steve helps her rediscover that part of her identity.

9. *Animal Farm*
- Boxer represents the honest working class, exploited by others.
- He is hard-working and loyal – first to Mr Jones, and then to the pigs.
- His naivety and trusting nature mean he is easily exploited.
- He is drawn sympathetically, though some readers might find him dull and frustrating.
- His death illustrates how little regard the pigs have for other animals.
- Without him the farm could not operate but he is not valued.

10. *Never Let Me Go*
- Tommy is shown from the start to be different from the others.
- His fits of temper and lack of 'creativity' mark him out.
- He does not actively rebel but he does not seem able to conform.
- For most of the novel Kathy does not understand his attitude but (unlike Ruth) she listens to him.

- Tommy is interested in finding out about the 'gallery' and other aspects of Hailsham before Kathy is.
- Like the others, his value to society is only as a donor – but he inspires friendship and love in Kathy.

11. *Anita and Me*
- Anita, as the title suggests, is the focus of the novel, though not the protagonist.
- She could be seen as an antagonist, in some ways the opposite of Meena.
- The changes in Meena's attitude to her show that Meena is growing up.
- She represents the white working-class culture of Tollington, which Meena is part of and yet not part of.
- Her troubled family helps to make her more sympathetic.
- She is a leader, looked up to by other children.
- Her association with Sam brings the community's racism into focus.

12. *Pigeon English*
- He is protagonist and narrator. We see things through his eyes. Is he a reliable narrator?
- His narration resembles a diary; its tone is chatty and colloquial.
- He is a young boy, a recent immigrant from Ghana. His speech reflects his background.
- He is keen to 'solve' the murder, not realising the danger he is in.
- His innocence leads him to see things in a positive light, treating most of life as a game, although he is in a very dangerous environment.

Pages 96–105 Revise Questions

Page 97 Quick Test
1. False. **2.** False. **3.** True. **4.** True.

Page 99 Quick Test
1. Yes. **2.** Yes. **3.** Yes. **4.** No.

Page 101 Quick Test
1. Onomatopoeia. **2.** Personification (or pathetic fallacy) **3.** Alliteration.
4. Persona.

Page 103 Quick Test
1. Rhyming couplet. **2.** Internal rhyme.
3. Ballad. **4.** Free verse.

Page 105 Quick Test
1. Similarity. **2.** Difference.
3. Difference. **4.** Similarity.

Pages 106–107 Review Questions

Give yourself 2 marks for each valid point supported by appropriate evidence. The points below are just suggestions. There are many other valid points to be made.

1. *An Inspector Calls*
- At the time the play is set, women did not have the vote.
- Eva, the working-class woman, represents different things in different people's eyes. Their ideas of her are shaped by gender and class.
- Mrs Birling fulfils the expected role of a middle-class wife, sitting on committees and giving charity.
- Sheila seems to do little but shop and get engaged – but she finds a voice at the end.
- There is a double standard in terms of sexual morality.

- The female characters are strong and opinionated.

2. *Blood Brothers*
- By starting with a tableau of the end, Russell shows the tragedy is inevitable.
- Mrs Johnstone is very superstitious: for example, she reacts angrily to seeing shoes put upon the table.
- Mrs Lyons does not believe in superstitions at first but becomes obsessed by escaping from fate.
- The narrator speaks about fate.
- The characters might think their lack of choice is because of fate, but is it the consequence of their actions?
- Or is it the result of economics and politics?

3. *The History Boys*
- Double/triple meaning in title – are the boys making history as well as studying history? Could this have happened only in the past?
- As far as the head teacher is concerned, the subject itself is not important. He just wants them to make the school look good.
- Mrs Lintott's approach to history is conventional and designed to equip pupils to pass exams.
- Irwin wants them to question everything – a different way of looking at history.
- However, Irwin's approach is also about passing exams – just different exams. He knows what they want.
- Irwin's idea that there is 'no need to tell the truth' can be applied to history, politics and life in general.
- Irwin ends up playing a part in history as a political adviser.

4. *DNA*
- When they think they are guilty of a crime, their reaction is to avoid blame.
- Some of the teenagers are nervous and scared but do not really accept their responsibility.
- They tend to look for 'leaders' – John Tate, Phil, Cathy – to absolve them from responsibility.
- Not taking responsibility for the crime they haven't committed leads them to pin the guilt on the innocent postman. They have no qualms about this.
- Later they plan the actual murder of Adam. By this time some of them have drifted off. Only Leah objects.
- Although they do not express guilty feelings or take responsibility, Leah reveals how guilt might have affected some of them – Brian on medication and John 'finding God'.

5. *The Curious Incident of the Dog in the Night-Time*
- Christopher's family is shown as being unusual, as he lives with his widowed father. Like Christopher, the audience would probably admire his father.
- Our perceptions are changed when we find Ed has lied and Judy is alive.
- We learn this when Christopher does, through the sympathetic character of Mrs Alexander.
- Christopher's relationships with his parents are difficult as he does not like physical contact and does not express emotion. He does not realise this is a problem.

- We see the strain this has put on his parents in different ways.
- Judy's letters give a nostalgic account of a happier family, as well as explaining her point of view about the difficulties of family life.

6. *A Taste of Honey*
- Helen is not interested in love. She is described as a 'semi-whore' and marries Peter for a comfortable life.
- Jo's relationship with the Boy seems romantic, especially because of his race.
- Jo does not seem to be too bothered about his not coming back. Perhaps because of her background, she has no idea of long-term relationships.
- The only relationship that seems loving is with her homosexual friend Geof. Maybe she cannot connect love and sex.
- The central relationship is that between Jo and Helen – a 'love–hate' relationship.
- Jo's relationships are all unconventional for the time, but the play is part of the fashion for 'kitchen sink drama', trying to show 'real life' on the stage.

7. *Lord of the Flies*
- The boys' background – British, public school – suggests they are the epitome of Western civilisation, so their savagery is shocking.
- They seek organisation and order at first, but they are constructing an idea of order.
- Strong leadership emerges in the form of Jack, showing that the idea of 'leadership' as a force for good is misplaced.
- Civilisation is a thin veneer. Given the opportunity, our instincts are to be savage, even evil.
- The beast is a symbol of savagery.
- The breakdown of 'civilisation' on the island is no worse than the wars being fought by the apparently civilised world.

8. *Telling Tales*
- The story is set in a community where the reality of death is ever-present. Accidental deaths in the mines are not uncommon.
- Elizabeth's father's attitude is practical. His first wife has died so he needs another one. He is not sentimental.
- The reactions of Walter's wife and mother are very different. His mother is distraught, while his wife seems to feel little emotion.
- The bringing in and laying out of the body are described in detail, giving a sense of the physicality of death.
- His death makes Elizabeth reflect on their relationship – his death 'restored the truth'.
- The chrysanthemums are symbolic, their significance changing.
- Elizabeth has to 'submit' to life and carry on but she is now aware that death is her 'ultimate master'.

9. *Animal Farm*
- The animals escape one form of oppression only to find another.
- They allow the pigs to change into oppressors by looking to them for leadership and naively trusting them.
- The pigs use slogans and songs as instruments of oppression.

- They change and manipulate language in order to oppress the other animals.
- The oppressors depend on spies and traitors to survive.
- *Animal Farm* is based on the events after the Russian Revolution but it is a 'fable' and its lessons can be applied to all kinds of oppressive regimes.

10. *Never Let Me Go*
- The novel centres on Kathy's friendship with Ruth and Tommy, seen through her eyes.
- Friendship may be more important to them because they do not have families.
- Their friendships are in many ways like those of any teenagers/ young adults, but they are more intense because of their being kept apart.
- Friendships often turn into sexual relationships. People want to be part of a couple.
- Kathy notices in the Cottages that behaviour is often copied from TV programmes. This might cast doubt on whether any of the clones really do have feelings for each other.
- The relationship between carer and donor is a form of friendship – Kathy is allowed to choose her donors.

11. *Anita and Me*
- Meena's family are a novelty in Tollington. As there are no other non-white children, Meena keeps her culture separate.
- Differences in culture are shown in dress and in food. Meena's mother and Mrs Worrall cook in completely different ways.
- The cultures are differentiated by language.
- Meena wants to belong and acts like the other children, exaggerating her accent to be accepted.
- There is an element of class difference as well as ethnic difference. Meena's family are well educated and middle-class.
- The visit of Nanima brings Meena closer to her Punjabi culture. She is protective of her grandmother and, by implication, her culture.
- Meena becomes aware of racism as she matures. When the novel

ends she moves away from Tollington and further into her Punjabi culture.

12. *Pigeon English*
- The novel focuses on the repercussions of a single violent act – a boy's murder.
- Harri is fascinated by the murder and tries to investigate it, treating it as an adventure rather than a dangerous reality.
- The school and area are dominated by gangs, who often commit violence.
- Harri's aunt has committed an act of violence on herself.
- Violence and petty crime seem to be part of everyday life on the estate.
- and drawn into the violence.
- The novel was inspired by a real-life murder and tries to understand the gang culture of Britain's cities.

Pages 108–109 Practice Questions

1. a) First person (plural). b) Past.
   c) They make us feel as if he is recounting an experience shared with others.
   d) In the trenches during the First World War (winter).
   e) Eight stanzas of equal length, each five lines, the last line being shorter.
   f) It is as if he has an extra thought (after the quatrain) or as if his thought is unfinished. It makes the refrain stand out, leaving a pause for thought.
   g) The refrain changes between 'but nothing happens' and variations on 'dying'. The first 'what are we doing here?' is like a stifled cry to which there is no answer as Owen returns to 'but nothing happens'. Stanzas 5–7 look for answers, but after he says that the love of God is dying, he returns to the hopelessness of nothing happening.
   h) 'east winds that knife us' identifies nature with violence; 'the mad gusts tugging on the wire' calls to mind the mental effect of the conflict as well as physical dangers of the wire.
   i) 'Gunnery rumbles' reflects the deep ominous sound of the guns.
   j) It is as if they are dreaming or even hallucinating about being at home, returning as 'ghosts' when they have died. The warmth contrasts with cold reality, but even this image is sad, as the houses are empty.
   [2 marks for each point]

2. a) First person – includes both singular and plural, as well as the second person singular. b) Past.
   c) It is about personal memories, addressed to the person he shared them with.
   d) Winter, by a lake.
   e) Four stanzas of four lines each (quatrains).
   f) *abba* The regularity of the rhyme scheme makes the memories seem organised and calm.
   g) 'as eyes that rove over tedious riddles'. It suggests that she is bored and perhaps does not understand him.
   h) It marks the end of the memory and suggests that a lot of things have passed since, fading away from him.
   i) 'Wrings with wrong' gives a sense of the almost physical pain she has caused him.
   j) The literal imagery paints a depressing picture. Nature is dead – cold and dry – reflecting the state of the relationship.
   [2 marks for each point]

3. a) A persona. An old mother.
   b) In a house, probably in a poor rural area, during the course of a day.
   c) Yes. There are four stressed syllables per line, though the number of unstressed syllables varies. The regularity could reflect the routine of her day. In spite of her hard life, it give the poem a cheerful tone.
   d) Yes. It is in rhyming couplets, regular and simple, reflecting a regular and simple life.
   e) Mostly, it is literal, describing what she sees, though the fire could be taken as a metaphor for life and the stars are personified as they 'blink and peep'.
   f) It is the story of an ordinary old woman's day and her life.
   g) Fire could be a symbol of life. Growing feeble and then cold is an image for old age.
   h) Old age. A woman's role. Death. Work. Envy of the young.
   i) He feels sympathy for the old woman. He sees life as pointless. He is saddened by the passing of time.
   j) All answers are valid.
   [2 marks for each point]

Pages 110–111 Review Questions

1.

Marks	Skills
26–30	• You have compared texts in an exploratory and critical way. • You have used precise, appropriate references to support your interpretation. • You have analysed the writer's methods using subject terminology appropriately. • You have explored the effects of the writer's methods. • You have explored links between text and ideas/context.
21–25	• You have made thoughtful, developed comparisons. • You have used appropriate references to support your interpretation. • You have examined the writer's methods using subject terminology effectively. • You have examined the effects of the writer's methods. • You have thoughtfully considered links between text and ideas/context.

[Maximum 30 marks]

a) Your answer might include:
- Ideas about who is affected by conflict and how – soldiers, relatives, civilians.
- Comparisons dealing with soldiers during and after the conflict: 'The Charge of the Light Brigade', 'Bayonet Charge', 'Exposure', 'Remains'.
- Comparisons of the effect on non-combatants: 'Poppies', 'The Émigrée', 'War Photographer'.
- Use of language, e.g. alliteration.

- Use of imagery and descriptions of nature.
- The use of the speaker to explore ideas and context.

b) Your answer might include:
- Ideas about what love means – 'I think of thee!',

- 'When We Two Parted', 'Winter Swans'.
- Different stages in love; the beginning and the end – 'Neutral Tones', 'Singh Song!', 'When We Two Parted'.
- The use of imagery of nature.

- Romantic ideas about love and relationships.
- Direct address to the loved one.
- Structure of a logical argument.

2. a)

Marks	Skills
21–24	• You have explored the text critically. • You have used precise references to support your interpretation. • You have analysed the writer's methods using appropriate subject terminology. • You have explored the effects of the writer's methods on the reader.
17–20	• You have responded thoughtfully to the text. • You have used appropriate references to support your interpretation. • You have examined the writer's methods using subject terminology effectively. • You have examined the effects of the writer's methods on the reader.

Your answer might include comments on:
- Clare's entirely positive view of nature.
- Repetition of 'I love'.
- Use of the sonnet form for a poem about nature.
- Hope and joy brought about by the season.

- Use of personification.
- Listing of all aspects of nature – animals, plants, the weather.
- The idea of nature being 'happy' and at 'play'.

- The lack of punctuation, giving a sense of freedom.
- Use of alliteration and onomatopoeia to create sounds – 'rustle like a wind shook wood'.

[Maximum 24 marks]

b)

Marks	Skills
7–8	• You have explored comparisons of the writers' use of language, structure and form, using appropriate subject terminology. • You have convincingly compared the effects of the writers' methods on the reader.
5–6	• You have thoughtfully compared the writers' use of language and/or structure and/or form, using effective subject terminology. • You have clearly compared the effects of the writers' methods on the reader.

Your answer might include comments on:
- Differing attitudes to nature.
- Difference in focus on one creature / all nature.

- Presence of speaker.
- Use of imagery.
- Use made of techniques such as alliteration.

- Differences in structure.

[Maximum 8 marks]

Pages 112–126 Mixed Exam-Style Questions

1. b, c , e, h [4]

2. See 'Skills' column of table on p. 128 (for pages 34–35 Practice Questions, Q2).

Marks	Examples of possible content
7–8	The writer writes at first as if he is explaining something to us, describing in detail something that is happening now. The phrase 'the spirit of the devil' makes us think of evil, and the descriptions of darkness and flames might also have connotations of hell and damnation. Yet there is a sense of excitement in the extended metaphor of the horse race. The paragraph ends with a comic contrast between the danger of the fire and the passengers' down-to-earth colloquial reaction: 'We're stopping where we are. Push on, George.'
5–6	He writes in the present tense and we can imagine ourselves there. The metaphor of the 'steeple-chase' makes the tram seem like a living thing and the experience like being on a horse. There is a contrast between the 'blackness' and 'heart of nowhere', which sound ominous, and the cheerful speech of the people.

[Maximum 8 marks]

3. See 'Skills' column of table on p. 129 (for p. 46–47 Practice Questions, Q1).

Marks	Examples of possible content
7–8	The writer moves from the general to the particular. The first three paragraphs move from describing the trams as something exotic and fantastical to telling us about particular people on them. The mood changes at the start of paragraph 2 with 'the reason for this', which leads into an account of what the trams are actually used for, contrasting with the fantastical imagery of the first paragraph…
5–6	At first the focus is on the tram ride and how exciting it is, at the same time telling us about the setting. The focus shifts to the passengers and how they feel about the tram service – more of the reality of it. In the third paragraph he gives a general description of drivers and conductors. Then we have some dialogue, which brings the focus to one conductor, Annie.

[Maximum 8 marks]

4. See 'Skills' column of table on p. 130 (for pages 56–57 Review Questions, Q2).

Marks	Examples of possible content
16–20	The writer only describes the men briefly, his main focus being the girl conductors. However, he gives a very vivid impression of the men in a few words. Although they are 'cripples and hunchbacks', who might be looked down on, especially because they are not at war, they have the 'spirit of the devil', a comparison which makes them seem exotic and exciting. The girls are introduced to us as 'fearless young hussies', implying that they do not behave in the way expected of women at the time. He goes on to compare them to non-commissioned officers. Coupled with a description of their unflattering uniform, this may not sound complimentary, but the tone of the description suggests admiration and respect…

| 11–15 | At first the people who work on the trams sound like misfits and are described in a quite insulting way – 'cripples and hunchbacks', but then the writer says they have 'the spirit of the devil in them'. This could mean they are wicked but, from what he then says, I think he means they are reckless and brave. The girls are different because they would not be at war anyway. They are young and very confident. He calls them 'fearless young hussies', which makes them sound attractive but a bit frightening. |

[Maximum 20 marks]

5. Look at the mark scheme for Question 3 on pages 46 and 47. This task is marked for content and organisation, and for technical accuracy.
[Maximum 40 marks]

6. b, d, f, g **[4]**

7. See 'Skills' column of table on p. 128 (for pages 34–35 Practice Questions, Q4).

Marks	Examples of possible content
7–8	Both writers say the city is beautiful. Dickens describes the view from outside the city and then the centre. Rackham describes tourist places, like the Ponte Vecchio, but says tourists are 'littering' it and also mentions graffiti and 'a very ugly souvenir stall'. Dickens does not say anything about other tourists. While Rackham focuses on the 'dilemma' facing the city, Dickens is most interested in the prison and the life of the 'blood-stained' inmates.
5–6	Dickens is very impressed by the 'magnificent' city and describes its beauty. Rackham also describes some of the attractions but talks about graffiti and an 'ugly' stall. Dickens sees a negative side of the city but for him it is the prison, next to the great castle, and the violence of a place where 'they are all blood-stained'. According to Rackham, the downside of Florence is all the tourists, who are spoiling what they come to see.

[Maximum 8 marks]

8. See 'Skills' column of table on p. 128 (for pages 34–35 Practice Questions, Q2).

Marks	Examples of possible content
10–12	In the first paragraph, Dickens uses images of light and richness to describe Florence: 'bright…glittering…like gold!' His exclamations and his use of the second person ('we') make us feel his wonder as if we were there with him. In the second paragraph, he moves into the city and his language reflects both the atmosphere and the architecture. He personifies the buildings, describing 'distrustful windows' and saying they 'frown, in their old sulky state'…
7–9	Dickens writes in the present tense and the first person ('we') as if he is telling us what happens as it happens. He describes the buildings as if they were people, saying they 'frown'. He contrasts the beautiful palaces with the prison, summing up how uncomfortable it is in the simile 'cells like ovens'.

[Maximum 12 marks]

9. See 'Skills' column of table on p. 130 (for pages 58–59 Practice Questions, Q2).

Marks	Examples of possible content
13–16	Dickens is writing about his personal experience of visiting Florence and the effect it had on him, whereas the purpose of Rackham's article is to examine the 'dilemma' of a city dependent on tourists being ruined by 'mass tourism and potential speculators'. Dickens uses hyperbolic, poetic images to describe the city 'shining in the sun like gold' but also 'stern and sombre'. Rackham starts almost by imitating Dickens as she describes a statue looking 'sternly', but for her this implies a judgement on the tourists, and from then on her focus is not on describing the city but on the issues.
9–12	Rackham writes about the issues of tourism and pollution and their effect on the city. Dickens does not mention this, perhaps because it was not a problem in his day. He describes the 'magnificent' city in detail, whereas she just sketches in a few details about the shops on the Ponte Vecchio in order to show us the 'dilemma of contemporary Florence'.

[Maximum 16 marks]

10. Look at the mark scheme for Question 3 on pages 46 and 47. This task is marked for content and organisation, and for technical accuracy.
[Maximum 40 marks]

Questions 11–16
For all questions, look at the mark scheme table on p.131 (for pages 70–71 Practice Questions).
[Maximum 30 marks]
This question is also marked for AO4 (spelling, punctuation and grammar).
For all questions, look at the mark scheme below.

Marks	Description of performance
4	• You have spelled and punctuated with consistent accuracy. • You have consistently used vocabulary and sentence structures to achieve effective control of meaning.
2–3	• You have spelled and punctuated with considerable accuracy. • You have consistently used a considerable range of vocabulary and sentence structures to achieve general control of meaning.

[Maximum 4 marks]

Your answers could include some of the following points.
11. *Julius Caesar*
  • Antony's use of rhetorical language.
  • His claim that he is not going to praise Caesar.
  • His praise of Brutus and the conspirators.
  • The way he seeks to portray himself as one of the people.
  • His position as Caesar's protégé.
  • His actions after he has got the people on his side.
  • His dealings with Octavius and Lepidus.
12. *Much Ado About Nothing*
  • Two meanings of honour – sexual reputation and the obligation to defend your reputation and that of your friends.
  • Benedick knows Hero has been 'wronged' and her honour questioned.
  • Benedick is not part of Hero's family so he is not obliged to defend her.
  • What Beatrice has in mind is 'a man's office' – different ideas of honour for men and women.
  • Defending Hero's honour shows Benedick's love for Beatrice.

- It also shows that he understands 'honour' as being a matter of right and wrong, not loyalty to friends.
- Honour is associated with the court and the aristocracy. Claudio has not acted as a man of his class should.

13. *Macbeth*
- Contrast between Macbeth's guilt and Lady Macbeth's lack of guilt.
- Lady Macbeth takes control.
- The knocking makes him nervous but she reacts in a practical way.
- She speaks to him as if telling off a child.
- She may be more ruthless, as she is happy to blame the grooms.
- Lady Macbeth persuades Macbeth to murder Duncan. She embraces evil; he knows he is doing wrong.
- He discusses his guilt but hers seems not to affect her until the sleepwalking scene.
- As a woman she can only have power through him, but she is dominant and taunts him about his role as a man.

14. *Romeo and Juliet*
- He falls in love at first sight.
- The audience might think he has got over Rosaline very quickly.
- Imagery of light and dark is used to express Juliet's beauty.
- Religious imagery is introduced.
- The effect of the soliloquy while the ball continues around him.
- Comparison with his ideas about love in the first scene.
- Mutual love is expressed in a sonnet.
- Portrayal of his love and their relationship in the balcony scene.
- His commitment to her and his actions after their marriage.
- Association of love and death.

15. *The Tempest*
- Prospero's power over Miranda is increased by his use of magic.
- Very unequal relationship – Miranda begs and kneels.
- Prospero is angry and not willing to listen.
- He uses her inexperience of the world to control her, lying to her.
- He is protective, has brought her up and educated her.
- He may be jealous of Ferdinand and/or unwilling to see Miranda grow up.
- However, he is won over by their love and welcomes Ferdinand – part of the general reconciliation at the end.
- Prospero seen as a father figure to Ariel and Caliban.
- Fatherhood as a metaphor for creativity/writing.

16. *The Merchant of Venice*
- Mercy seen as God-given and natural.
- Imagery used to express its 'quality'.
- Mercy contrasted with power, symbolised in the sceptre, but seen as necessary in a ruler.
- It is not the opposite of justice but 'seasons' it.
- Portia's use of rhetorical language to convince Shylock.
- The failure of her appeal to Shylock and what this says about him.
- Is the outcome of the trial just?
- How far would differences in Elizabethan and modern attitudes influence an audience's reaction to the trial?

Questions 17–23:
See mark scheme above for Questions 11–16. This question does not carry additional marks for spelling, punctuation and grammar.
Your answers could include some of the following points.

17. *Frankenstein*
- Frankenstein's reaction and his language reflect his terror.
- The readers see the monster through Frankenstein's narration. They might think his reaction unfair.
- The monster's speech is calm, whereas we, like Frankenstein, might expect him to be aggressive.
- The monster is humble and even servile in his approach – 'I am thy creature'.
- He uses gentle language – 'mild', 'clemency' – contrasting with Frankenstein's violent language.
- He uses logic, and refers to ideas of justice and to the Bible, suggesting he is intelligent and educated.
- This chapter marks a turning point, leading to the monster's narration.
- His narrative helps us see him as a victim of Frankenstein.
- His story shows the potential he had for good and how this was destroyed.

18. *The Sign of Four*
- As Watson is the narrator, we see her through his eyes.
- He describes her appearance in great detail, as he would describe anything else in the book.
- He draws conclusions about her character, which do not have the logical basis of conclusions that Holmes might make, and show he is attracted to her.
- She is drawn as a sympathetic character and a victim who needs protecting: 'her lip trembled'.
- Watson declares his admiration in hyperbolic terms.
- Her main purpose is to introduce the plot. The note she has been sent leads into the mystery and adventure.
- Her romance with Watson forms a sub-plot, which contrasts with the main plot.
- The reactions of Watson and Holmes to her differ sharply – Watson is shocked at Holmes's misogyny; Holmes lacks Watson's empathy.
- The reader might suspect that Watson is foolish in falling for her and she could be tricking him, but he is proved right.

19. *Jane Eyre*
- The passage starts with 'Unjust!' Jane feels that she does not belong and is used as a scapegoat.
- Her adult narrator's voice analyses her position at Gateshead, seeing it partly as a result of the situation but also as owing to her own nature.
- Even as a child, Jane does not conform to her expected role.
- The Red Room is a powerful symbol of isolation from society, which Jane refers to throughout the novel.
- The description of the room and the weather build fear and mystery.
- This can be related to the Gothic tradition, although the supernatural elements are not real – here they are the result of a child's fears.

- Jane looks for love and substitute families throughout the novel – at Lowood, at Thornfield, with the Rivers family. Her position as governess is neither servant nor family.
- She thinks of herself as different – in her looks and her nature.

20. *Pride and Prejudice*
- The importance of the setting – Darcy's home, which reveals a lot about him.
- Pemberley is described as elegant, tasteful and beautiful. This says something about its owner which surprises Elizabeth.
- The idea of being its mistress appeals to her – she would not marry just for money but wants a 'good' marriage.
- The presence of the Gardiners reminds her why she refused Darcy.
- She had already begun to change her feelings after receiving Darcy's letter.
- Now she is given an account of his character by someone who can be seen as reliable and honest.
- The housekeeper maintains he is not proud and has other qualities.
- The way he treats and reacts to Wickham are central to Elizabeth's changing feelings. At first she was misled by Wickham. Now she sees Darcy's side.
- We are given access to Elizabeth's feelings through Austen's narrative style.

21. *Great Expectations*
- The strangeness of the setting and the contrast between Miss Havisham and Estella.
- How Dickens describes Estella's appearance.
- Pip as a naive/unreliable narrator.
- Estella's attitude towards Pip – her insults and her contempt for him – and how far this is due to Miss Havisham.
- Pip's love for Estella in spite of this.
- Issues of class and gender.
- Pip's reaction to Estella when he meets her after her marriage.
- The ending – is it ambiguous?

22. *The Strange Case of Dr Jekyll and Mr Hyde*
- Utterson is introduced as a reliable, logical, professional man.
- His profession gives him access to Lanyon, Jekyll and their documents.
- Utterson and Enfield are described as 'dull', making the contrast with the events Enfield describes greater.
- Stevenson uses their walk to describe the contrast between the 'thriving' street and 'sinister' building, like Jekyll and Hyde.
- Use of imagery to create atmosphere.
- Utterson is inquisitive but also discreet – information is gradually revealed to him.

23. *A Christmas Carol*
- The readers are taken with Scrooge to see an 'ordinary', poor family celebrate Christmas.
- The importance of family life and being with loved ones – contrast with Scrooge's situation.
- Dickens's characteristic use of lists to build descriptions of plenty.
- A sense of excitement and anticipation built.
- Bob refers to Tiny Tim's words about Christ.

- A sense throughout the novel that celebration and caring for others go together.
- The ghost shows Scrooge a range of people celebrating Christmas.
- Dickens's use of a popular genre to put across a serious message about society.

Questions 24–35

Use the mark scheme for Questions 19–23 (above). This question is also marked on your spelling, punctuation and grammar.

Your answers could include some of the following points.

24. *An Inspector Calls*
- Description of Mr Birling in the opening stage directions.
- His physical presence and bombastic style of speech.
- His social position as a rich, self-made man.
- His views on politics, society and the future.
- His traditional role in the family and relations with his wife and children.
- His reaction to the Inspector's arrival.
- His contact with Eva Smith and what it tells us about industrial relations.
- The difference hindsight makes to an assessment of his character (both from the 1940s and a modern perspective).

25. *Blood Brothers*
- Narrator makes it sound like the re-telling of a legend or myth.
- Narrator comments on action.
- Narrator enters action as various minor characters.
- Comic effect of narrator's intervention.
- Narrator used to move story forward.
- Narrator's musings on fate, superstition etc.
- How the narrator becomes sinister.
- Does he control as well as comment on the action?
- Narrator as a Brechtian alienation (distancing) technique.

26. *The History Boys*
- Irwin as stereotypical young, keen supply teacher.
- Headmaster's use of Irwin to get results and to undermine Hector.
- Contrast with Mrs Lintott's approach to history.
- Comparison with Hector's teaching style and ideas.
- His disregard for the truth.
- His sexuality / interest in Dakin and comparisons with Hector's 'groping'.
- Significance of the revelation that he lied about his background.
- His subsequent career as 'spin doctor'.
- His use as a framing device to start the acts from the 'present'.

27. *DNA*
- Characters come mostly in pairs, in established friendships.
- Their action demands group loyalty.
- In the first part the focus is entirely on the friendship group – the outside world is not important.
- Reported sentimental outpouring of friendship and grief for the 'dead' boy.
- Contrast this with their responsibility and guilt.
- How friendships fall apart.
- How some are leaders and some followers – and how leadership of the group changes.

- What is meant by friendship? Is it meaningful in this context?
- Writer says performers can change names and even genders of characters – would this change the dynamics of the group?

28. *The Curious Incident of the Dog in the Night-Time*
- She is a special needs teacher – we know little about her beyond this.
- Scenes between her and Christopher show how he reacts to others in school.
- Her role shows us his personality/ character as a 'special need', which is how society sees it.
- She is a sounding board for Christopher's thoughts/ideas/plans.
- She has a professional understanding/ distance which helps her deal with him without the emotional frustrations of his parents.
- She reads out the letters and is therefore a channel through which we hear Judy's point of view.
- She tells him that he cannot live with her because she is not his mother.
- There is sympathy but maybe a lack of emotional attachment – this might make it easier for Christopher to deal with her.

29. *A Taste of Honey*
- Description of Helen as 'semi-whore' implies casual attitude to sex and society's disapproval.
- Helen more interested in money/ security than love – not certain if she is actually a prostitute.
- Jo has grown up without the usual parental attitudes to sex of the period.
- Unlike Helen she does associate sex with love – she craves affection.
- Characters discuss sexual matters openly, even quite crudely.
- Attitudes to pre-marital sex / single mothers and homosexuality then and now.

30. *Lord of the Flies*
- The Lord of the Flies – the sow's head – symbolising evil and lack of civilisation.
- Symbolism of the conch–democracy and civilisation.
- How they come to worship the Lord of the Flies – its association with the devil through Beelzebub.
- The Beast – an imaginary thing that becomes a powerful symbol.
- Symbolism of place – the forest glade, the mountain, the beach, the island as a whole.
- Piggy's glasses, symbolising intellect and reason, and the conch, symbolising democracy and civilisation, are both destroyed.
- Character can be symbolic of themes/ attitudes.
- Symbols related to the Bible / other literary sources and traditions.
- How the meaning of symbols can change and/or be ambiguous.

31. *Telling Tales*
- The narrator's version of his parents' happy family life.
- His interpretation of the relationship between Mother and Ralph, and what their relationship might really be like.
- Tensions between narrator and Ralph / Grandfather and Ralph – competing for Mother's affection?

- Compare Mother's reaction to husband's death with 'The Darkness Out There' / 'The Odour of Chrysanthemums' / 'A Family Supper'.
- Narrative viewpoint – compare with 'My Polish Teacher's Tie' – unreliable/ reliable viewpoint.
- Ideas about marriage – 'The Odour of Chrysanthemums', 'A Family Supper'.
- Use of symbolism and imagery – 'The Odour of Chrysanthemums'.

32. *Animal Farm*
- At the beginning the pigs are on the side of the other animals, opposed to the farmer, and act with them.
- From early on they are seen as leaders – more intelligent than others.
- Old Major's and Snowball's deaths change things. Napoleon is shown as power-hungry.
- Do they fill a power vacuum? Does someone have to take a lead in all societies?
- All power corrupts.
- Parallels with USSR and other totalitarian regimes.
- Symbolism of pigs walking on their hind feet.
- Final chapter where pigs are indistinguishable from humans and accepted by humans.
- Do they change or do they just show their true natures?

33. *Never Let Me Go*
- Tommy is seen through Kathy's eyes.
- She is tries to understand him, giving us anecdotes about him to try to work out why he behaves as he does.
- He is seen as different from other pupils – an outsider, picked on.
- His 'tantrums' seem to come from nowhere, expressions of anger that no-one understands.
- His conversations with Miss Lucy help him and Kathy to understand more about their situation.
- His relationship with Ruth and Kathy's view of it.
- How he changes as he gets older – what he is like as a donor.
- Kathy's love for him and her feelings after his 'completion'.

34. *Anita and Me*
- She lies to her parents and disobeys them. However, she loves and looks up to both of them.
- They allow her a lot of freedom, which she sometimes abuses.
- She is fascinated by their past lives in India and their love story.
- She sees them as devoted to each other – a love match, not an arranged marriage.
- She idealises them – the only slight implied criticism is that they are a bit pushy and her mother wants to interfere in people's lives.
- The relationship changes a bit after the birth of her brother, when she does not get as much attention.
- They are seen as different from other parents in the village, because of their culture and their class.

35. *Pigeon English*
- Gang culture is seen through Harri's innocent eyes and its extent is gradually revealed to readers.
- Harri's desire to belong makes him want to join the Dell Farm Crew.

- At first he seems to see them just as a group who rule the school – it's like a game.
- Harri and Dean do not see the danger of 'investigating' the crime, not understanding what gangs are really about.

- Harri feels sick when he sees the reality of them attacking an old man.
- Tension between gang culture and the family and community's Christianity. Harri thinks gang members can be brought to God.

- Rules are important in gangs and in family life – gangs as perversion of family.
- Language used to show culture and membership of the group.
- Novel inspired by real-life crime – how this context influences its reception.

36. For both questions, look at the mark scheme table on p.136 (for pages 110–111 Review Questions, Q1).

  a) Your answer might include:
  - Who is in danger and from what? – 'Exposure', 'Bayonet Charge', 'Remains', 'Poppies'.
  - Soldiers put in danger by those above them – 'Bayonet Charge', 'Exposure'.
  - The brigade seen as one – other poems focus on individual reactions.
  - Rhythm and metre.
  - Sense of excitement and bravery – 'Remains'; contrast 'Bayonet Charge', 'Exposure'.

  - Use of imagery, literal and figurative.
  - Use of language, e.g. alliteration in 'Exposure'.
  - Voice/speaker not in danger – 'War Photographer', 'Poppies'; contrast with 'Exposure', 'Remains'.

  b) Your answer might include:
  - The nature of the parting – here 'sorrow and tears', bitterness in 'Neutral Tones', death in 'Porphyria's Lover'.
  - The nature of the relationship – parents in 'Eden Rock'.

  - Reasons for the parting – she has broken her vows but the details are not given.
  - The use of imagery of nature – 'Neutral Tones'.
  - Romantic ideas about love and relationships.
  - Direct address to the loved one.
  - Feelings of poet/voice towards subject – 'love–hate relationship' or love turning to hate?
  - Regular structure with simple rhyme scheme – apparent simplicity expresses deep feelings.

37. See mark scheme table on p.136 (for pages 110–111 Review Questions, Q2a).

a) Your answer might include comments on the following:
- He gives a voice to an ordinary soldier.
- Persona's motives for becoming a soldier – poverty, unemployment.
- The ballad form tells a story in a simple, traditional form – appropriate to subject.

- Rhythm and rhyme give it a cheerful tone in contrast with the subject.
- The language is colloquial, the voice working-class.
- His attitude to his enemy – he sees him as the same kind of man.
- References to the 'inn' and 'nipperkin' make it seem homely and everyday.

- Reference to 'traps' places him in the country, perhaps as gamekeeper, perhaps as poacher. He is used to killing animals.
- The nature of the deed contrasts with the friendly language.
- Makes a strong point about war through a naive voice who sees his 'foe' as an individual like himself.

b)

Marks	Skills
7–8	• You have explored comparisons of the writers' use of language, structure and form, using appropriate subject terminology. • You have convincingly compared the effects of the writers' methods on the reader.
5–6	• You have thoughtfully compared the writers' use of language and/or structure and/or form, using effective subject terminology. • You have clearly compared the effects of the writers' methods on the reader.

Your answer might include comments on:
- Differing situations – one going to war, the other having returned.
- Past tense / future tense.
- Difference in focus – one on killing, the other on dying.

- Contrast in language.
- Sense of patriotism in 'The Soldier' absent from 'The Man He Killed'.
- One matter-of-fact, the other emotional.

- Use of imagery in 'The Soldier'.
- Difference in tone created by rhythm/ metre and language.

Glossary and Index

a

abbreviation   a shortened form of a word or phrase (52)

abstract noun   a noun which names something you cannot touch or feel, such as an idea or emotion (26)

accent   a way of pronouncing words, usually associated with a region or area (90)

act   a division of a play (91)

active voice   when the subject is the person or thing doing: for example, 'the dog bit the boy' (10)

adjective   a word used to describe a noun and add more detail (26)

adverb   a word used to describe verbs, often ending in 'ly', such as 'swiftly', 'anxiously' (26)

alliteration   repetition of a sound at the beginning of two or more words (29, 100)

alphabetical order   the arrangement of information according to the alphabet (A–Z) (31)

ambiguity   when something has more than one meaning (adjective – **ambiguous**) (87, 98)

anecdote   a short account of an interesting or humorous story, often used to reinforce a point being made (53)

antagonist   the person who opposes the protagonist (40)

apostrophe (')   punctuation mark used to show possession or omission (9)

archaic   old-fashioned, no longer in use (101)

argument   a reasoned point of view (53)

article   a short piece of writing, usually in a newspaper or magazine (50)

aside   a line or lines addressed to the audience while other actors are on stage (65)

associate   connect mentally (7)

assonance   repetition of a vowel sound within words (29, 100)

atmosphere   the tone or mood of the text (39)

attitude   a writer's feelings or opinions about something (98)

audience   a group of people who hear, watch or read something (52)

authorial voice   the writer speaking directly to the reader (75)

authority   power or influence, often because of knowledge or expertise (adjective – **authoritative**) (61, 79)

autobiographical   describes writing about the author's own experiences (50)

autobiography   the story of the author's life (49)

b

ballad   a form of poetry which tells a story, usually in quatrains with a regular metre and rhyme scheme (97)

Bildungsroman   a novel that tells the story of someone growing up (76)

biography   the story of someone's life (49)

blank verse   poetry which has a regular metre but does not rhyme (103)

blog   a dairy or journal published on the internet (short for weblog; **blogger** – a person who writes a blog) (31)

broadsheet   a 'serious' newspaper, so-called because they used to be published on large sheets of paper (54)

bullet point   a typographical symbol used to introduce an item in a list (31)

c

caesura   a pause in a line of poetry, sometimes denoted by a punctuation mark (66)

chapter   a division within a book (31)

character   a fictional person (38)

chronological order   order of time, starting with the earliest event (31)

clause   a phrase (group of words) which could stand alone as a sentence, having a main verb (10)

climax   the dramatic high point of a story, usually at the end (37)

colloquial   conversational or chatty (noun – **colloquialism**) (79)

colon (:)   a punctuation mark used to introduce a list or an explanation (8)

comma (,)   a punctuation mark used to separate clauses or items in a list (8)

complex sentence   a sentence containing more than one clause (but not a compound sentence) (11)

compound sentence   a sentence consisting of two clauses of equal importance, joined by a conjunction (10)

conceit   an elaborate or far-fetched simile or (extended) metaphor (67)

conclusion   end (30)

concrete noun   a noun that names something you can touch or feel (also **common noun**) (26)

conjunction   a word used to join two words, clauses or phrases and show the relationship between them: for example, 'and', 'but', 'because' (10, 27)

connective   any word or phrase used to join phrases, sentences or paragraphs (13)

connotation   a meaning that is suggested by the use of a word or phrase (28)

consonant   any letter that is not a vowel (6)

content   subject matter; what something contains (22)

context   circumstances (60)

contraction   making two words into one by leaving out letters and using an apostrophe: for example, 'doesn't', 'I'm', 'who's' (6)

counter-argument   an argument that answers one that has already been given (53)

court   the people surrounding a king or queen (61)

d

deduction   working something out or coming to a conclusion (73)

determiner   a short word that comes before a noun and helps to define it, including the definite article ('the') and indefinite article ('a') (27)

diagram   a plan, sketch, drawing, or outline designed to demonstrate or explain how something works (86)

dialect   words or phrases particular to a region (14)

dialogue   speech between two or more people; conversation (63, 91)

diarist   a person who writes a diary (48)

diction   the choice of words and phrases used (26)

difference   a way in which two or more things are not alike (22)

direct address   speaking directly to the audience, usually using 'you' (53)

direct speech   the actual words spoken, put in inverted commas (41)

director   a person who directs plays (87)

discourse marker   a word or phrase that connects sentences or paragraphs (13, 53)

divine right   the idea that the right to rule comes from God (61)

dramatic monologue   a long poem in which a fictional character speaks to a reader or an audience (96)

e

ellipsis (…)   punctuation indicating that something has been left out (9)

embed   with reference to a quotation, to place it within sentences so that the whole sentence makes sense (24)

emotive language   language used to provoke emotions, such as shock or pity, in readers (28)

end-stopping   ending a line of verse with a punctuation mark (also called lineation) (102)

enjambment   when lines are not end-stopped but the sense runs on between lines or even stanzas (102)

evidence   information referred to in order to support a point being made (21)

exclamation mark (!)   a punctuation mark used to denote extreme emotion (8)

explicit open, obvious (18)

exposition setting the scene or giving background information at the beginning of a story (36)

extended metaphor a series of similar metaphors combining to create one image (67)

f

fable a story, often about animals, that gives a moral lesson (85)

feature a newspaper or magazine article that is not a news report (50)

figurative imagery the use of an image of one thing to tell us about another (39)

form a type of writing or the way it is presented (48)

formal language language that is similar to Standard English and used in situations where it is not appropriate to be too conversational (79)

fragment another word for a 'minor sentence', one which does not contain a main verb (10)

free verse poetry that does not have a regular metre or rhyme scheme (103)

full stop (.) a punctuation mark that marks the end of a sentence (8)

function what something is used for (76)

g

genre a kind or type of literature: for example, detective story or romance (48)

grammar the study or rules of how words relate to each other (14)

headline heading at the top of a newspaper or magazine article (54)

homophone a word that sounds the same as another word but is spelled differently and has a different meaning (6)

hyperbole exaggeration (adjective – **hyperbolic**) (28, 53)

iambic pentameter a line of poetry consisting of ten syllables with the stress on every second syllable (66)

identify select; name (19)

image a picture, also used metaphorically of 'word pictures' (63, 87)

imagery when words are so descriptive that they paint a picture in your mind. Imagery is used to allow the reader to empathise or imagine the moment being described. (29, 42)

imply to suggest something that is not expressly stated (noun – **implication**; adjective – **implicit**) (20)

inciting incident an event that starts the action of a story (36)

indent to start writing a little way in from the margin: for example, to start a new paragraph (12)

indirect speech speech that is reported rather than quoted: for example, He said that she was there (41)

infer to deduce something that is not openly stated (noun – **inference**) (20)

informal language conversational language that is spoken between people who are usually familiar with one another (48)

interpret when you infer meaning and explain what you have inferred, you are interpreting implicit information or ideas (noun – **interpretation**) (20, 87)

interval a break during a performance (91)

intrusive narrator a narrator who is outside the action but comments on it (37)

inverted commas (' ') punctuation marks used to indicate quotations, titles etc. (9)

irony when words are used to imply an opposite meaning, or sarcastic language that can be used to mock or convey scorn (adjective – **ironic**) (79)

isolate separate; place apart (7)

issue a subject being discussed (63, 75)

journal a form of diary (48)

journalism writing in a newspaper or magazine (50)

l

literal imagery the use of description to convey mood or atmosphere (39)

location place (85)

lyric a short poem about feelings (97)

m

medium means of communication (plural – **media**) (87)

metaphor an image created by directly comparing one thing to another, such as 'my brother is a little monkey' (29, 101)

metre the pattern of stressed and unstressed syllables in poetry (66, 103)

minor sentence a 'sentence' that does not contain a verb – also known as a 'fragment' (10)

mnemonic a way of remembering information, especially spellings (7)

modal verb a verb that shows the mood or state of another verb: for example, 'could', 'might' (14)

mood the general feeling conveyed (see **atmosphere**) (39)

morality ideas of good and bad behaviour, or right and wrong (61)

motif an idea or image that is repeated at intervals in a text (75)

motivation the reason(s) for doing something (64)

movement a group of writers who share similar ideas about literature and/or write in a similar style (96)

musical theatre a form of drama including music (85)

n

naive narrator a narrator who does not understand what is going on, often a child (76, 89)

narrative story (37, 40)

narrator the person telling a story (37)

non-fiction text a text that is mainly based on facts and not made up (48)

noun a naming word (10, 26)

o

object (in grammar) the thing or person to whom something is done (in the active voice) (10)

octave a set of eight lines of verse (102)

omission missing out (9)

omniscient narrator a narrator who is outside the action and knows everything (37, 89)

onomatopoeia the use of a word that sounds like what it describes (29, 100)

opening start, beginning (30)

opinion what someone thinks (18)

oxymoron two contradictory words placed together: for example, 'bitter sweet' (67)

p

paragraph a section of a piece of prose writing, shown by indentation or leaving a line (12, 31)

parallel phrasing repeating the structure and some of the words, phrases, clauses or sentences (43)

paraphrase to put something in your own words (24)

parenthesis a word or phrase inserted into a sentence to explain something (plural – **parentheses**) (9)

passive voice where the subject has the action done to him or her: for example, 'the boy was bitten by the dog' (10)

past continuous tense the tense used to convey an action that continued for some time in the past, e.g. 'he was talking for hours' (15)

past perfect tense the tense used to describe events that happened before those being described in the past tense, using 'had' (15)

past tense the tense used to described something that has happened (7)

pathetic fallacy either a form of personification, giving nature human qualities, or using a description of the surroundings to reflect the mood of a character (29)

perfect tense a form of the past tense, using 'has' or 'have' (15)

period an amount of time (84)

persona a fictional voice used by a poet (98, 100)

personal pronoun   a pronoun that stands in for the names of people (14)

personification   when an inanimate object or idea is given human qualities (29)

perspective   point of view (48, 75)

Petrarchan or Italian sonnet   a form of sonnet consisting of an octave and a sestet (102)

playwright   a person who writes plays (89)

plot   the main events of a story (63)

plural   more than one (6, 14)

possession   belonging or ownership (9)

preposition   a short word showing the relationship of one thing to another: for example, 'to', 'under' (10, 27)

present tense   the tense used to describe things happening now (15)

pronoun   a short word which replaces a noun ('I', 'you', 'he', 'she' etc.) (26)

proper noun   a noun that names an individual person or thing, such as a place or day, and has a capital letter (26)

prose   any writing that is not poetry (66, 87)

protagonist   the main character, the person whom the story is about (37, 40)

psychology   the study of the human mind (73)

pun   word play, when words are organised in an amusing way to suggest other meaning (54)

q

quatrain   a set of four lines of verse (102)

question mark (?)   a punctuation mark used at the end of a question (8)

quotation   words or phrases taken directly from the text (verb – **quote**) (24)

quotation marks   inverted commas when used around a quotation (9)

r

recipient   the person who receives something, especially a letter (49)

refer   mention or allude to something (noun - **reference**) (24)

refrain   a repeated line or lines, usually at the end of stanzas, in poetry (100)

register   the form of language used in particular circumstances (26)

relative pronoun   a word such as 'who', 'which' or 'that', used to connect clauses (11)

repetition   when words, phrases, ideas or sentences are used more than once – this can be used to highlight key issues and make important sections more memorable (28)

report   an account of something that has happened, often in a newspaper (50)

reported speech   see **indirect speech** (41)

reverse chronological order   ordering events by putting the most recent first and working backwards (31)

review   an article that gives an opinion on, for example, a film, play or book (50)

rhetoric   the art of speaking (adjective – **rhetorical**) (28)

rhetorical device   a language technique used to influence an audience (53)

rhetorical question   a question that does not require an answer, used to make the reader think about the possible answer and involve them in the text (28)

rhyme   the use of words with the same endings to make patterns (102)

rhyming couplet   two successive lines of poetry that rhyme (66, 102)

rhythm   the beat of the writing, usually in poetry (103)

s

scene   a division of a play, often within an act (91)

script   the text of a play (87)

semantic field   the area from which words and phrases have been taken (26)

semi-colon (;)   punctuation mark used to connect clauses, also used in lists (8)

sentiment   feeling (73)

sestet   a set of six lines of verse (102)

setting   where and when the action takes place (39, 75)

Shakespearean or English sonnet   a form of sonnet popularised by Shakespeare, consisting of four quatrains and a rhyming couplet (102)

sibilance   repetition of 's' sounds (29)

significance   what something means or stands for (77)

silent letter   a letter within a word which is not pronounced (7)

similarity   a way in which two or more things are alike (22)

simile   a comparison of one thing to another using the words 'like' or 'as', such as 'the raindrops fell like tears' (29, 101)

simple past tense   the form of the past tense usually formed by adding '-ed' (15)

simple sentence   a sentence that only contains a main clause (10)

singular   one (14)

skim read   to read quickly in order to find something in the text (22)

slang   informal language, often local and changing quickly (14)

social order   where people are 'placed' in society, with some more important than others (61)

soliloquy   a speech to the audience, expressing a character's thoughts or feelings (plural **soliloquies**) (65)

sonnet   a form of poetry, usually a love poem, of 14 lines (67)

source   the origin of something, used by examiners to describe texts used in exams (51)

speech marks   inverted commas when used around direct speech (9)

Standard English   the variety of English generally accepted as the correct form for writing and formal speech (14)

stanza   a section of a poem, often called a verse (31, 102)

strapline   a subheading under a headline, which explains or expands on the headline (54)

stress   (in poetry) emphasis (103)

subheading   used to break up the text and guide the reader through various sections (54)

subject   the person or thing that a sentence is about (10)

subordinate clause   a clause that contains extra information (11)

summarise   give a shortened account of something, retaining the meaning (noun – **summary**) (22)

supernatural   not belonging to the natural world; magical (73)

syllable   a unit of pronunciation (103)

symbol   an object that represents something else: for example, an idea or emotion (adjective – **symbolic**) (29, 79, 100)

synthesis   the combining of two or more things (verb – **synthesise**) (22)

t

tabloid   a type of newspaper, less serious and easier to read than a broadsheet, traditionally in a smaller format (54)

terminology   use of appropriate, often specialised, words (105)

text box   a box which contains text (31)

theme   subject matter: what the text is about rather than what happens in it (62)

third person   he, she, it (singular); they (plural) (15)

tone   the overall feel or attitude of the writing (79)

topic sentence   a sentence, usually the first in the paragraph, which tells you what the paragraph is about (12)

turning point   an event that changes the direction of a story (37, 91)

u

unreliable narrator   a narrator who cannot always be trusted (89)

v

verb   a doing, thinking, feeling or being word (7, 26)

verse   poetry (66)

viewpoint   point of view (48)

vocabulary   words used (26)

voice   the narrator or speaker; his or her characteristic style (41, 98)

volta   a turn or change in a poem, especially between the octave and sestet in a Petrarchan sonnet (102)

vowel   a, e, i, o, u (6)

Collins

AQA GCSE 9-1
English Language & Literature

Workbook

Paul Burns

Preparing for the GCSE Exam

Revision That Really Works

Experts have found that there are two techniques that help you to retain and recall information and consistently produce better results in exams compared to other revision techniques.

It really isn't rocket science either – you simply need to:

- **test yourself** on each topic as many times as possible
- **leave a gap** between the test sessions.

Three Essential Revision Tips

1. Use Your Time Wisely

- Allow yourself plenty of time.
- Try to start revising at least six months before your exams – it's more effective and less stressful.
- Don't waste time re-reading the same information over and over again – it's not effective!

2. Make a Plan

- Identify all the topics you need to revise (this Complete Revision & Practice book will help you).
- Plan at least five sessions for each topic.
- One hour should be ample time to test yourself on the key ideas for a topic.
- Spread out the practice sessions for each topic – the optimum time to leave between each session i about one month but, if this isn't possible, just make the gaps as big as realistically possible.

3. Test Yourself

- Methods for testing yourself include: quizzes, practice questions, flashcards, past papers, explaining a topic to someone else, etc.
- This Complete Revision & Practice book provides seven practice opportunities per topic.
- Don't worry if you get an answer wrong – provided you check what the correct answer is, you are more likely to get the same or similar questions right in future!

Visit **collins.co.uk/collinsGCSErevision** to download your free flashcards, for more information about the benefit of these techniques, and for further guidance on how to plan ahead and make them work for you.

Command Words Used in Exam Questions

This table shows the meanings of some of the most commonly used command words in GCSE exam questions.

Command word	Meaning
List…	Pick out words or phrases and copy them. Do not comment on them.
Choose…	Pick the correct statements and fill in the box.
Look in detail…	Carefully re-read the appropriate part of the text before giving a detailed answer.
Focus on…	Your answer should be about the section of text indicated and not about the rest of the source.
How…?	Write about the writer's methods, e.g. use of language and structure.
How far…?/To what extent…?	You are free to agree, disagree or partly agree. Answer the question in detail using appropriate references.
Describe/Write a description…	Describe something; do NOT write a story.
Refer to both…	Write equally about both sources.
Explore/Explain…	Write a detailed answer using appropriate references and terminology.
Starting with the extract, explore/explain…	About half your answer should be a detailed analysis of the extract you are given.
Compare…	Write equally about the two texts, focusing on their similarities and differences

Contents

Key Technical Skills: Writing

Spelling

Grade 2–3

1 Insert the correctly spelled word in each of the following pairs of sentences:

a) your/you're

Is that _____ coat?

_____ in the wrong place.

b) there/ they're/ their

_____ all in the yard eating

_____ lunches, over

_____ by the tree.

c) where/ wear/ were

What do you think I should

_____ for the party?

_____ did you say they

_____ going?

d) hear/here

Come over _____. I can't

_____ you very well.

e) to/ too/ two

You have _____ choose

_____ of the five

options. Three would be

_____ many.

f) its/it's

The cat's eaten _____ food

and now _____

asleep.   [15

Grade 3–5

2 The following passage contains ten incorrect spellings. Underline them and then write the correct spellings below.

If you are going to improve your preformance in any area, weather in a sport, a hobby or in you're studys, you must practice. Succesfull people who have acheived great things in life always say it is becos of hard work just as much as talent. You mite not want to be an Olympic champion but you can still get a lot of satisfaction from nowing you have improved.

_____

_____

_____

_____   [10

Grade 4–6

3 Put the following words into their plural forms:

a) tornado _____

b) woman _____

c) antibody _____

d) antithesis _____

e) soliloquy _____   [5

Total Marks = _____ / 30

Key Technical Skills: Writing

Punctuation

1 Punctuate the following passage using only full stops and insert a capital letter after each one. There should be five full stops.

Anita and Me is a novel based on the author's own childhood It is the story of a family who come from India they settle in a village in the English Midlands the narrator makes friends with a girl called Anita their friendship is the focus of the book

_____

_____

_____ [5]

2 Add five commas and five apostrophes to the passage below.

Pride and Prejudice is Jane Austens most popular book. Elizabeth one of five sisters meets a man called Mr Darcy who is very rich and rather snobbish. Darcys best friend whose name is Mr Bingley falls in love with Elizabeths older sister. The sisters relationships dont go smoothly.

_____

_____

_____ [10]

3 Add a question mark, an exclamation mark, a colon, a semi-colon or brackets to the following pairs of clauses so that they make sense.

a) Where did they come from nobody knows.

_____

b) What a lovely surprise it was just what I wanted.

_____

c) Pip the hero of the story meets Magwitch on the marshes.

_____

d) Kai had rice pudding Ellie chose the cheese.

_____

e) We love Birmingham it has everything a city should have.

_____ [5]

Total Marks = _____ / 20

Key Technical Skills: Writing

> ### Sentence Structure

Grade 1–3 **1** Combine the following simple sentences to form compound sentences using the conjunctions **and** or **but**.

a) Jo lives next door to me. Mo lives next door to her.

_____

b) Mo has a dog. Jo does not have any pets.

_____ [2

Grade 3–5 **2** Combine the following simple sentences to form complex sentences using the conjunctions **because** or **although.**

a) He worked as quickly as he could. He did not finish on time.

_____

b) I missed the bus. I stopped to talk to someone on the way.

_____ [2

Grade 3–5 **3** Combine the following sentences to form a complex sentence using a relative pronoun.

Tom is my best friend. He lives on the main road.

_____ [1

Grade 5+ **4** Identify whether the sentences below are simple, complex, compound or minor sentences.

a) Bella jumped for joy. _____

b) Nana cut the cake and everyone sang 'Happy Birthday'. _____

c) Brilliant! _____

d) Trying my best to be cheerful, despite my misgivings, I joined in with

the celebrations. _____

e) Do not leave this room until you have tidied up. _____ [5

> **Total Marks =** _____ / 10

Key Technical Skills: Writing

Text Structure and Organisation

1 Rearrange the following paragraphs so that the passage makes sense. Put the paragraphs in the correct order.

a) These groups have achieved a lot but their efforts have had little impact on the behaviour of people passing through on their way to the shops and bars on the main road.

b) The residents of Manningham Drive say they have had enough of noise, litter and generally anti-social behaviour in their neighbourhood.

c) We asked both the council and the police for their response to Ms Braithwaite's comments but, so far, they have not replied.

d) They have had a number of meetings and have organised an army of volunteers to deal with the litter and graffiti problem. They go out regularly in groups every week to pick up rubbish and clean up.

e) Spokesperson Lizzie Braithwaite said, 'We are doing everything we can to improve our neighbourhood but we can only do so much. We are calling on the police and the local council to deal with anti-social behaviour in the street. So far they have done nothing.' [5]

2 Insert each of these five discourse markers or connectives into the passage so that it makes sense:

nevertheless   **after**   **therefore**   **despite**   **however**

a) _____ I got your letter, I decided to visit Manningham Drive.

b) _____ serving as your councillor for six months, I am sorry to say that I

was unaware of the extent of the problem. Thanks to your group, **c)** _____,

I now appreciate how the residents feel. I have, **d)** _____, contacted

the appropriate council department and the Chief Constable. They have not yet replied.

e) _____, I shall continue to pursue the matter on your behalf. [5]

Total Marks = _____ / 10

Key Technical Skills: Writing

Standard English and Grammar

Grade 3–6

1 In the following sentences, insert the correct form of the verb 'to be' or 'to do'.

Present tense

a) You _____ taller than me.

b) They _____ brothers.

Simple past tense

c) We _____ the first to arrive.

d) She _____ all her homework.

Perfect tense

e) He _____ in my class for three years.

f) They _____ all the cooking for the party.

Simple past + Past perfect

g) We _____ pleased with the result because

we _____ everything asked of us.   [8

Grade 4–6

2 Which of the following is correct in Standard English? Circle the correct words.

a) They have **got/gotten** their **invites/invitations** to the party.

b) He's one of the **only/few** people to have **broke/broken** the sound barrier.   [4

Grade 5+

3 Rewrite the following passage using Standard English.

I was stood in the street minding me own business when I seen Zaki. He come over to me acting dead casual. Me and Zaki was best mates. I was gonna ask him how he done in his exams. I never said nothing though. I could see he done good. Then I clocked Kirsty sat on the wall. 'Did you guys flunk your exams again?' she shouted.

_____

_____

_____

_____

_____   [8

Total Marks = _____ / 20

Key Technical Skills: Reading

Explicit Information and Ideas

1 Read the passage below.

> The Muncaster family has been farming on Windle Top for over a hundred years. In their dairy farm they have over 150 cattle. In the summer, the cattle stay out in the fields and are brought in for milking twice a day. Gerry and Annie Muncaster say it's a hard life but very rewarding. They hope that their children will follow them into farming one day.

Which of the statements below contain information that is explicitly stated in the text? Tick the correct answers.

a) The Muncasters are farmers. ☐

b) Gerry inherited the farm from his father. ☐

c) There are over 150 cattle on the farm. ☐

d) Gerry and Annie do not enjoy farming. ☐

e) The cattle are milked twice a day. ☐

f) The Muncasters have a lot of children. ☐

g) Windle Top is in Yorkshire. ☐

h) According to the Muncasters, farming is a rewarding job. ☐ [4]

2 Read the passage below.

> He was a very nice looking old gentleman, and he looked as if he were nice, too, which is not at all the same thing. He had a fresh-coloured, clean-shaven face, and white hair, and he wore rather odd-shaped collars and a top hat that wasn't exactly the same kind as other people's.
>
> From *The Railway Children* by E. Nesbit

List four things that we learn about the old gentleman's appearance.

_____

_____

_____

_____ [4]

Total Marks = _____ / 8

Key Technical Skills: Reading

> ## Implicit Information and Ideas

 1 Which of the following statements...

A imply that the writer enjoys living on a farm?
B imply that the writer does not enjoy living on a farm?
C give no indication of the writer's feelings.

Write the appropriate letter in the boxes.

a) I know one thing. I will never set foot on a farm again. ☐

b) There's something special about working with animals and growing crops. ☐

c) We grow wheat, barley and corn on the farm. ☐

d) My sister hates farming. ☐

e) I miss shopping, nights out in town, my family and my friends. ☐

f) I was a real townie and it took a while, but I'm really glad I moved here. ☐

g) It is three miles from the farm to the nearest village. ☐

h) Every night on the farm I go to bed feeling that I've achieved something worthwhile. ☐ [8.

2 Read the following passage.

The narrator has just seen some Martians that have arrived on Earth.

> I turned and, running madly, made for the first group of trees, perhaps a hundred yards away; but I ran slantingly and stumblingly, for I could not avert my eyes from these things.
>
> From *The War of the Worlds* by HG Wells.

Which of the following statements are TRUE? Tick the statements that are implied by what the narrator says.

a) The narrator is frightened. ☐

b) The narrator has never seen a Martian before. ☐

c) The narrator is old. ☐

d) The narrator thinks the Martians are friendly. ☐

e) The narrator is fascinated by the Martians. ☐

f) The narrator is a Martian. ☐

g) The narrator thinks he will be safer amongst the trees. ☐

h) The narrator runs very fast. ☐ [4

Total Marks = _____ / 12

Key Technical Skills: Reading

> ## Synthesis and Summary 1

1 Reduce each of the following sentences to five words by crossing out, in order to give the necessary information without losing sense.

a) Jackie, who has long dark hair, won the sack race.

b) I must insist that you give me the letter now.

c) A vengeful wind blew over the two much-loved trees.   [3]

2 Read the following statement from someone who has witnessed an accident.

> I spent most of the day at my nan's house, number 5 Roland Street. I love going there because she always spoils me with sweets and presents. When I left at four o'clock, it was very windy. It was cold as well but I was well wrapped up so it didn't bother me. When I was at the front gate, I saw a car coming round the corner from Bilton Road. Just as it turned, a tree in the garden of the corner house was blown right over and landed across the car's bonnet. The driver braked suddenly. I ran over to see if anyone was hurt. As I approached, I could see two people inside, though my view wasn't clear because of the tree being in the way. By the time I got there they were getting out of the car. They must have had a terrible shock, but they seemed okay. Nan came down the street then and so did a few of the neighbours. It's a very close community.

If you were investigating the accident, which **five** of the following pieces of information would be most relevant to understanding what had happened? Tick the correct answers.

a) The witness was in Roland Street at four o'clock. ☐

b) The witness's nan spoils them with sweets and presents. ☐

c) The witness was dressed for cold and windy weather. ☐

d) The car came round the corner from Bilton Road. ☐

e) The wind blew over a tree in the garden of the corner house. ☐

f) The tree landed across the car's bonnet. ☐

g) The witness thinks the people in the car must have had a shock. ☐

h) Two people got out of the car and appeared unhurt. ☐

i) People came out of their houses. ☐

j) People in Roland Street are very friendly. ☐   [5]

3 On a separate piece of paper, write a summary of the witness's statement. Aim for 50 words or fewer.   [12]

Total Marks = _____ / 20

Key Technical Skills: Reading

Synthesis and Summary 2

1 Read the two passages below.

A This text is adapted from a letter written by 'JDS' to *The Liverpool Mercury* in 1832. A turnpike road was a private road which people had to pay tolls to use.

> GENTLEMEN, I should feel particularly obliged to you or any of your readers if you could inform me by whose authority the turnpike on the Aigburth road was established, and why the public at large are required to pay tolls there when the inhabitants of that neighbourhood are exempted. I think it not only a nuisance, but a complete imposition, which calls loudly for inquiry. I have heard, a few interested individuals round there had in a former period been at an expense (mark, for their own convenience) in repairing the road, but it has long since paid itself over and over again; and, let me ask, who pockets the money collected there now? The road is kept in excellent repair for about one-quarter of a mile beyond the gate, but on approaching Garston it is very bad.

B This is an email sent to a local council about the roads near the writer, Amina's, home.

> Hi, I really am getting fed up with this now. I've written umpteen emails and texts to you about the state of the High Street. There are two main problems: parking and that road surface. There are double yellow lines along a fair proportion of the road. Why do so many people ignore them or, worse still, think it's okay to park either half-on and half-off the pavement or even entirely on the pavement, creating an obstacle course for prams and wheelchairs? This is against the law. And as for the road surface… it's pothole city outside my shop. I've lived and worked here for ten years; every year it gets worse and nobody does anything about it. What are we paying our council tax and business rates for?

Pick out as many similarities and differences as you can between the contents of the two sources. Write them in the table below or on a separate piece of paper. There may be more differences than similarities. Do not comment on language or style.

Similarities	Differences

[10

2 Now sum up the similarities and differences in the texts above, writing in proper sentences. Do not comment on language or style. Continue on a separate piece of paper.

_____

_____

_____

_____

[8

Total Marks = ... / 18

Key Technical Skills: Reading

Referring to the Text

1 Match each statement **a)–c)** with its paraphrase **x)–z)**:

a) I was proceeding towards the location from which the sound emanated.

b) I am anxious to ascertain the identity of the perpetrator.

c) At 21.30 we took our leave of the apartment which was our home.

x) At half past nine we left our flat.

y) I was going to the place the noise came from.

z) I want to find out who did it.

[3]

2 The following sentences all include quotations from *Romeo and Juliet,* which have not been set out correctly. Set them out correctly using colons and/or quotation marks where appropriate.

a) Romeo refers to Juliet as a bright angel. _____

_____

_____

b) Romeo rejects his family Henceforth I never will be Romeo. _____

_____

_____

c) When Juliet asks how he found her, Romeo replies By love, that first did prompt me to enquire. He lent me counsel, and I lent him eyes. _____

_____

[6]

3 Here are two examples of the use of PEE. Use different colours to highlight the point, the evidence and the explanation (or exploration).

a) Gratiano insults Shylock, calling him 'an inexecrable dog', a metaphor that implies that he considers Shylock less than human.

b) By the end of the novel, Scrooge is a reformed character, shown by his gift of the turkey to the Cratchits, a generous gesture that the old Scrooge would never have made. [6]

Total Marks = _____ / 15

Key Technical Skills: Reading

Analysing Language 1

Grade 2–3

1 Read the passage below and identify the word class (part of speech) of the bold words.

> Apparently, the vegetable **kingdom** in Mars, instead of having green for a **dominant** colour, is of a vivid blood-red tint. At any rate, **the** seeds which the Martians (intentionally **or accidentally**) **brought with them** gave rise in all cases to red-coloured growths.
>
> From *The War of the Worlds* by HG Wells

Choose from: **pronoun   adjective   verb   adverb   noun   conjunction   determiner   preposition**

a) kingdom _____

b) dominant _____

c) the _____

d) or _____

e) accidentally _____

f) brought _____

g) with _____

h) them _____   [8

Grade 2–3

2 a) Give an example from the passage of a proper noun. _____

b) There are two sentences in the passage above. What sort of sentence are they?

_____

c) Give an example of a relative pronoun from the passage. _____

d) Are the sentences in the active or passive voice? _____   [4

Grade 4–6

3 a) Which two of these terms could be used to describe the register of the passage above?

formal   colloquial   technical   dialectical

_____ and _____   [2

b) Explain why you have chosen these two words.

_____

_____

_____

_____

_____

[4

Total Marks = _____ / 18

Key Technical Skills: Reading

> ## Analysing Language 2

1 Read the following sentence and give an example of each of the language techniques used in the table below.

The great grinning giant's feet squelched in the mud as he looked danger in the face.

a) alliteration	
b) personification	
c) onomatopoeia	

[3]

2 State whether each of the following sentences contains a metaphor or a simile and describe the effect of the comparison.

	Metaphor or simile?	Effect
She came into the room like a tornado.		
You are my rock.		

[4]

3 Read the following passage from *Wuthering Heights* by Emily Brontë. Here, the narrator visits his landlord's house, Wuthering Heights.

> On that bleak hill-top the earth was hard with a black frost, and the air made me shiver through every limb. Being unable to remove the chain[1], I jumped over, and, running up the flagged causeway[2] bordered with straggling gooseberry bushes, knocked vainly for admittance, till my knuckles tingled, and the dogs howled.
>
> [1] a chain fastening the gate   [2] the path

How does the writer use language to convey an unwelcoming atmosphere?

On a separate piece of paper comment on:

- the writer's choice of words and phrases
- language features and techniques
- sentence forms.

[8]

Total Marks = _____ / 15

Key Technical Skills: Reading

Analysing Form and Structure

Grade 3–5

1 Match the endings **a)–c)** with the descriptions **x)–z)**.

a) And without hesitation he laid the ancient timepiece in the hands of its rightful owner.

b) Go to your wide futures, you said.

c) Do not play tricks on people unless you can stand the same treatment yourself.

x) Readers might find this ending inspiring.

y) This ending draws a lesson from the story.

z) This is a neat ending that would satisfy the reader.

[3

Grade 4–6

2 Here is the opening of a short story, 'To Please His Wife', by Thomas Hardy. Read it and answer the questions below.

> The interior of St. James's Church, in Havenpool Town, was slowly darkening under the close clouds of a winter afternoon. It was Sunday: service had just ended, the face of the parson in the pulpit was buried in his hands, and the congregation, with a cheerful sigh of release, were rising from their knees to depart.
>
> For the moment the stillness was so complete that the surging of the sea could be heard outside the harbour-bar. Then it was broken by the footsteps of the clerk going towards the west door to open it in the usual manner for the exit of the assembly. Before, however, he had reached the doorway, the latch was lifted from without, and the dark figure of a man in a sailor's garb appeared against the light.

a) What has just taken place?

b) What do we learn about the story's setting?

c) What is the effect of the phrase, 'slowly darkening under the close clouds of a winter afternoon'?

d) What is the effect of the phrase, 'the stillness was so complete that the surging of the sea could be heard'?

e) Why do you think none of the three people mentioned are given names?

f) What do you think might happen next?

[12

Total Marks = ... / 15

English Language 1

Creative Reading 1

1 Read the extracts below and state which is narrated by...

A A naïve or unreliable narrator

B An omniscient narrator

C A reliable first-person narrator

D An intrusive narrator

a)

> Adam, you perceive, was by no means a marvellous man, nor, properly speaking, a genius, yet I will not pretend that his was an ordinary character among workmen…
>
> From *Adam Bede* by George Eliot

b)

> Feeling the importance of not interrupting Sergeant Cuff's examination of the boy, I received the clerk in another room. He came with bad news of his employer. The agitation and excitement of the last two days had proved too much for Mr Bruff.
>
> From *The Moonstone* by Wilkie Collins

c)

> The Mole was bewitched, entranced, fascinated. By the side of the river he trotted as one trots, when very small, by the side of a man, who holds one spellbound by exciting stories; and when tired at last, he sat on the bank…
>
> From *The Wind in the Willows* by Kenneth Grahame

d)

> After supper she got out her book and learned me about Moses and the Bullrushers; and I was in a sweat to find out all about him; but by and by she let it out that Moses had been dead a considerable long time; so then I didn't care no more about him; because I don't taken no stock in dead people.
>
> From *The Adventures of Huckleberry Finn* by Mark Twain

[4]

Total Marks = _____ / 4

English Language 1

 1 Look at the quotations in the table below. Each is taken from one of the set texts, but you do not need to have studied the text to answer the question.

In the third column, enter how we learn about the character, choosing from:

- Narrator's description

- What the character does

- What the character says

- How others react to the character

- What others say to/about the character.

In the fourth column, state what we learn about the character from the quotation.

Character	Quotation	How we learn about the character	What we learn about the character
Lady Catherine de Burgh *Pride and Prejudice*	Her air was not conciliating, nor was her manner of receiving them such as to make her visitors forget their inferior rank.		
Mary Morstan *The Sign of Four*	…I found myself in dream-land, with the sweet face of Mary Morstan looking down upon me.		
Mrs Fairfax *Jane Eyre*	She conducted me to her own chair, and then began to remove my shawl and untie my bonnet strings: I begged she would not give herself so much trouble.		
Fezziwig *A Christmas Carol*	'Yo ho, my boys!' said Fezziwig. 'No more work tonight. Christmas-eve, Dick. Christmas, Ebenezer! Let's have the shutters up…'		
Hyde *The Strange Case of Dr Jekyll and Mr Hyde*	'There must be something else,' said the perplexed gentleman. 'There is something more if I could find a name for it. God bless me, the man hardly seems human!'		

[15]

Total Marks = _____ / 15

English Language 1

Narrative Writing

Imagine you have been set the following task in your exam:

Your school or college is holding a creative writing competition and has invited people to write a short story with the title 'The New Neighbour'.

Use the following questions and guidelines to help you plan your story.

a) What person will you write the story in: first or third?_____ [1]

b) If you are writing in the first person, is the narrator also the protagonist?_____ [1]

c) Who is your protagonist? Make notes about the protagonist:

   i) gender_____

   ii) age_____

   iii) appearance _____

   _____

   iv) background _____

   _____

   v) relationships _____

   _____ [5]

d) Where is the story set? _____ [1]

e) When is it set? (Now, in the past or in the future?) _____ [1]

f) How long does the story take? (A day, a month, a year?) _____ [1]

2 How will your story be structured? Make brief notes on your:

a) exposition _____

_____

b) inciting incident _____

c) turning point(s) _____

d) climax _____

e) coda _____ [10]

> **Total Marks = _____ / 20**

English Language 1

Descriptive Writing

Imagine you have been set the following task in your exam:

Your school or college is holding a creative writing competition and has invited people to write a piece of descriptive writing about a place that holds happy memories for them.

Use the following questions and guidelines to help you plan your story.

1

  a) What person will you write the story in: first or third? _____ [1

  b) Are you going to write in the past or present tense? _____ [1

  c) Make brief notes on the place as seen from:

    i) long distance

    _____

    _____

    ii) middle distance

    _____

    _____

    iii) close up

    _____

    _____ [6

2 Using an adjective and a noun for each, jot down at least two things you can:

  a) see _____

  b) hear _____

  c) smell _____

  d) taste _____

  e) touch _____ [1

3 Write down an appropriate:

  a) simile _____

  b) metaphor _____ [

Total Marks = _____ / 20

English Language 2

Reading Non-fiction

1 Read the following two reviews and use the table below to list differences in the writers' points of view and how they are expressed.

A

As soon as I saw Holcombe Manor I felt at home. Of course, it was nothing like our home – rather, it is a quaint half-timbered Tudor house nestling among the gentle hills, surrounded by ancient oaks. There is even a moat. Entering the magnificent hall, heated by a huge welcoming fire, we felt like royalty, and our hosts, Audrey and Frank, treated us like royalty. They gave us a cosy bedroom overlooking the moat, which featured a splendid four-poster bed and led into a delightfully old-fashioned ensuite. Breakfast the next morning was superb, everything sourced from local producers and served in his own inimitable and rather eccentric manner by Frank. Miles from the nearest village, the place exuded tranquillity. It's the perfect place to recharge your batteries.

B

Unless you're some kind of time-traveller and want to experience life in the uncivilised past, avoid Holcombe Manor! For a start, it's miles from the nearest village, which itself doesn't even have a pub or shop. The phone signal is terrible and the ever-so-posh owners haven't even heard of WiFi. Our room was cramped, dominated by a massive ancient, creaky bed, and wasn't as clean as it might be. The bathroom didn't even have a shower. After a poor night's sleep we were treated to a barely adequate breakfast, served up by the bumbling and inefficient 'Lord of the Manor', Frank. We won't be going back.

	Text A	Text B
What is the text about?		
What is the writer's attitude to Holcombe Manor?		
What impression do you get of the writer?		
How would you describe the general tone and style?		
Comment on any interesting language features.		

[20]

Total Marks = _____ / 20

English Language 2

Writing Non-fiction

 1 Imagine that in your exam you have been asked to argue for or against the following statement:

'Working hard at school is pointless when you can achieve fame and fortune simply by appearing on reality television.'

In the table, list four or five points that support the statement and four or five points that disagree with the statement.

For	Against

[10

 2 Imagine that the question asked you to write a letter on the subject to a broadsheet newspaper. Write the beginning (salutation) and first paragraph of your letter.

[

 3 Imagine that the question asked you to write an article for a teenage magazine. Write the first part of your answer.

[

Total Marks = _____ / 20

Shakespeare

Context and Themes

1 Think about the Shakespeare play you have studied (*Macbeth, Romeo and Juliet, The Merchant of Venice, Much Ado About Nothing, The Tempest* or *Julius Caesar*). Write a sentence or two explaining how each of the following themes is reflected in it. An example has been done for you.

a) Power and ambition – **Example:** Macbeth and Lady Macbeth ruthlessly achieve their ambition to make Macbeth king but Macbeth is corrupted by his power.

b) Love and marriage _____

_____

c) Order and chaos _____

_____

d) Fate _____

_____

e) Revenge _____

_____

f) Appearance and reality _____

_____ [10]

2 Think about the play you have studied and write a sentence or two explaining how each of the following aspects of social and historical context is reflected in it. An example has been done for you.

a) The place where the play is set – **Example:** Venice was a great port and commercial centre, its success founded on the risks taken by merchants, as in *The Merchant of Venice*.

b) Religion _____

_____

c) Male and female roles _____

_____

d) Cultural context _____

_____

e) Wealth and poverty/social class _____

_____

f) Real historical events _____

_____ [10]

Total Marks = _____ / 20

Shakespeare

Characters, Language and Structure

Grade 3–6

1 Choose two characters from the play you have studied. Find a quotation (either words spoken by the character or words spoken about the character) which tells us something about each character.

Put the characters' names, quotations and a brief explanation of what you think the quotations tell us about the character in the table below. An example has been done for you.

Character	Quotation	Explanation
Cassius	CAESAR: Yon Cassius has a lean and hungry look. He thinks too much. Such men are dangerous. (*Julius Caesar* Act 1 Scene 2)	Having said that he prefers men who are 'fat' because they are content, Caesar says that 'lean' Cassius, who is 'hungry' or ambitious, cannot be trusted.

[8

Grade 3–6

2 Here are some quotations from Shakespeare that use the following literary techniques: **metaphor, oxymoron, simile, rhetorical question**.

For each quotation, state which technique is being used and its effect.

a) Shall I lay perjury upon my soul?
No, not for Venice. (*The Merchant of Venice* Act 4 Scene 1)

Technique: _____   **Effect:** _____

_____

b) O heavy lightness, serious vanity (*Romeo and Juliet*, Act 1 Scene 1)

Technique: _____   **Effect:** _____

_____

c) The strongest oaths are straw
To the fire i' the blood (*The Tempest* Act 4 Scene 1)

Technique: _____   **Effect:** _____

_____

d) DUNCAN: Dismayed not this our captains, Macbeth and Banquo?
CAPTAIN: Yes, as sparrows eagles, or the hare the lion! (*Macbeth* Act 1 Scene 2)

Technique: _____   **Effect:** _____

[12

_____

Total Marks = _____ / 20

The 19th-Century Novel

Context and Themes

1 a) On a separate piece of paper, write down five themes that occur in the novel that you have studied. Here are some examples to get you started:

Frankenstein – science; *Pride and Prejudice* – family life; *A Christmas Carol* – the spirit of Christmas; *Jane Eyre* – marriage; *Great Expectations* – money; *The Strange Case of Dr Jekyll and Mr Hyde* – good and evil; *The Sign of Four* – treasure. [5]

b) Now write a sentence or two about each theme that you have identified, for example:

Frankenstein explores the possible consequences of scientific discovery, as Frankenstein unwittingly creates an evil 'creature'. [10]

2 Read the following statements about nineteenth-century society and write a sentence or two explaining how each one is reflected in the novel you have studied.

a) Almost everyone was Christian so writers could assume that readers shared Christian beliefs and values.

Example: Jane Eyre is horrified at the idea of marrying a man who is already married. The fact that she discovers Rochester is married in church emphasises the sinful nature of what he is doing.

_____

_____

b) Nineteenth-century writers were interested in both personal feelings and moral responsibility.

_____

_____

c) Nineteenth-century women had fewer rights than men and fewer opportunities.

_____

_____

d) The nineteenth century was a time of exploration, discovery and scientific advances.

_____

_____

e) While a few people were very rich in nineteenth-century Britain, many lived in poverty.

_____

_____ [10]

Total Marks = _____ / 25

The 19th-Century Novel

Characters, Language and Structure

Grade 4–6

1 Identify five significant characters from the novel you have studied. For each one, draw up a chart like the one below and fill it in.

Name	
Description/ Appearance	
Background	
Personality	
Relationships	
Function	

[25]

Grade 4–6

2 Here are five quotations from nineteenth-century novels. Each uses a linguistic/literary technique. Match each quotation **a)–e)** with a description of its use **v)–z)**.

a) [I] managed to compound a drug by which these powers should be dethroned from their supremacy. (*The Strange Case of Dr Jekyll and Mr Hyde*)

b) 'Bah!' said Scrooge, 'Humbug!' (*A Christmas Carol*, Stave 1)

c) '… the offered olive-branch.' (*Pride and Prejudice*, Chapter 13)

d) 'Hold her arms, Miss Abbot; she's like a mad cat.' (*Jane Eyre*, Chapter 2)

e) How can I describe my emotions at this catastrophe, or how delineate the wretch whom with such infinite pains and care I had endeavoured to form? (*Frankenstein*, Chapter 5)

v) The character uses a colloquial metaphor to express his strong feelings.

w) The speaker uses a simile to describe the violent resistance of someone being restrained.

x) The narrator uses a rhetorical question before attempting to answer it himself.

y) The narrator combines scientific language and personification to describe his attempt to change his nature.

z) The letter-writer uses a symbol that is commonly recognised as representing an offer of peace.

[5]

Total Marks = _____ / 30

Modern Texts

Context and Themes

1 Think about the text you have studied and its social and cultural context. In answer to each of these questions, circle the most appropriate answer. If you have studied the anthology you may be able to answer these questions for individual stories.

a) When was the text written?   **1940s   1950s   1980s   1990s   2000s   2010s**

b) When is it set?   **At the time it was written   Before the time it was written   After the time it was written**

c) Where is it set? (more than one answer possible)
Northern England   The Midlands   London/Southern England   On a farm   In a town/city   In a village   In a school

d) How would you describe its genre/form? (more than one answer possible)
Musical theatre   Science fiction   Allegory   Novel   Drama   Short story   Bildungsroman

e) For what audience was it written?   **Adults   Children/teenagers**   [5]

2 a) Write a paragraph about the 'world' of the text you have studied, referring to where and when it is set, how the characters live and how their attitudes reflect the time and place in which they live.

_____

_____

_____

_____   [5]

b) Write a paragraph explaining how the world of the text differs from the world in which you live.

_____

_____

_____

_____   [5]

3 In the table below, write three themes that occur in your text and a sentence or two about each theme.

Theme	Explanation

[9]

Total Marks = _____ / 24

Modern Texts

Characters, Language and Structure

Grade 3–5

1 If you have studied a novel or short stories, answer only questions **a)–e)** about language and structure. (If you have studied the stories in the anthology, answer separately on each story you have studied.) If you have studied a play, answer only questions **f)–j)**.

a) How is your text divided? _____

b) How would you describe the narrator? _____

c) How would you describe the language/register used by the narrator? _____

_____

d) Have you noticed anything interesting about how any of the characters speak?

_____

e) Find an example of the use of figurative language in your text. _____

_____ **[5]**

f) How is the play divided? _____

g) What do we learn from the stage directions? _____

_____

h) Which characters, if any, speak directly to the audience? _____

_____

i) Are there any notable differences between the ways in which different characters speak?

_____

j) Find an example of the use of figurative language in your text. _____

_____ **[5]**

Grade 4–6

2 Identify five significant characters from the text you have studied. For each one, draw up a chart like the one below and fill it in.

Name	
Description/Appearance	
Background	
Personality	
Relationships	
Function	

[25]

Total Marks = _____ **/ 30**

Poetry

Context and Themes

If you have studied the 'Love and Relationships' cluster in the anthology, answer only questions **1** and **3**.
If you have studied 'Power and Conflict' answer only questions **2** and **4**.

1 Match poems a)–e) with the descriptions of aspects of their context v)–z).

a) 'Follower'   v) Nineteenth-century interest in psychology.

b) 'Before You Were Mine'   w) Twentieth-century rural Ireland.

c) 'Porphyria's Lover'   x) Twentieth-century Scotland.

d) 'Singh Song!'   y) Women's experience in rural England.

e) 'The Farmer's Bride'   z) The Sikh community in England.

_____ [5]

2 Match poems a)–e) with the descriptions of aspects of their context v)–z).

a) 'London'   v) The history of the Caribbean.

b) 'The Charge of the Light Brigade'   w) Poverty and revolution.

c) 'Checking Out Me History'   x) The Romantic movement.

d) 'Poppies'   y) Remembrance Sunday.

e) Extract from 'The Prelude'   z) The Crimean War.

_____ [5]

3 In which poems in 'Love and Relationships' are these themes present? Try to name three.

a) Marriage _____

b) Parents and children _____

c) Romantic love _____

d) Nature _____

e) Death _____[15]

4 In which poems in 'Power and Conflict' are these themes present? Try to name three.

a) Soldiers at war _____

b) The effect of war on non-combatants _____

c) The abuse of power _____

d) Memories _____

e) Nature _____[15]

Total Marks = _____ / 20

Poetry

> ## Language, Form and Structure

If you have studied the 'Love and Relationships' cluster in the anthology, answer only questions **1** and **3**. If you have studied 'Power and Conflict', answer questions **2** and **4**.

1 Which poems in 'Love and Relationships' feature the following aspects of form and structure?

   a) Sonnet form _____

   b) Ballad form _____

   c) Rhyming couplets _____

   d) Half rhyme _____ [4]

2 Which poems in 'Power and Conflict' feature the following aspects of form and structure?

   a) Iambic pentameter _____

   b) Ballad form _____

   c) Rhyming couplets _____

   d) Refrain _____ [4]

3 Look at these quotations from poems in 'Love and Relationships'. On a separate piece of paper, identify the literary techniques they use and explain their effect. Pick from these techniques: **alliteration; archaic language; metaphor; onomatopoeia; pathetic fallacy; repetition; sibilance.**

Some quotations may include more than one technique.

   a) And a few leaves lay on the starving sod ('Neutral Tones')

   b) …Anchor. Kite. ('Mother, any distance')

   c) Long, long shall I rue thee ('When We Two Parted')

   d) …your ghost clatters towards me… ('Before You Were Mine') [16]

4 Look at these quotations from poems in 'Power and Conflict'. On a separate piece of paper, identify the literary techniques they use and explain their effect. Pick from these techniques: **assonance; dialect; pathetic fallacy; repetition; simile.**

Some quotations may include more than one technique.

   a) His foot hung like/Statuary in mid-stride. ('Bayonet Charge')

   b) And, as I rose upon the stroke, my boat
   Went heaving through the water like a swan. (Extract from 'The Prelude')

   c) Dem tell me/Dem tell me/Wha dem want to tell me. ('Checking Out Me History')

   d) leaves and branches/can raise a tragic chorus in a gale. ('Storm on the Island') [16]

Total Marks = _____ / 20

Poetry

Unseen Poetry

1 Read the poem below and answer the questions that follow. Continue on a separate piece of paper if needed.

> **A Birthday** by Christina Rossetti
>
> My heart is like a singing bird
>   Whose nest is in a watered shoot;
> My heart is like an apple-tree
>   Whose boughs are bent with thick-set fruit;
> My heart is like a rainbow shell
>   That paddles in a halcyon sea;
> My heart is gladder than all these
>   Because my love is come to me.
>
> Raise me a dais of silk and down;
>   Hang it with vair[1] and purple dyes;
> Carve it in doves and pomegranates,
>   And peacocks with a hundred eyes;
> Work it in gold and silver grapes,
>   In leaves and silver fleurs-de-lys;
> Because the birthday of my life
>   Is come, my love is come to me.
>
> [1] a bluish grey fur

a) What is the poem about according to the title? _____

b) What is it actually about? _____

c) Is there a regular rhythm and/or rhyme scheme? If so, what effect does it have?

_____

d) What does the poet mean by her 'heart'? _____

e) What is the effect of the repetition of 'my heart' in the first stanza? _____

f) Which three things does she use similes to compare her 'heart' to and what links them?

_____

g) What general impression do the images of the second stanza give? _____

h) Identify three imperatives in the second stanza and describe their effect. _____

i) How would you describe the poet's mood? _____

j) What is meant by the final two lines? _____

_____ [10]

Poetry

2 Read this poem. Then re-read the poem on page 175 and compare the poems using the table below.

> **On His Eightieth Birthday** by Robert Savage Landor
>
> To my ninth decade I have tottered on,
> And no soft arm bends now my steps to steady;
> She, who once led me where she would, is gone,
> So when he calls me, Death shall find me ready.

	'A Birthday'	'On His Eightieth Birthday'
Speaker or voice		
Structure		
Rhythm/metre		
Rhyme		
Vocabulary/register		
Use of sound		
Imagery		
Themes		
The poet's attitude		

[36]

Total Marks = _____ / 46

English Language Paper 1

Explorations in Creative Reading and Writing

You are advised to spend about 15 minutes reading through the source and all five questions.
You should make sure you leave sufficient time to check your answers.

Section A: Reading

Answer all questions in this section.
You are advised to spend about 45 minutes on this section.

Source

This extract is taken from 'The Postmaster', a short story by Rabindranath Tagore, first published in 1891. The story, about a man who runs the post office, is set in a village in India.

Our postmaster belonged to Calcutta[1]. He felt like a fish out of water in this remote village. His office and living-room were in a dark thatched shed, not far from a green, slimy pond, surrounded on all sides by a dense growth.

The postmaster's salary was small. He had to cook his own meals, which he used to share with
5   Ratan, an orphan girl of the village, who did odd jobs for him.

When in the evening the smoke began to curl up from the village cowsheds, and the cicadas[4] chirped in every bush; when the mendicants of the Baül sect[3] sang their shrill songs in their daily meeting-place, when any poet, who had attempted to watch the movement of the leaves in the dense bamboo thickets, would have felt a ghostly shiver run down his back, the postmaster would
10 light his little lamp, and call out "Ratan."

Ratan would sit outside waiting for this call, and, instead of coming in at once, would reply, "Did you call me, sir?"

"What are you doing?" the postmaster would ask.

"I must be going to light the kitchen fire," would be the answer.

15 And the postmaster would say: "Oh, let the kitchen fire be for awhile; light me my pipe first."

At last Ratan would enter, with puffed-out cheeks, vigorously blowing into a flame a live coal to light the tobacco. This would give the postmaster an opportunity of conversing. "Well, Ratan," perhaps he would begin, "do you remember anything of your mother?" That was a fertile subject. Ratan partly remembered, and partly didn't. Her father had been fonder of her than her mother;
20 him she recollected more vividly. He used to come home in the evening after his work, and one or two evenings stood out more clearly than others, like pictures in her memory. Ratan would sit on the floor near the postmaster's feet, as memories crowded in upon her. She called to mind a little brother that she had—and how on some bygone cloudy day she had played at fishing with him on the edge of the pond, with a twig for a make-believe fishing-rod. Such little incidents
25 would drive out greater events from her mind. Thus, as they talked, it would often get very late, and the postmaster would feel too lazy to do any cooking at all. Ratan would then hastily light the fire, and toast some unleavened bread, which, with the cold remnants of the morning meal, was enough for their supper.

On some evenings, seated at his desk in the corner of the big empty shed, the postmaster too
30 would call up memories of his own home, of his mother and his sister, of those for whom in his
exile his heart was sad,—memories which were always haunting him, but which he could not talk
about with the men of the factory, though he found himself naturally recalling them aloud in the
presence of the simple little girl. And so it came about that the girl would allude to his people
as mother, brother, and sister, as if she had known them all her life. In fact, she had a complete
35 picture of each one of them painted in her little heart.

One noon, during a break in the rains, there was a cool soft breeze blowing; the smell of the
damp grass and leaves in the hot sun felt like the warm breathing of the tired earth on one's body.
A persistent bird went on all the afternoon repeating the burden of its one complaint in Nature's
audience chamber.

40 The postmaster had nothing to do. The shimmer of the freshly washed leaves, and the banked-
up remnants of the retreating rain-clouds were sights to see; and the postmaster was watching
them and thinking to himself: "Oh, if only some kindred soul were near—just one loving human
being whom I could hold near my heart!" This was exactly, he went on to think, what that bird
was trying to say, and it was the same feeling which the murmuring leaves were striving to express.
45 But no one knows, or would believe, that such an idea might also take possession of an ill-paid
village postmaster in the deep, silent mid-day interval of his work.

The postmaster sighed, and called out "Ratan." Ratan was then sprawling beneath the guava-
tree, busily engaged in eating unripe guavas. At the voice of her master, she ran up breathlessly,
saying: "Were you calling me, Dada?" "I was thinking," said the postmaster, "of teaching you to
50 read." And then for the rest of the afternoon he taught her the alphabet.

[1] now called Kolkata

[2] insects, which make a loud buzzing noise

[3] a group of religious wandering musicians

---

1 Read again the beginning of the source from line 1 to 5.

List four things you learn about the postmaster from this part of the source.   **[4 mark**

---

2 Look in detail at this extract from line 6 to 10 of the source.

> When in the evening the smoke began to curl up from the village cowsheds, and the cicadas[4]
> chirped in every bush; when the mendicants[3] of the Baül sect sang their shrill songs in their daily
> meeting-place, when any poet, who had attempted to watch the movement of the leaves in the
> dense bamboo thickets, would have felt a ghostly shiver run down his back, the postmaster would
> light his little lamp, and call out "Ratan."

How does the writer use language here to create an impression of evening in the village?

You could include the writer's choice of:

- words and phrases
- language features and techniques
- sentence forms.   **[8 mark**

3 You now need to think about the whole source.

This text is from the beginning of a short story.

How has the writer structured the text to interest you as a reader?

You could write about:

- what the writer focuses your attention on at the beginning of the source
- how and why the writer changes this focus as the source develops
- any other structural features that interest you. **[8 marks]**

4 A student said, 'The writer has created a touching story about two lonely people helping each other. Ratan appears to get more out of the relationship than the postmaster.'

To what extent do you agree?

In your response you could:

- consider your own impressions of the postmaster, Ratan and their relationship
- evaluate how the writer conveys ideas about, and attitudes to, loneliness
- support your response with references to the text. **[20 marks]**

Section B: Writing

You are advised to spend about 45 minutes on this section.
You are reminded of the need to plan your answers.
Write in full sentences.
You should leave enough time to check your work at the end.

5 A local newspaper is running a creative writing competition and intends to publish the winning entries.

EITHER

a) Write a description of a place suggested by this picture.

OR

b) Write a story that begins 'Suddenly the quiet of the evening was interrupted by an unfamiliar sound.'

[24 marks for content and organisation and 16 marks for technical accuracy: total 40 marks]

English Language Paper 2

Writers' Viewpoints and Perspectives

You are advised to spend about 15 minutes reading through the source and all five questions.
You should make sure you leave sufficient time to check your answers.

Section A: Reading

Answer all questions in this section.
You are advised to spend about 45 minutes on this section.

Source A

This extract is taken from *Domestic Manners of the Americans* by Frances Trollope, published in 1832. In this chapter the writer, an Englishwoman living in the USA, gives her reaction to what she sees as the 'familiarity' of Americans.

The extraordinary familiarity of our poor neighbours startled us at first, and we hardly knew how to receive their uncouth advances, or what was expected of us in return; however, it sometimes produced very laughable scenes. Upon one occasion two of my children set off upon an exploring walk up the hills; they were absent rather longer than we expected, and the rest of

5 our party determined upon going out to meet them; we knew the direction they had taken, but thought it would be as well to enquire at a little public-house at the bottom of the hill, if such a pair had been seen to pass. A woman, whose appearance more resembled a Covent Garden market-woman than any thing else I can remember, came out and answered my question with the most jovial good humour in the affirmative, and prepared to join us in our search. Her look,

10 her voice, her manner, were so exceedingly coarse and vehement, that she almost frightened me; she passed her arm within mine, and to the inexpressible amusement of my young people, she dragged me on, talking and questioning me without ceasing. She lived but a short distance from us, and I am sure intended to be a very good neighbour; but her violent intimacy made me dread to pass her door; my children, including my sons, she always addressed by their Christian

15 names, excepting when she substituted the word "honey;" this familiarity of address, however, I afterwards found was universal throughout all ranks in the United States.

My general appellation amongst my neighbours was "the English old woman," but in mentioning each other they constantly employed the term "lady;" and they evidently had a pleasure in using it, for I repeatedly observed, that in speaking of a neighbour, instead of saying

20 Mrs. Such-a-one, they described her as "the lady over the way what takes in washing," or as "that there lady, out by the Gulley, what is making dip-candles." Mr. Trollope was as constantly called "the old man," while draymen, butchers' boys, and the labourers on the canal were invariably denominated "them gentlemen;" nay, we once saw one of the most gentlemanlike men in Cincinnati introduce a fellow in dirty shirt sleeves, and all sorts of detestable et cetera, to one of

25 his friends, with this formula, "D— let me introduce this gentleman to you." Our respective titles certainly were not very important; but the eternal shaking hands with these ladies and gentlemen was really an annoyance, and the more so, as the near approach of the gentlemen was always redolent of whiskey and tobacco.

Source B

A newspaper article in which the writer expresses his opinion about customer service in restaurants.

CALL ME (SIR OR) MADAM

Sean Boyle wants to be served by a waiter, not a new best friend.

'Hey, guys! How are you doing?'

The first time I was greeted like this by a waiter in a (fairly upmarket) restaurant, I was outraged.
5   Obviously not a very classy joint, I thought, and not one I would care to set foot in again. But it's got to
the point now that if I stuck to my guns and boycotted every establishment where I was spoken to like
a New York delinquent rather than a middle-aged British gentleman, I would never leave the house.

And what is it about the word 'guys'? Suddenly, it's everywhere, applied to people of both genders and
all ages. It started with children's T.V. presenters, ever notorious for using Americanisms to 'get down
10   with the kids', and now it's everywhere. On television it's used to address not just hip young men from the
streets but elderly ladies buying antiques, minor celebrities learning to dance and even elected politicians.
Go into any school nowadays and you're likely to hear the appalling Americanism, 'Listen up, guys' rather
than, 'Pay attention, children' or 'Be quiet, Class Four'. Whenever more than one person is addressed they
are called 'you guys'. It's as if nobody is aware that the plural form of the pronoun 'you' is 'you'.

15   This kind of over-familiarity seems to have been imported from America – or copied from American
films and television. Yet – to bring us back to restaurants – friends who have lived in the USA tell me
that Americans are often more polite and formal than we are: being addressed as 'Sir' or 'Madam' is the
norm. Of course, you can get the forced friendliness of 'Hi, my name's Heidi. I'll be your server tonight.'
That's another irritating trend that's gaining a foothold over here – we don't need to know her name
20   and we already know what her job is. We're not here to get chummy with the staff; we just want them to
bring us our food. And when it happens in a British restaurant it just seems false. What we've imported
is a stereotypical idea of Stateside friendliness rather than genuine warmth and good manners.

I wonder if this need to embrace informality has something to do with a British dislike of
servility. I used to work in a shop in London and – like most of my colleagues – was quite happy to
25   address customers as 'Sir' or 'Madam'. Yet I knew people who said they found this demeaning, as if
by addressing people in this way we were accepting that they were somehow superior to us.

It has been said this discomfort with the idea of serving others is a reaction to the time when huge
numbers of working-class Britons spent their lives 'in service', often in 'Downton Abbey' style big
houses, where they were never allowed to forget their lowly status. Twenty-first-century Britons bow to
30   no-one. In contrast, in countries like France and Italy, serving people is not considered demeaning. To
serve is not to be servile. Walk into almost any restaurant in these countries and you will be greeted by
'bonjour' or 'buona sera' and addressed as 'Monsieur/Madame' or 'Signore/Signora'. In return, you are
expected to greet not only the staff but the people sitting near you. When you've done that, you can get
on with eating your meal, efficiently served by a professional waiter – not by your new best friend, Luigi.

35   I don't want waiting staff and bar staff to touch their forelocks and grovel to me. But nor do I
want my evening out to turn into some kind of pseudo-American sitcom. There's a happy medium
here, 'guys'. By all means be friendly – there's nothing wrong with a cheerful smile as you say
'good evening' or even a brief chat about the weather – but treat your customers with respect,
starting with the use of 'Sir' and 'Madam'. And for the sake of good customer relations, the English
40   language and my blood pressure, please never, ever call us 'you guys'.

Practice Exam Papers

1 Read again the first paragraph of **Source A** (lines 1 to 16).

Choose **four** statements below which are TRUE.

- Shade the boxes of the ones that you think are true.
- Choose a maximum of four statements.

A. The neighbours are very unfriendly.

B. Frances Trollope has more than two children.

C. She knows which way the children went.

D. The woman says she has not seen the children.

E. The woman is quiet and gentle.

F. Trollope's children find the incident funny.

G. The neighbour calls Trollope's children by their first names.

H. The woman's familiarity is unusual in America.

[4 marks]

2 You need to refer to **Source A** and **Source B** for this question.

Use details from both sources. Write a summary of the differences and similarities between the behaviour described by Trollope and by Boyle. [8 marks]

3 You now need to refer **only** to **Source A**, the extract from *Domestic Manners of the Americans*.

How does the writer use language to inform and entertain the reader? [12 marks]

4 For this question, you need to refer to both **Source A** and **Source B**.

Compare how the writers convey their attitudes to good manners and over-friendliness. In your answer you should:

- compare their attitudes
- compare the methods they use to convey these attitudes
- support your ideas with quotations from both texts. [16 marks]

Section B: Writing

You are advised to spend about 45 minutes on this section.
You are reminded of the need to plan your answers.
Write in full sentences.
You should leave enough time to check your work at the end.

5 'People claim that they have hundreds or even thousands of friends – but they've never met most of them. In real life, nobody has more than two or three true friends.'

Write an article for a magazine in which you explain your point of view on this statement.

[24 marks for content and organisation and 16 marks for technical accuracy: total 40 marks]

English Literature Paper 1

Shakespeare and the 19th-Century Novel

You should spend a total of 1 hour 45 minutes on this paper.
Answer **one** question from **Section A** and **one** question from **Section B**.
The maximum mark for the paper is 64.
Spelling, punctuation and grammar (AO4) will be assessed in **Section A**. There are four additional marks available.

Section A: Shakespeare

Choose the question from this section on your chosen text.

1 *Macbeth*

Read the following extract from Act 4 Scene 3 and then answer the question that follows.

At this point in the play, Malcolm has just told Macduff that his family has been killed on Macbeth's orders.

	MACDUFF	He has no children. All my pretty ones!
		Did you say all? O hell-kite! All?
		What, all my pretty chickens and their dam
		At one fell swoop?
5	MALCOLM	Dispute it like a man.
	MACDUFF	I shall do so,
		But I must also feel it as a man.
		I cannot but remember such things were
		That were most precious to me. Did heaven look on
10		And would not take their part? Sinful Macduff,
		They were all struck for thee. Naught that I am,
		Not for their own demerits but for mine
		Fell slaughter on their souls. Heaven rest them now.
	MALCOLM	Be this the whetstone of your sword. Let grief
15		Convert to anger: blunt not the heart, enrage it.
	MACDUFF	O, I could play the woman with mine eyes
		And braggart with my tongue! But gentle heavens
		Cut short all intermission. Front to front
		Bring thou this fiend of Scotland and myself.
20		Within my sword's length set him. If he 'scape,
		Heaven forgive him too.

Starting with this extract, explore how Shakespeare presents Macduff's character in *Macbeth*.

Write about:

how Shakespeare presents Macduff in this extract
how Shakespeare presents Macduff in the play as a whole.   **[30 marks + AO4 4 marks]**

2 *Romeo and Juliet*

Read the following extract from Act 2 Scene 3 and then answer the question that follows.

Here, Friar Laurence reacts to the news that Romeo has fallen in love with Juliet.

	FRIAR LAURENCE	Holy Saint Francis, what a change is here!
		Is Rosaline that thou didst love so dear,
		So soon forsaken? Young men's love then lies
		Not truly in their hearts but in their eyes.
5		Jesu Maria, what a deal of brine
		Hath washed thy sallow cheek for Rosaline!
		How much salt water thrown away in waste
		To season love, that of it doth not taste!
		The sun not yet thy sighs from heaven clears.
10		Thy old groans yet ring in my ancient ears.
		Lo, here upon thy cheek the stain doth sit
		Of an old tear that is not washed off yet.
		If e'er thou wast thyself, and those woes thine,
		Thou and these woes were all for Rosaline.
15		And art thou changed? Pronounce this sentence then:
		Women may fall when there's no strength in men.
	ROMEO	Thou chidd'st me oft for loving Rosaline.
	FRIAR LAURENCE	For doting, not for loving, pupil mine.

Starting with this extract, explore how Shakespeare presents attitudes to love in *Romeo and Juliet*.

Write about:

- how Shakespeare presents attitudes to love in this extract
- how Shakespeare presents attitudes to love in the play as a whole.

[30 marks + AO4 4 marks

3 *The Tempest*

Read the following extract from Act 2 Scene 2 and then answer the question that follows.

In this scene, Stefano and Trinculo have made Caliban drunk and he has sworn to serve Stefano instea of Prospero.

	CALIBAN	I prithee, let me bring thee where crabs grow,
		And I with my long nails will dig thee pig-nuts.
		Show thee a jay's nest, and instruct thee how
		To snare the nimble marmoset. I'll bring thee
5		To clust'ring filberts, and sometimes I'll get thee
		Young seamews from the rock. Wilt thou go with me?

STEFANO	I prithee now, lead the way, without any more talking. Trinculo, the King and all our company else being drowned, we will inherit here. Here, bear my bottle. Fellow Trinculo, we'll fill him by and by again.
10 **CALIBAN** (*sings drunkenly*)	Farewell, master, farewell, farewell!
TRINCULO	A howling monster, a drunken monster!
CALIBAN (*sings*)	No more dams I'll make for fish.
	Nor fetch in firing.
	At requiring,
15	Nor scrape trenchering, nor wash dish.
	'Ban, 'ban, Cacaliban.
	Has a new master. Get a new man!
	Freedom, high-day! High-day, freedom! Freedom, high-day, freedom!

Starting with this extract, explore how Shakespeare writes about slavery and freedom in *The Tempest*.

Write about:

* how Shakespeare presents ideas about slavery and freedom in this extract
* how Shakespeare presents ideas about slavery and freedom in the play as a whole.

[30 marks + AO4 4 marks]

4 | *Much Ado About Nothing*

Read the following extract from Act 1 Scene 3 and then answer the question that follows.

Here, Don John discusses his sad mood and discontent with Conrad.

DON JOHN	I cannot hide what I am. I must be sad when I have cause, and smile at no man's jests; eat when I have stomach, and wait for no man's leisure; sleep when I am drowsy, and tend on no man's business; laugh when I am merry, and claw no man in his humour.
5 **CONRAD**	Yea, but you must not make the full show of this till you may do it without controlment. You have of late stood out against your brother, and he hath ta'en you newly into his grace, where it is impossible you should take true root but by the fair weather that you make yourself. It is needful that you frame the season for your own harvest.
10 **DON JOHN**	I had rather be a canker in a hedge than a rose in his grace, and it better fits my blood to be disdained of all than to fashion a carriage to rob love from any. In this, though I cannot be said to be a flattering honest man, it must not be denied but I am a plain-dealing villain. I am trusted with a muzzle, and enfranchised with a clog. Therefore I have decreed not to sing in my cage. If I had my mouth I would bite. If I had my liberty I would do my liking. In the meantime, let me be that I am, and seek not to alter me.

Starting with this extract, explore how Shakespeare presents Don John as a villain in *Much Ado About Nothing.*

Write about:

- how Shakespeare presents Don John in this extract
- how Shakespeare presents Don John in the play as a whole.

[30 marks + AO4 4 marks]

5 *The Merchant of Venice*

Read the following extract from Act 3 Scene 2 and then answer the question that follows.

Here, Portia explains her feelings to Bassanio before he chooses a casket.

PORTIA   I pray you tarry. Pause a day or two
Before you hazard, for in choosing wrong
I lose your company; therefore forbear a while.
There's something tells me, but it is not love.
5   I would not lose you; and you know yourself
Hate counsels not in such a quality.
But lest you should not understand me well –
And yet a maiden hath no tongue but thought –
I would detain you here some month or two
10   Before you venture for me. I could teach you
How to choose right, but then I am forsworn.
So will I never be. So may you miss me;
But if you do, you'll make me wish a sin,
That I had been forsworn. Beshrew your eyes!
15   They have o'erlooked me and divided me:
One half of me is yours, the other half yours –
Mine own, I would say—but if mine, then yours,
And so all yours. O these naughty times
Put bars between the owners and their rights!
20   And so though yours, not yours. Prove it so.
Let Fortune go to hell for it, not I.

Starting with this extract, explore how Shakespeare presents the role of women in *The Merchant of Venice.*

Write about:

- how Shakespeare presents the role of women in this speech
- how Shakespeare presents the role of women in the play as a whole.

[30 marks + AO4 4 marks]

6 *Julius Caesar*

Read the following extract from Act 5 Scene 5 and then answer the question that follows.

At this point in the play, after losing the final battle, Brutus has killed himself.

MESSALA	How died my master, Strato?
STRATO	I held his sword, and he did run upon it.
MESSALA	Octavius, then take him to follow thee,
	That did the latest service to my master.
5 ANTONY	This was the noblest Roman of them all.
	All the conspirators save only he
	Did that they did in envy of great Caesar.
	He only in a general honest thought
	And common good to all made one of them.
10	His life was gentle, and the elements
	So mixed in him that nature might stand up
	And say to all the world 'This was a man'.
OCTAVIUS	According to his virtue let us use him,
	With all respect and rites of burial.
15	Within my tent his bones tonight shall lie,
	Most like a soldier, ordered honourably.

Starting with this extract, explore how Shakespeare presents Brutus as 'the noblest Roman of them all' in *Julius Caesar*.

Write about:

- how Shakespeare presents Brutus in this extract
- how Shakespeare presents Brutus in the play as a whole.

[30 marks + AO4 4 marks]

Section B: The 19th-Century Novel

Choose the question from this section on your chosen text.

7 | **Robert Louis Stevenson: *The Strange Case of Dr Jekyll and Mr Hyde***

Read the following extract from Chapter 7 and then answer the question that follows.

In this extract, Mr Utterson and Mr Enfield see Dr Jekyll at his window.

The court was very cool and a little damp. And full of premature twilight, although the sky, high up overhead, was still bright with sunset. The middle one of the three windows was halfway open; and sitting close beside it, taking the air with an infinite sadness of mien, like some disconsolate prisoner, Utterson saw Dr Jekyll.

5   'What! Jekyll!' he cried. 'I trust you are better.'

'I am very low, Utterson,' replied the doctor drearily, 'very low. It will not last long, thank God.'

'You stay too much indoors,' said the lawyer. 'You should be out, whipping up the circulation, like Mr Enfield and me. (This is my cousin – Mr Enfield – Dr Jekyll.) Come now; get your hat and take a quick turn with us.'

Practice Exam Papers

10   'You are very good,' sighed the other. 'I should like to very much; but no, no, no, it is quite impossible; I dare not, But indeed, Utterson, I am very glad to see you; this is really a great pleasure; I would ask you and Mr Enfield up, but the place is really not fit.'

   'Why then,' said the lawyer, good-naturedly, 'the best thing we can do is to stay down here and speak to you from where we are.'

15   'That is just what I was about to venture to propose,' returned the doctor with a smile. But the words were hardly uttered, before the smile was struck out of his face and succeeded by an expression of such abject terror and despair, as froze the very blood of the two gentlemen below. They saw it but for a glimpse, for the window was instantly thrust down; but that glance had been sufficient, and they turned and left the court without a word.

Starting with this extract, write about how sympathetically Stevenson presents the character of Dr Jekyll in *The Strange Case of Doctor Jekyll and Mr Hyde*.

Write about:

- how Stevenson writes about Jekyll and how others react to him in this extract
- how he writes about Jekyll in the novel as a whole.

[30 marks]

8   **Charles Dickens: *A Christmas Carol***

Read the following extract from Stave (Chapter) 4 and then answer the question that follows.

In this extract, Scrooge is watching the Cratchits after the 'death' of Tiny Tim.

She hurried out to meet him; and little Bob in his comforter – he had need of it poor fellow – came in. His tea was ready for him on the hob, and they all tried who should help him to it most. Then the two young Cratchits got upon his knees, and laid, each child, a little cheek against his face, as if they said, 'Don't mind it, father. Don't be grieved!'

5   Bob was very cheerful with them, and spoke pleasantly to all the family. He looked at the work upon the table, and praised the industry and speed of Mrs Cratchit and the girls. They would be done long before Sunday, he said.

   'Sunday! You went today, then, Robert?' said his wife.

   'Yes, my dear,' returned Bob. 'I wish you could have gone. It would have done you good to see 10 how green a place it is. But you'll see it often. I promised him that I would walk there on a Sunday. My little, little child!' cried Bob. 'My little child!' He broke down all at once. He couldn't help it. If he could have helped it, he and his child would have been farther apart, perhaps, than they were.

   He left the room, and went upstairs into the room above, which was lighted cheerfully, and hung with Christmas. There was a chair set close beside the child, and there were signs of 15 someone having been there lately. Poor Bob sat down in it, and, when he had thought a little and composed himself, he kissed the little face. He was reconciled to what had happened, and went down again quite happy.

They drew about the fire, and talked; the girls and mother working still. Bob told them of
20 the extraordinary kindness of Mr Scrooge's nephew, whom he had scarcely seen but once, and
who, meeting him in the street that day, and seeing that he looked a little – 'just a little down,
you know,' said Bob, inquired what had happened to distress him. 'On which,' said Bob, 'for he
is the pleasantest-spoken gentleman you ever heard, I told him. "I am heartily sorry for you, Mr
Cratchit." He said, "and heartily sorry for your good wife." By-the-bye, how he ever knew that I
25 don't know.'

Starting with this extract, explore how Dickens writes about the Cratchit family and their importance
in the novel.

Write about:

- how Dickens writes about the Cratchits in this extract
- how Dickens writes about the Cratchits in the novel as a whole.

[30 marks]

9 **Charles Dickens: *Great Expectations***

Read the following extract from Chapter 1 and then answer the question that follows.

In this extract, Pip meets Magwitch for the first time.

'Hold your noise!' cried a terrible voice, as a man started up from among the graves at the side of
the church porch. 'Keep still, you little devil, or I'll cut your throat!'

A fearful man, all in coarse gray, with a great iron on his leg. A man with no hat, and with broken
shoes, and with an old rag tied round his head. A man who had been soaked in water, and smothered in
5 mud, and lamed by stones, and cut by flints, and stung by nettles, and torn by briars; who limped, and
shivered, and glared and growled; and whose teeth chattered in his head as he seized me by the chin.

'Oh! Don't cut my throat, sir,' I pleaded in terror. 'Pray, don't do it, sir.'

'Tell us your name!' said the man. 'Quick!'

'Pip, sir.'

10 'Once more,' said the man, staring at me, 'Give it mouth!'

'Pip. Pip, sir.'

'Show us where you live,' said the man. 'Pint out the place!'

I pointed to where our village lay, on the flat inshore among the alder-trees and pollards, a
mile or more from the church.

15 The man, after looking at me for a moment, turned me upside-down, and emptied my pockets.
There was nothing in them but a piece of bread. When the church came to itself – for he was so
sudden and strong that he made it go head over heels before me, and I saw the steeple under my
feet – when the church came to itself, I say, I was seated on a high tombstone, trembling, while he
ate the bread ravenously.

20 'You young dog,' said the man, licking his lips, 'what fat cheeks you ha' got.' I believe they were
fat, though I was at that time undersized for my years, and not strong. 'Darn me if I couldn't eat
'em,' said the man, with a threatening shake of his head, 'and if I han't half a mind to't!'

Starting with this extract, write about how Dickens presents the character of Magwitch and his relationship with Pip.

Write about:

- how Dickens writes about Magwitch and the impression he makes on Pip in this extract
- how Dickens writes about Magwitch and his relationship with Pip in the novel as a whole.   **[30 marks]**

10   **Charlotte Brontë: *Jane Eyre***

Read the following extract from Chapter 17 and then answer the question that follows.

In this extract, Jane leaves the room where Mr Rochester is entertaining his friends.

I then quitted my sheltered corner and made my exit by the side-door, which was fortunately near. Thence a narrow passage led into the hall: in crossing it, I perceived my sandal was loose; I stopped to tie it, kneeling down for that purpose on the mat at the foot of the staircase. I heard the dining-room door unclose; a gentleman came out; rising hastily, I stood face to face with him:

5   it was Mr Rochester. 'How do you do?' he asked.

'I am very well, sir.'

'Why did you not come and speak to me in the room?' I thought I might have retorted the question on him who put it: but I would not take that freedom. I answered –

'I did not wish to disturb you, as you seemed engaged, sir.'

10   'What have you been doing during my absence?'

'Nothing in particular; teaching Adele as usual.'

'And getting a great deal paler than you were – as I saw at first sight. What is the matter?'

'Nothing at all, sir.'

'Did you take any cold that night you half drowned me?'

15   'Not the least.'

'Return to the drawing-room: you are deserting too early.'

'I am tired, sir.'

He looked at me for a minute. 'And a little depressed,' he said. 'What about? Tell me.'

'Nothing – nothing, sir. I am not depressed.'

20   'But I affirm that you are: so much depressed that a few more words would bring tears to your eyes – indeed, they are there now, shining and swimming; and a bead has slipped from the lash and fallen on the flag. If I had time, and was not in mortal dread of some prating prig of a servant passing, I would know what all this means. Well, tonight I excuse you; but understand that so long as my visitors stay, I expect you to appear in the drawing-room every evening; it is my wish; don't

25   neglect it. Now go, and send Sophie for Adele. Good-night, my –' He stopped, bit his lip, and abruptly left me.

Starting with this extract, explore how Brontë writes about Jane's position as a governess and her awareness of social class.

Write about:

- how Brontë writes about Jane's position as a governess in this extract
- how Brontë writes about Jane's position as a governess and her awareness of social class in the novel as a whole.
 [30 marks]

11 **Mary Shelley: *Frankenstein***

Read the following extract from Chapter 4 and then answer the question that follows.

In this extract, Victor Frankenstein describes his work as he begins to create the creature.

No-one can conceive the variety of feelings which bore me onwards, like a hurricane, in the first enthusiasm of success. Life and death appeared to me ideal bounds, which I should first break through, and pour a torrent of light into our dark world. A new species would bless me as its creator and source; many happy and excellent natures would owe their being to me. No father

5 could claim the gratitude of his child so completely as I should deserve theirs. Pursuing these reflections, I thought that if I could bestow animation upon lifeless matter, I might in process of time (although I now found it impossible) renew life where death had apparently devoted the body to corruption.

These thoughts supported my spirits, while I pursued my undertaking with unremitting ardour.

10 My cheek had grown pale with study, and my person had become emaciated with confinement. Sometimes, on the very brink of certainty, I failed; yet still I clung to the hope which the next day or the next hour might realize. One secret which I alone possessed was the hope to which I had dedicated myself; and the moon gazed on my midnight labours, while, with unrelaxed and breathless eagerness, I pursued nature to her hiding-places. Who shall conceive the horrors of my

15 secret toil as I dabbled among the unhallowed damps of the grave or tortured the living animal to animate the lifeless clay? My limbs now tremble, and my eyes swim with the remembrance; but then a resistless and almost frantic impulse urged me forward; I seemed to have lost all soul or sensation but for this one pursuit. It was indeed but a passing trance, that only made me feel with renewed acuteness so soon as, the unnatural stillness ceasing to operate, I had returned to

20 my old habits. I collected bones from charnel- houses and disturbed with profane fingers, the tremendous secrets of the human frame.

Starting with this extract, explore how Shelley writes about Frankenstein's feelings about his work in *Frankenstein*.

Write about:

- how Shelley writes about Frankenstein's feelings about his work in this extract
- how Shelley writes about Frankenstein's feelings about his work in the novel as a whole. **[30 marks]**

12 **Jane Austen:** *Pride and Prejudice*

Read the following extract from Chapter 29 (vol. 2 Chapter 6) and then answer the question that follows.

In this extract, Mr Collins expresses his delight at receiving an invitation from Lady Catherine de Burgh.

Mr Collins's triumph in consequence of this invitation was complete. The power of displaying the grandeur of his patroness to his wondering visitors, and of letting them see her civility towards himself and his wife was exactly what he had wished for, and that an opportunity of doing it should be given so soon was an instance of Lady Catherine's condescension as he knew
5 not how to admire enough.

'I confess,' he said, 'that I should not have been at all surprised by her Ladyship's asking us on Sunday to drink tea and spend the evening at Rosings. I rather expected, from my knowledge of her affability, that it would happen. But who could have foreseen such an attention as this? Who could have imagined that we should receive an invitation to dinner there (an invitation moreover
10 including the whole party) so immediately after your arrival!'

'I am the less surprised at what has happened,' replied Sir William, 'from that knowledge of what the manners of the great really are, which my situation in life has allowed me to acquire. About the Court, such instances of elegant breeding are not uncommon.'

15 Scarcely anything was talked of the whole day or next morning, but their visit to Rosings. Mr Collins was carefully instructing them in what they were to expect, that the sight of such rooms, so many servants, and so splendid a dinner might not wholly overpower them.

When the ladies were separating for the toilette, he said to Elizabeth, 'Do not make yourself uneasy, my dear cousin, about your apparel. Lady Catherine is far from requiring that elegance
20 of dress in us, which becomes herself and her daughter. I would advise you merely to put on whatever of your clothes is superior to the rest, there is not occasion for anything more. Lady Catherine will not think the worse of you for being simply dressed. She likes to have the distinction of rank preserved.'

Starting with this extract, explore how Austen writes about snobbery in *Pride and Prejudice*.

Write about:

- how Austen writes about snobbery in this extract
- how Austen writes about snobbery in the novel as a whole.

[30 marks]

13 **Sir Arthur Conan Doyle:** *The Sign of Four*

Read the following extract from Chapter 11 and then answer the question that follows.

In this extract, Watson and Miss Morstan open the box that is supposed to contain the Great Agra Treasure.

'That is all over,' I answered. 'It was nothing. I will tell you no more gloomy details. Let us turn to something brighter. There is the treasure. What could be brighter than that? I got leave to bring it with me, thinking that it would interest you to be the first to see it.'

'It would be of the greatest interest to me,' she said. There was no eagerness in her voice,
5 however. It had struck her, doubtless, that it might seem ungracious upon her part to be indifferent to a prize which had cost so much to win.

'What a pretty box!' she said, stooping over it. 'This is Indian work, I suppose?'

'Yes, it is; Benares metal-work.'

'And so heavy!' she exclaimed, trying to raise it. 'The box alone must be of some value. Where
10 is the key?'

'Small threw it into the Thames,' I answered. 'I must borrow Mrs Forrester's poker.' There was in the front a thick and broad hasp, wrought in the image of a sitting Buddha. Under this I thrust the end of the poker and twisted it outward as a lever. The hasp sprang open with a loud snap. With trembling fingers I flung back the lid. We both stood gazing in astonishment.

15   The box was empty!

No wonder that it was heavy. The iron-work was two thirds of an inch thick all round. It was massive, well made, and solid, like a chest constructed to carry things of great price, but not one shred or crumb of metal or jewellery lay within it. It was absolutely and completely empty.

'The treasure is lost,' said Miss Morstan calmly.

20   As I listened to the words and realized what they meant, a great shadow seemed to pass from my soul. I did not know how this Agra treasure had weighed me down, until now that it was finally removed. It was selfish, no doubt, disloyal, wrong, but I could realize nothing save that the golden barrier was gone from between us.

Starting with this extract, explore how Conan Doyle writes about wealth and its effect on people in *The Sign of Four*.

Write about:

• how Conan Doyle writes about the treasure in this extract
• how Conan Doyle writes about the treasure and wealth in general in the novel as a whole. **[30 marks]**

English Literature Paper 2

Modern Texts and Poetry

You should spend a total of 2 hour 15 minutes on this paper.
Answer **one** question from **Section A, one** from **Section B** and **both** questions in **Section C**.
The maximum mark for the paper is 96.
Spelling, punctuation and grammar (AO4) will be assessed in **Section A**. There are four additional marks available.

Section A: Modern Prose or Drama

Answer one question from this section on your chosen text.

J. B. Priestley: *An Inspector Calls*

EITHER

1   How does Priestley write about social problems in *An Inspector Calls*?

Write about:
- the social problems that Priestley writes about in *An Inspector Calls*
- how Priestley presents these problems by the way he writes.   **[30 marks + AO4 4 marks]**

OR

2   How does Priestley write about the role and significance of Inspector Goole in *An Inspector Calls*?

Write about:
- the role and significance of Inspector Goole
- how Priestley presents the Inspector.   **[30 marks + AO4 4 marks]**

Willy Russell: *Blood Brothers*

EITHER

3   To what extent do Mickey and his mother create their own tragedy in *Blood Brothers*?

Write about:
- what Mickey and Mrs Johnstone do and what happens to them
- how Russell writes about what they do and what happens to them.   **[30 marks + AO4 4 marks]**

OR

4   How does Russell write about the character of Linda and her relationship with Mickey and Edward in *Blood Brothers?*

Write about:
- the character of Linda and her relationship with Mickey and Edward
- how Russell presents Linda and her relationship with Mickey and Edward.   **[30 marks + AO4 4 marks]**

Alan Bennett: The History Boys

EITHER

5 How does Bennett use the Headmaster to present ideas about education and authority in *The History Boys*?

Write about:
- what the Headmaster does and says
- how Bennett presents the Headmaster in the play.   **[30 marks + AO4 4 marks]**

OR

6 How does Bennett write about friendships between teachers and pupils in *The History Boys*?

Write about:
- the friendships between teachers and pupils in the play
- how Bennett presents these friendships.   **[30 marks + AO4 4 marks]**

Dennis Kelly: *DNA*

EITHER

7 How does Kelly write about the way teenagers can behave in *DNA*?

Write about:
- the actions taken by the teenage characters in *DNA*
- how Kelly presents their actions in the play.   **[30 marks + AO4 4 marks]**

OR

8 How does Kelly present the character of Cathy as a leader in *DNA*?

Write about:
- the character of Cathy and her role as a leader
- how Kelly presents the character Cathy.   **[30 marks + AO4 4 marks]**

Simon Stephens: *The Curious Incident of the Dog in the Night-Time*

EITHER

9 How does Stephens present Christopher as being different from other people in *The Curious Incident of the Dog in the Night-Time*?

Write about:
- things Christopher does and says that indicate his 'difference'
- how Stephens presents Christopher as being different from other characters.   **[30 marks + AO4 4 marks]**

OR

10 'Wellington's death causes Christopher to change in many ways.' How far do you agree with this statement?

Write about:
- to what extent Christopher changes after the death of Wellington
- how Stephens presents these changes.   **[30 marks + AO4 4 marks]**

Shelagh Delaney: *A Taste of Honey*

EITHER

11 'In *A Taste of Honey* the female characters regard the male characters as weak and unreliable.' How far do you agree with this statement?

Write about:
- how Delaney presents male characters and what they say and do
- how Helen and Jo react to and talk about men.   [30 marks + AO4 4 marks]

OR

12 How does Delaney write about motherhood in *A Taste of Honey*?

Write about:
- different ideas about motherhood in the play
- how Delaney presents these ideas.   [30 marks + AO4 4 marks]

William Golding: *Lord of the Flies*

EITHER

13 Is Simon an important character in *Lord of the Flies*?

Write about:
- the significance of Simon in *Lord of the Flies*
- how Golding presents the character of Simon.

[30 marks + AO4 4 marks]

OR

14 How does Golding write about the idea of 'Britishness' in *Lord of the Flies*?

Write about:
- ideas about how being British is presented in the novel
- how Golding presents these ideas.   [30 marks + AO4 4 marks]

AQA Anthology: *Telling Tales*

EITHER

15 How do writers explore relationships between people of different generations in 'Korea' and one other story from *Telling Tales*?

Write about:
- the relationships described in the two stories
- how the writers present these relationships.   [30 marks + AO4 4 marks]

OR

16 How do writers explore how people change in 'The Darkness Out There' and one other story from *Telling Tales*?

Write about:
- how people change in the two stories
- how the writers present these changes.   [30 marks + AO4 4 marks]

George Orwell: *Animal Farm*

EITHER

17 'Orwell uses old Major and his dream to write about idealism in *Animal Farm.*' How far do you agree with this statement?

Write about:
- how Orwell presents old Major's ideals
- to what extent Orwell uses old Major's ideals to explore the results and limits of idealism.

[30 marks + AO4 4 marks]

OR

18 How does Orwell write about the pigs becoming more like humans and the other animals' reaction to this in *Animal Farm*?

Write about:
- the ways in which the pigs change and the reaction of the other animals
- how Orwell writes about these changes.

[30 marks + AO4 4 marks]

Kazuo Ishiguro: *Never Let Me Go*

EITHER

19 How does Ishiguro present Kathy and what difference does her role as narrator make to our reading of *Never Let Me Go*?

Write about:
- how Ishiguro presents Kathy's character in *Never Let Me Go*
- how she uses language as the narrator of *Never Let Me Go*.

[30 marks + AO4 4 marks]

OR

20 How does Ishiguro write about what it means to be human in *Never Let Me Go*?

Write about:
- ideas about what it means to be human presented in the novel
- how Ishiguro presents these ideas.

[30 marks + AO4 4 marks]

Meera Syal: *Anita and Me*

EITHER

21 How does Syal present Indian culture and traditions in *Anita and Me*?

Write about:
- examples of Indian culture and traditions in *Anita and Me*
- how Syal writes about Indian culture and traditions.

[30 marks + AO4 4 marks]

OR

22 How does Syal write about Meena and her family's feelings about Tollington in *Anita and Me*?

Write about:
- how Meena and her family feel about Tollington
- how Syal presents these feelings.

[30 marks + AO4 4 marks]

Stephen Kelman: *Pigeon English*

EITHER

23 How does Kelman present violence and danger in *Pigeon English*?

Write about:
- examples of violent and dangerous behaviour in *Pigeon English*
- how Kelman presents violent and dangerous behaviour.   **[30 marks + AO4 4 marks]**

OR

24 How does Kelman present female characters in *Pigeon English*?

Write about:
- examples of female characters in *Pigeon English*
- how Kelman presents female characters.   **[30 marks + AO4 4 marks]**

Section B: Poetry

Answer **one** question from this section.

AQA Anthology: Poems Past and Present

EITHER

Love and Relationships

25 Compare the way poets write about family relationships in 'Before You Were Mine' and one other poem from 'Love and Relationships'.

Before You Were Mine

I'm ten years away from the corner you laugh on
with your pals, Maggie McGeeney and Jean Duff.
The three of you bend from the waist, holding
each other, or your knees, and shriek at the pavement.
5   Your polka-dot dress blows round your legs. Marilyn.

I'm not here yet. The thought of me doesn't occur
in the ballroom with the thousand eyes, the fizzy, movie tomorrows
the right walk home could bring. I knew you would dance
like that. Before you were mine, your Ma stands at the close
10 with a hiding for the late one. You reckon it's worth it.

The decade ahead of my loud, possessive yell was the best one, eh?
I remember my hands in those high-heeled red shoes, relics,
and now your ghost clatters toward me over George Square
till I see you, clear as scent, under the tree,
15 with its lights, and whose small bites on your neck, sweetheart?

Cha cha cha! You'd teach me the steps on the way home from Mass,
stamping stars from the wrong pavement. Even then
I wanted the bold girl winking in Portobello, somewhere
in Scotland, before I was born. That glamorous love lasts
20 where you sparkle and waltz and laugh before you were mine.

Carol Ann Duffy

[30 marks]

OR

Practice Exam Paper

Power and Conflict

26 Compare the way poets write about how people are changed by experience in 'Remains' and one other poem from 'Power and Conflict'.

[30 marks]

Remains

On another occasion, we get sent out
to tackle looters raiding a bank.
And one of them legs it up the road,
probably armed, possibly not.

5   Well myself and somebody else and somebody else
are of the same mind,
so all three of us open fire.
Three of a kind all letting fly, and I swear

I see every round as it rips through his life –
10   I see broad daylight on the other side.
So we've hit this looter a dozen times
and he's there on the ground, sort of inside out,

pain itself, the image of agony.
One of my mates goes by
15   and tosses his guts back into his body.
Then he's carted off in the back of a lorry.

End of story, except not really.
His blood-shadow stays on the street, and out on patrol
I walk right over it week after week.
20   Then I'm home on leave. But I blink

and he bursts again through the doors of the bank.
Sleep, and he's probably armed, and possibly not.
Dream, and he's torn apart by a dozen rounds.
And the drink and the drugs won't flush him out –

25   he's here in my head when I close my eyes,
dug in deep behind enemy lines,
not left for dead in some distant, sun-stunned, sand-smothered land
or six-feet-under in desert sand,

but near to the knuckle, here and now,
30   his bloody life in my bloody hands.

Simon Armitage

Section C: Unseen Poetry

Answer **both** questions in this section.

The Darkling Thrush

I leant upon a coppice gate
    When Frost was spectre-grey,
And Winter's dregs made desolate
    The weakening eye of day.
The tangled bine-stems scored the sky
5   Like strings of broken lyres,
And all mankind that haunted nigh
    Had sought their household fires.

The land's sharp features seemed to be
    The Century's corpse outleant,
10 His crypt the cloudy canopy,
    The wind his death-lament.
The ancient pulse of germ and birth
    Was shrunken hard and dry,
And every spirit upon earth
15   Seemed fervourless as I.

At once a voice arose among
    The bleak twigs overhead
In a full-hearted evensong
    Of joy illimited;
20 An aged thrush, frail, gaunt, and small,
    In blast-beruffled plume,
Had chosen thus to fling his soul
    Upon the growing gloom.

So little cause for carolings
25   Of such ecstatic sound
Was written on terrestrial things
    Afar or nigh around,
That I could think there trembled through
    His happy good-night air
30 Some blessed Hope, whereof he knew
    And I was unaware.

Thomas Hardy

7.1 In 'The Darkling Thrush' how does the poet use natural imagery to present his mood and feelings?   **[24 marks]**

Spellbound

The night is darkening round me,
The wild winds coldly blow;
But a tyrant spell has bound me
And I cannot, cannot go.

5   The giant trees are bending
Their bare boughs weighed with snow.
And the storm is fast descending,
And yet I cannot go.

Clouds beyond clouds above me,
10 Wastes beyond wastes below;
But nothing drear can move me;
I will not, cannot go.

Emily Brontë

27.2 In both 'The Darkling Thrush' and 'Spellbound', the poets write about nature and their own feelings.

What are the similarities and/or differences between the ways the poets present nature and their feelings?   **[8 marks]**

Answers

Key Technical Skills: Writing – pages 148–152

Page 148 Spelling

1. a) Is that **your** coat? **You're** in the wrong place.
   b) **They're** all in the yard eating **their** lunches, over **there** by the tree.
   c) What do you think I should **wear** for the party? **Where** did you say they **were** going?
   d) Come over **here**. I can't **hear** you very well.
   e) You have **to** choose **two** of the five options. Three would be **too** many.
   f) The cat's eaten **its** food and now **it's** asleep.
      [1] for each correct answer up to a maximum of [15]

2. If you are going to improve your **performance** in any area, **whether** in a sport, a hobby or in **your studies**, you must **practise**. **Successful** people who have **achieved** great things in life always say it is **because** of hard work just as much as talent. You **might** not want to be an Olympic champion, but you can still get a lot of satisfaction from **knowing** you have improved.
      [1] for each correct answer up to a maximum of [10]

3. a) tornadoes
   b) women
   c) antibodies
   d) antitheses
   e) soliloquys   [maximum 5]

Page 149: Punctuation

1. *Anita and Me* is a novel based on the author's own childhood. [1] It is the story of a family who come from India. [1] They settle in a village in the English Midlands. [1] The narrator makes friends with a girl called Anita. [1] Their friendship is the focus of the book. [1]   [maximum 5]

2. *Pride and Prejudice* is Jane Austen's [1] most popular book. Elizabeth, [1] one of five sisters, [1] meets a man called Mr Darcy, [1] who is very rich and rather snobbish. Darcy's [1] best friend, [1] whose name is Mr Bingley, [1] falls in love with Elizabeth's [1] older sister. The sisters' [1] relationships don't [1] go smoothly.   [maximum 10]

3. a) Where did they come from? Nobody knows.
   b) What a lovely surprise! It was just what I wanted.
   c) Pip (the hero of the story) meets Magwitch on the marshes.
   d) Kai had rice pudding; Ellie chose the cheese.
   e) We love Birmingham: it has everything a city should have.
      [1] for each correct answer up to a maximum of [5]

Page 150: Sentence Structure

1. a) Jo lives next door to me **and** Mo lives next door to her. [1]
   b) Mo has a dog **but** Jo does not have any pets. [1]
2. a) **Although** he worked as quickly as he could, he did not finish on time. [1]
   b) I missed the bus **because** I stopped to talk to someone on the way. [1]
3. Tom, **who** is my best friend, lives on the main road. [1]
4. a) simple   b) compound   c) minor
   d) complex   e) complex
      [1] for each correct answer up to a maximum of [5]

Page 151: Text Structure and Organisation

1. b), d), a), e), c)   [maximum 5]
2. a) After   b) Despite   c) however   d) therefore
   e) Nevertheless   [maximum 5]

Page 152: Standard English and Grammar

1. a) are b) are c) were d) did e) has been
   f) have done g) were; had done   [maximum 8]

2. a) got; invitations   b) few; broken   [maximum 4]
3. I was **standing** in the street minding **my** own business when I saw Zaki. [1] He **came** over to me acting **very (or really) casual**. [1] Zaki **and I** were best mates (or **friends**). [1] I was **going to** ask him how he **did (or had done)** in his exams. [1] I **did not say anything** though. [1] I could see he **had done well**. [1] Then I **noticed (or saw)** Kirsty **sitting** on the wall. [1] 'Did you (or **you two**) **fail** your exams again?' she shouted. [1]
      [1] for each sentence re-written in correct Standard English up to a maximum of [8]

Key Technical Skills: Reading – pages 153–160

Page 153: Explicit Information and Ideas

1. a) ✓ c) ✓ e) ✓ h) ✓   [maximum 4]
2. **Any four from:** He was very nice looking. He had a fresh-coloured face. He was clean shaven. He had white hair. He wore oddly shaped collars. He wore a top hat.   [maximum 4]

Page 154: Implicit Information and Ideas

1. a) B b) A c) C d) C e) B f) A
   g) C h) A   [maximum 8]
2. a) ✓ b) ✓ e) ✓ g) ✓   [maximum 4]

Page 155: Synthesis and Summary 1

1. a) Jackie won the sack race. b) Give me the letter now.
   c) Wind blew over two trees.   [maximum 3]
2. a) ✓ d) ✓ e) ✓ f) ✓ h) ✓   [maximum 5]
3. The summary below is a suggestion only. You should have included details of what exactly happened (the tree being blown onto the car) and when and where it happened. When I left number 5 Roland Street [1], at four o'clock [1], it was very windy [1]. A car [1] came round the corner [1] from Bilton Road [1]. Just then, a tree [1] was blown over [1] and landed across its bonnet [1]. The driver braked suddenly [1]. Two people got out of the car [1] unhurt [1].   [maximum 12]

Page 156: Synthesis and Summary 2

1.

Similarities	Differences
They are both about roads.	The road in A is a private road and JDS does not know who owns it, but the one in B is the responsibility of the council.
They both think the state of the roads are poor.	B talks about parking while A is only about the state of the road.
They both mention the fact that they are paying for the roads.	JDS mentions part of the road being in 'excellent repair'. Amina comments on all of the road being bad.
They both want something done about the roads.	JDS wants an 'inquiry'. Amina wants action from the council.
	The road in B is in a 'busy town centre' but the one in A appears not to be, as it is 'approaching Garston'.
	Amina lives and has a shop on the road; JDS does not live there (he complains that residents do not have to pay).

[1] for each similarity or difference pointed out up to a maximum of [10].

2. Look at the mark scheme below, decide which description is closest to your answer and decide what mark to give it up to a maximum of [8].

Marks	Skills
7–8	You have given a perceptive interpretation of both texts. You have synthethised evidence from the texts. You have used appropriate quotations from both texts.
5–6	You have started to interpret both texts. You have shown clear connections between the texts. You have used relevant quotations from both texts.

Page 157: Referring to the Text

1. a)–y); b)–z); c)–x)   [maximum 3]
2. a) Romeo refers to Juliet as a 'bright angel'. [2]
   b) Romeo rejects his family: 'Henceforth I never will be Romeo.' [2]
   c) When Juliet asks how he found her, Romeo replies:
      By love, that first did prompt me to enquire.
      He lent me counsel, and I lent him eyes. [2]
3. a) Gratiano insults Shylock, [P] calling him 'an inexecrable dog', [E] a metaphor that implies that he considers Shylock less than human. [Ex] [3]
   b) By the end of the novel, Scrooge is a reformed character, [P] shown by his gift of the turkey to the Cratchits, [E] a generous gesture that the old Scrooge would never have made. [Ex] [3].

Page 158: Analysing Language 1

1. a) kingdom – noun   b) dominant – adjective
   c) the – determiner   d) or – conjunction
   e) accidentally – adverb   f) brought – verb
   g) with – preposition   h) them – pronoun   [maximum 8]
2. a) Mars   b) complex   c) which   d) active   [maximum 4]
3. a) Formal and technical   [maximum 2]
   b) Up to [2] marks for each reasonable explanation, e.g. 'The language is associated with science and reads like an explanation in a school text book' and 'It is written in Standard English'.   [maximum 4]

Page 159: Analysing Language 2

1. a) alliteration – great grinning giant's
   b) personification – looked danger in the face
   c) onomatopoeia – squelched   [maximum 3]

2.
She came into the room like a tornado.	simile	A tornado is a strong wind. The comparison implies she entered suddenly and quickly and might have been frightening. (Or a similar explanation.)
You are my rock.	metaphor	The person addressed is seen as strong and solid like a rock, implying reliability. (Or a similar explanation.)

      [maximum 4]

3. Look at the mark scheme below, decide which description best fits your answer and decide what mark to give it up to a maximum of [8]

Marks	Skills Examples of possible content
7–8	**Skills** • You have analysed the effects of the writer's choice of language. • You have used an appropriate range of quotations. • You have used sophisticated subject terminology appropriately.

Example of possible content
In the first sentence the narrator uses three adjectives to build a picture of an unpleasant winter's day: 'bleak', 'hard' and 'black'. This literal imagery can be viewed as a simple description of the environment and its physical effect on the narrator, making him 'shiver through every limb' but readers might see it as pathetic fallacy, reflecting the coldness of the welcome he is about to receive. The narrator reacts to being locked out with a spurt of physical activity as he jumps over the chained gate and runs up the path. However, his positivity is not reflected in what he sees – the chain clearly showing that visitors are unwelcome, 'straggling gooseberry bushes' indicating neglect. After describing what he can see (though he does not seem to get the message) he turns to the sound coming from the house: 'the dogs howled'. The onomatopoeic 'howled' vividly conveys both neglect and hostility.

Marks	Skills
5–6	**Skills** • You have clearly explained the effects of the writer's choice of language. • You have used a range of relevant quotations. • You have used subject terminology appropriately. **Example of possible content** The writer uses the adjectives 'bleak', 'hard' and 'black' to show how cold and unfriendly the place is. The narrator shivers 'through every limb'. The verbs 'jumped' and 'running' show that the narrator is very active and is not easily put off by the bad weather or the chain that is keeping him out. The 'straggling gooseberry bushes' show neglect. His hands are 'tingling', which again emphasises how cold he feels. This reflects the metaphorically cold unfriendliness of the house.

Page 160: Analysing Form and Structure

1. a)–z); b)–x); c)–y)   [maximum 3]
2. a) A church service   b) It is winter/it takes place near the sea. c) It creates a gloomy/mysterious atmosphere. d) The silence might lead to a feeling that something is about to break it/The storminess of the sea creates an atmosphere of danger. e) The important thing about them is their jobs/The writer is deliberately holding back the information. f) Any reasonable answer mentioning the sailor and what he is doing there. Up to [2] marks for each answer to a maximum of [12]

English Language 1 – pages 161–164

Page 161: Creative Reading 1

1. a) D (also accept B)   b) C   c) B   d) A   [maximum 4]

Page 162: Creative Reading 2

1. [1] for each correct answer in the second column and up to [2] for each answer similar to those given in column 3.

Character	How we learn about the character	What we learn about the character
Lady Catherine de Burgh	Narrator's description	She is snobbish, domineering/ intimidating.
Mary Morstan	How others react to the character	She is attractive/perhaps concerned about the narrator/The narrator is in love with her.

Mrs Fairfax	What the character does	She is kind-hearted/caring/practical.
Fezziwig	What the character says	He is in charge/He is generous/He enjoys himself/He is outgoing.
Hyde	What others say to/about the character	There is something odd and mysterious about him, almost inhuman.

Page 163: Narrative Writing

The following are examples of the sort of thing you might write. Your answers are likely to be completely different.

1. a) First
   b) No
   c) i) Male ii) Impossible to tell
      iii) Green, antennae, one large eye
      iv) From outer space v) Has a pet
   d) An ordinary street in England.
   e) Next year
   f) A year
   [1] for each reasonable answer up to a maximum of [10].
2. a) My family and our street. b) A new neighbour arrives.
   c) We find out he is from Mars and wants to return but his spaceship is lost. d) We find the spaceship and he goes home. e) Life is almost back to normal but we're expecting another new neighbour. [2] for each reasonable answer up to a maximum of [10]

Page 164: Descriptive Writing

These answers are examples only. Your answers are likely to be completely different.

1. a) Third [1] b) Past [1] c) i) A narrow Victorian street in town. [2] ii) A neat house with flowers in the window boxes. [2] iii) The fire in the back room. [2]
2. a) Flickering flames [2] b) Crackling logs [2] c) Freshly baked bread [2] d) Raspberry jam [2] e) Soft cushions [2]
3. a) As welcoming as a warm hug. [1] b) The house was an enchanted castle. [1]

English Language 2 – pages 165–166

Page 165: Reading Non-fiction

Up to [2] for each answer similar to the following, to a maximum of [20]

	Text A	Text B
What is the text about?	Staying at a hotel/guest house called Holcombe Manor.	Staying at a hotel/guest house called Holcombe Manor.
What is the writer's attitude to Holcombe Manor?	Felt 'at home'. Thought it was welcoming and cosy. Enthusiastic about hosts. Enjoyed the stay.	Thought it was cut off, cramped and unclean. Disliked host. Did not enjoy the stay.
What impression do you get of the writer?	Likes peace and quiet. Interested in history.	Likes modern facilities. Might be prejudiced against 'posh' people. High standards or a bit intolerant?
How would you describe the general tone and style?	Enthusiastic/positive.	Negative/insulting.
Comment on any interesting language features.	Uses a lot of positive but quite clichéd adjectives. Fairly formal tone.	Starts by addressing readers. Colloquial tone.

Page 166: Writing Non-fiction

The following are only suggestions. There are many other points you could make. [1] for each up to as maximum of [10]

For	Against
There are many examples of people who are successful without qualifications.	There are different types of success and fame/celebrity culture is shallow.
'Instant' success on reality shows can lead to other opportunities ordinary people don't often get.	Instant success can lead to great stress, unhappiness and mental health issues.
You could work really hard and even be successful academically but still not be well-paid or happy.	Academic work is not just about success. It broadens the mind and is interesting in itself.
The sort of work you do in school does not always help you afterwards.	Even if you gain fame and fortune easily, it's a good idea to have a 'back up' in case things go wrong.
Reality shows are too easily dismissed. Many who appear on them have worked hard and are still working hard to achieve their ambitions.	The two things are not mutually exclusive.

2. [1] for each of the following up to a maximum of [5].
   • Opening with 'Dear Sir/Madam/Editor'.
   • Setting out the opening correctly.
   • Using a formal tone.
   • Clearly stating the purpose of your letter.
   • Presenting your point of view clearly.
   • Using a literary or rhetorical device.
   • Accurate punctuation and spelling.
3. [1] for each of the following up to a maximum of [5]
   • Using an intriguing or amusing headline.
   • Using a strapline.
   • Using an appropriate informal tone.
   • Clearly stating the purpose of your article.
   • Presenting your point of view clearly.
   • Using a literary or rhetorical device.
   • Accurate punctuation and spelling.

Shakespeare – pages 167–168

Page 167: Context and Themes

1. Up to [2] for each reasonable answer up to a maximum of [10]
2. Up to [2] for each reasonable answer up to a maximum of [10]

Page 168: Characters, Language and Structure

1. [2] for each quotation and [2] for a reasonable interpretation up to a maximum of [8]
2. [1] for each correct answer and [2] for a reasonable explanation similar to the suggestions below up to a maximum of [12]
   a) Rhetorical question. The speaker expresses outrage and disbelief at the suggestion that he thinks had been made, answering the question in the negative.
   b) Oxymoron. Its use suggests both Romeo's confusion about love and how themes of love and hate are intertwined in the play.
   c) Metaphor. By comparing oaths to straw that could be destroyed by fire, the speaker emphasises how weak and worthless they are.
   d) Simile. The Captain expresses how much stronger than their enemies Banquo and Macbeth are by comparing them to powerful animals and their enemies to their prey.

The 19th-Century Novel – pages 169–170

Page 169: Context and Themes

1. a) [1] for each reasonable answer up to a maximum of [5]
   b) Up to [2] for each reasonable answer up to a maximum of [10]
2. Up to [2] for each reasonable answer up to a maximum of [10]

Page 170: Character, Language and Structure

1. [1] for every box completed with a reasonable answer for each character up to a maximum of [25]
2. a)–y), b)–v), c)–z), d)–w), e)–x) [5]

Modern Texts – pages 171–172

Page 171: Context and Themes

1. Check your answers against the text you have studied and give yourself [1] mark for each correct answer up to a maximum of [5]
2. Below are examples of the kind of answer that you might have given. Give yourself up to [5] marks for each reasonable answer similar to these, depending on how full your answer is.
   a) *An inspector Calls* is set shortly before the First World War, in 1912, in a 'large city' in the Midlands. The family is middle-class and wealthy, Mr Birling being a self-made man who has married someone from a higher social class. They are 'comfortable' and smug, but the Inspector reveals the dark side of their world.
   b) The world of *Never Let Me Go* seems to be just like the real world of just a few years ago, However, there are aspects of this world which are not real. Breeding people to provide spare parts is not something that is done officially now, although there are cases of people having children to provide genetic material for existing children who are sick.
3. [1] for each theme up to a maximum of [3]. Up to [2] for each reasonable explanation up to a maximum of [6].

Page 172: Characters, Language and Structure

1. [1] for each appropriate answer up to a maximum of [5]
2. [1] for every box completed with a reasonable answer for each character up to a maximum of [25]

Poetry – pages 173–176

Page 173: Context and Themes

1. a)–w), b)–x), c)–v), d)–z), e)–y)   [maximum 5]
2. a)–w), b)–z), c)–v), d)–y), e)–x)   [maximum 5]
3. The following answers are suggestions. You may have listed other poems.
   a) 'Eden Rock', 'The Farmer's Bride', 'Singh Song!', 'Winter Swans'.
   b) 'Eden Rock', 'Follower', 'Walking Away', 'Before You Were Mine', 'Mother, any distance'.
   c) 'When We Two Parted', 'Neutral Tones', Singh Song!', 'Love's Philosophy', Sonnet 29, 'Winter Swans'.
   d) 'The Farmer's Bride', 'Letters From Yorkshire', 'Winter Swans','Follower', 'Love's Philosophy', 'Neutral Tones'.
   e) 'Eden Rock', 'Porphyria's Lover', Sonnet 29, 'When We Two Parted'.   [maximum 15]
4. The following answers are suggestions. You may have listed other poems.
   a) ''The Charge of the Light Brigade', 'Exposure', 'Bayonet Charge', 'Remains', 'Poppies'.
   b) 'Poppies', 'War Photographer', 'The Emigree', 'Kamikaze'.

c) 'Ozymandias', 'London', 'My Last Duchess', 'Checking Out Me History', 'The Charge of the Light Brigade'.
d) 'Checking Out Me History', 'The Emigree', 'Poppies', 'Remains', Extract from 'The Prelude', 'Kamikaze'.
e) Extract from 'The Prelude', 'Bayonet Charge', 'Kamikaze', 'Poppies'.   [maximum 15]

Page 174: Language, Form and Structure

1. a) Sonnet 29 b) 'Neutral Tones' c) 'The Farmer's Bride' d) 'Follower' [4]
2. a) Extract from 'The Prelude'/'My Last Duchess'/'Checking Out Me History' b) 'London' c) 'My Last Duchess' d) 'The Charge of the Light Brigade'/'Exposure' [4]
3. a) Alliteration and pathetic fallacy. The alliteration of 'l' and 's' (also called sibilance) helps to make the line sound gentle and sad. The image of the earth starving adds to the sense of bleakness and despair.
   b) Metaphor. The metaphors give a picture of the nature of the relationship. The poet is flying away but his mother is holding him to the ground.
   c) Repetition and archaic language. The repetition of 'long' increases the sense of the future stretching ahead. The archaic language perhaps makes it sound more important, almost religious.
   d) Onomatopoeia. 'Clatters' creates a vivid picture through sound of the poet's mother walking along the pavement.   [maximum 16]
4. a) Simile. By comparing the soldier's foot to a statue, the poet creates a sense of him being frozen in time, emphasising the importance of the moment.
   b) Assonance and simile. The repetition of the long 'o' gives a sense of calm regularity. The comparison to a swan gives a sense that the poet and his boat are part of nature.
   c) Dialect and repetition. The use of dialect gives a sense of the speaker's heritage and identity. Repetition emphasises his point, highlighting how 'dem' are different from the poet but are in charge.
   d) Pathetic fallacy. The poet creates mood and atmosphere by giving human feelings to the wind and trees.   [maximum 16]

Pages 175–176: Unseen Poetry

1. [1] for each answer similar to those given below up to a maximum of [10]. Other answers might be equally valid.
   a) The poet or speaker's birthday.
   b) The poet or speaker celebrating being in love and how her life has changed.
   c) Yes. Two stanzas, each of which contains two quatrains. Each line has four stressed syllables. Each quatrain rhymes *abcb* but the final line ends in a half-rhyme. The regularity contains the poet's emotions. The change in the final line gives a strong ending on 'me'.
   d) The heart is a common symbol for love or emotion.
   e) It creates a strong focus on the poet's emotional state as she tries to explain it in a series of images.
   f) A singing bird, an apple tree, a shell. They are all beautiful, natural things.
   g) A sense of beauty, richness and luxury.
   h) 'Raise', 'carve' and 'work'. They make the poet seem in command, like a queen giving orders.
   i) Happy, elated, excited, joyful, looking forward to her future.
   j) The arrival of her love is like a new birthday, signifying that her life is about to change forever.
2. The answers below are suggestions. There may be other valid responses. Up to [2] for every box completed with a valid answer up to a maximum of [36]

	A Birthday	On His Eightieth Birthday
Speaker or voice	A person, possibly the poet, who has fallen in love.	An old man, probably the poet.
Structure	Two stanzas of eight lines (octaves).	One stanza of four lines (quatrain).
Rhythm/metre	Tetrameter, with variation in stress.	Iambic pentameter.
Rhyme	Regular until final line, which is a half-rhyme.	*Abab* – regular with no variation.
Vocabulary/register	Formal but personal using language of nature and riches. Second stanza in second person.	Formal but personal.
Use of sound	Repetition. Brief alliteration ('because...birthday').	Alliteration in 'steps...steady' and 'where... would'.
Imagery	Series of similes taken from nature, followed by a series of images of richness and luxury.	Literal imagery describing the past. Personification of 'Death'.
Themes	Celebration of being in love. The future.	Old age. Memories of love. The past. Death.
The poet's attitude	Positive and joyful. Excited – perhaps a bit self-centred.	Thoughtful/melancholy. Content.

Practice Exam Papers – pages 177–202

Page 177 English Language Paper 1 – Section A: Reading

1. Any four from:
    - He came from Calcutta.
    - He felt like a fish out of water.
    - He lived and worked in a shed.
    - His salary was small.
    - He cooked his own meals.
    - He shared his meals with Ratan.
    - Ratan did odd jobs for him.

    [1] for each up to a maximum of [4]

2. Look at the mark scheme below, decide which description is closest to your answer and then decide what mark to give it up to a maximum of [8].

Marks	Skills	Examples of possible content
7–8	• You have analysed the effects of the choice of language. • You have chosen an appropriate range of examples. • You have used a range of subject terminology appropriately.	The paragraph consists of one complex sentence, in which the writer uses details of sights, sounds and the feelings they invoke to build a picture of life in an Indian village. 'The village cowsheds' give a sense of ordinary everyday life in contrast with the natural sound of the cicadas and the mysterious spiritual song of the Baül sect, its harshness reflected in the alliteration of 'sect sang their shrill songs'. A sense of mystery, almost fear, is created in 'ghostly shiver' running down the back of the imagined poet before the writer brings us down to earth with the alliterative but prosaic image of the postmaster lighting his 'little lamp', the size of the lamp reflecting his own insignificance.
5–6	• You have clearly explained the effects of the choice of language. • You have chosen relevant examples. • You have used subject terminology appropriately.	The paragraph is one long sentence, describing the sights and sounds of the village. The alliteration in 'cicadas chirping' and 'sang their shrill songs' brings the noises to life and makes them sound a bit frightening. The poet feels a 'shiver' in his back. At the end we focus on the postmaster. His 'little lamp' describes his own smallness in the forest.

3. Look at the mark scheme below, decide which description is closest to your answer and then decide what mark to give it up to a maximum of [8].

Marks	Skills	Examples of possible content
7–8	• You have analysed the use of structural features. • You have chosen an appropriate range of examples. • You have used a range of subject terminology appropriately.	The extract starts with a very brief description of the protagonist and how he fits into the village. The third paragraph focuses on the sights and sounds of the village to build an atmosphere and give a sense of the postmaster's environment. A new character, Ratan, is introduced and the writer uses the modal verb 'would' to introduce an account of their routine. A short passage of dialogue gives a sense of their relationship as the focus shifts to Ratan and her background is filled in through what she tells the postmaster. Then the focus shifts from general exposition to a particular time ('one noon') and back to the protagonist and his loneliness. The final paragraph describes a turning point in their relationship as he offers to teach Ratan to read, making the reader wonder what difference this might make to them and their relationship.
5–6	• You have clearly explained the effects of structural features. • You have chosen relevant examples. • You have used subject terminology appropriately.	The extract starts by telling us where the protagonist comes from and who he is. It then describes the village where he lives. Focus moves to Ratan, and we are told about how she and the postmaster interact. The phrase 'one noon' marks the beginning of the story after the exposition. We learn that the postmaster is lonely. In the final paragraph, he offers to teach Ratan to read and we wonder where this will lead for both of them.

4. Look at the mark scheme below, decide which description is closest to your answer and then decide what mark to give it up to a maximum of **[20]**.

Marks	Skills	Examples of possible content
16–20	• You have critically evaluated the text in a detailed way. • You have used examples from the text to explain your views convincingly. • You have analysed a range of the writer's methods. • You have developed a convincing response to the focus of the statement.	The immediate impression given of the postmaster is of someone alone in an unfamiliar place, emphasised by the common simile 'like a fish out of water' and the literal imagery of the slimy pond and ramshackle house, which give the impression of an unwelcoming environment. His only friend is also alone in the world, but she is very different from him and their relationship is not equal. She calls him 'sir' and does 'odd jobs' for him. However, as they talk to each other about their past they become closer. Ratan chooses to remember happy times rather than 'greater things', which the reader might infer are sad or even tragic. The postmaster's own memories are described as 'haunting', the adjective with its connotations of the supernatural, suggesting mystery and sadness. The postmaster is still lonely, however, his mood beautifully evoked by the image of the bird and the 'murmuring leaves' expressing his feelings for him. His response to his need for companionship is to draw closer to Ratan. He starts to teach her to read, showing that she is a lot more to him than a servant. She calls him 'Dada', suggesting he has now replaced her lost family.
11–15	• You have clearly evaluated the text. • You have used examples from the text to explain your views clearly. • You have clearly explained the effect of the writer's methods. • You have made a clear and relevant response to the focus of the statement.	The postmaster is described in a simile as 'like a fish out of water'. He has come from Calcutta and does not know anyone so is very lonely. Ratan is also on her own. She is an 'orphan girl' who helps him out doing 'odd jobs'. At first, she is like a servant to him but they get to know each other and talk about their past lives. The postmaster's memories are 'haunting' him which makes him seem sad and the reader feel sorry for him. The writer uses pathetic fallacy to show his mood. He thinks the birds and the leaves are talking about his loneliness. He wants a special person to share his life with. He becomes closer to Ratan and she thinks of him as her family. They have not got much in common, but their friendship is touching and they are both less lonely.

Section B: Writing

5. Look at the mark scheme below, decide which description is closest to your answer and then decide which mark to give yourself. This task is marked for content and organisation, and for technical accuracy.
   Content and Organisation [maximum 24]:

22–24	**Content** • You have communicated convincingly and compellingly throughout. • Your tone, style and register assuredly match purpose, form and audience. • You have used an extensive and ambitious vocabulary with sustained crafting of linguistic devices. **Organisation** • Your writing is highly structured and developed, including a range of integrated and complex ideas. • Your paragraphs are fluently linked with integrated discourse markers. • You have used a variety of structural features in an inventive way.
19–21	**Content** • You have communicated convincingly. • Your tone, style and register consistently match purpose, form and audience. • You have used an increasingly sophisticated vocabulary with a range of appropriate linguistic devices. **Organisation** • Your writing is structured and developed, including a range of engaging ideas. • You have used paragraphs consistently with integrated discourse markers. • You have used a variety of structural features effectively.
16–18	**Content** • You have communicated clearly and effectively. • Your tone, style and register match purpose, form and audience. • You have used an extensive vocabulary with a range of linguistic devices. **Organisation** • Your writing is engaging, including a range of detailed, connected ideas. • You have used paragraphs coherently with integrated discourse markers. • You have used structural features effectively.
13–15	**Content** • You have communicated clearly. • Your tone, style and register generally match purpose, form and audience. • You have used vocabulary for effect with a range of linguistic devices. **Organisation** • Your writing is engaging, including a range of connected ideas. • You have used paragraphs coherently with a range of discourse markers. • You have usually used structural features effectively.

Technical Accuracy [maximum 16]:

13–16	• You have consistently demarcated sentences accurately. • You have used a wide range of punctuation with a high level of accuracy. • You have used a full range of sentence forms for effect. • You have used Standard English consistently and accurately, with secure control of grammatical structures. • You have achieved a high level of accuracy in spelling, including ambitious vocabulary. • Your use of vocabulary is extensive and ambitious.
9–12	• You have usually demarcated sentences accurately. • You have used a range of punctuation, usually accurately. • You have used a variety of sentence forms for effect. • You have used Standard English appropriately with control of grammatical structures. • You have spelled most words, including complex words, correctly. • Your use of vocabulary is increasingly sophisticated.

Page 180 English Language Paper 2 – Section A: Reading

1. B C F G **[maximum 4]**
2. Look at the mark scheme below, decide which description is closest to your answer and then decide what mark to give it up to a maximum of **[8]**.

Marks	Skills	Examples of possible content
7–8	• You have given a perceptive interpretation of both texts. • You have synthesised evidence from the texts. • You have used appropriate quotations from both texts.	Both writers describe behaviour they consider to be 'familiarity' (Trollope) or 'over-familiarity' (Boyle). The former criticises the behaviour of a particular neighbour before talking about Americans in general, while the latter mentions waiters, TV presenters and teachers. Trollope acknowledges the woman is helpful and intends to be friendly, and concludes her 'violent intimacy' is the norm in the USA. Boyle does not think the behaviour he describes is genuine and thinks it is copied from an idea of American friendliness. Both are concerned with forms of address. Trollope says that she and her husband are called 'the old man' and 'the English old woman' while ordinary working people such as 'draymen, butchers' boys and labourers' are referred to as 'them gentlemen'. Boyle is concerned with service rather than class and says staff in restaurants in France and Italy behave properly in contrast with those serving in Britain.
5–6	• You have started to interpret both texts. • You have shown clear connections between the texts. • You have used relevant quotations from both texts.	Trollope writes about the manners of Americans, Boyle about British people who imitate American manners. The behaviour Trollope describes is mostly from a woman who is over friendly, using first names and calling the children 'honey'. Boyle writes mostly about waiters. He says they now say, 'You guys' instead of 'Sir/Madam'. He says others, like teachers, do the same thing.

3. Look at the mark scheme below, decide which description is closest to your answer and then decide what mark to give it up to a maximum of **[12]**.

Marks	Skills	Examples of possible content
10–12	• You have analysed the effects of the choice of language. • You have used an appropriate range of quotations. • You have used sophisticated subject terminology appropriately.	Trollope starts with an anecdote to illustrate her point. She describes the situation in an understated, undramatic way ('absent rather longer than we expected') so it is clear that the search is not in itself the point of the story. Her later use of hyperbole, for example, 'exceedingly coarse and vehement' and 'violent intimacy', and the idea that the woman 'almost frightened' her (when you might think she'd be more frightened about her children being missing) suggests she wants to both shock and amuse, as does her reference to the 'amusement' of her children. In the second paragraph she uses a lot of direct speech to give the reader a flavour of American manners. She quotes the dialect of the Americans: 'That there lady… what is making dip-candles'. Here both the juxtaposition of the term 'lady' (in England usually someone who did not work) and 'making dip-candles' and the use of the non-standard 'that there' and 'what is' add both to the vividness of the picture and its humorous tone. Yet the tone seems affectionate, with a hint of self-deprecation, so you do not feel that she is 'making fun' of her neighbours.
7–9	• You have clearly explained the effects of the choice of language. • You have used a range of relevant quotations. • You have used subject terminology appropriately.	The narrative is formal, with long sentences and formal, old-fashioned Standard English: 'our party determined' and 'such a pair had been seen to pass'. When she meets the woman whom she compares to a market woman to give readers an idea of her appearance, her language becomes more dramatic. The woman is 'coarse and vehement' and Trollope does not like her 'violent intimacy'. She wants to put across how Americans speak so she uses a lot of quotations in the second half. Phrases like 'them gentlemen' and 'that there lady' convey both their dialect and their attitude.

4. Look at the mark scheme below, decide which description is closest to your answer and then decide what mark to give it up to a maximum of **[16]**.

Marks	Skills	Examples of possible content
13–16	• You have compared ideas and perspectives in a perceptive way. • You have analysed methods used to convey ideas and perspectives. • You have used a range of appropriate quotations.	The two writers have broadly similar attitudes to manners. They both prefer a degree of formality. Trollope uses the word 'familiarity' and Boyle 'over–familiarity' in the same pejorative way. Trollope is shocked ('almost frightened') by some of the ways of Americans while Boyle is 'outraged' by being addressed in a familiar, American-style way by a waiter. However, Trollope's purpose in writing is to inform her audience of the ways of Americans, remarking that such manners are 'universal' in the USA, while Boyle assumes his audience is familiar with the behaviour he is complaining about. He is putting forward an argument about the Americanisation of manners in Britain and expressing his distaste. Consequently, his tone is one of comic exaggerated outrage ('I would never leave the house'; 'never, ever') mixed with a serious attempt to analyse what he sees. Trollope too uses comedy but she is concerned more with reporting what she sees than analysis.
9–12	• You have compared ideas and perspectives in a clear and relevant way. • You have explained clearly methods used to convey ideas and perspectives. • You have used relevant quotations from both texts.	The two writers both dislike 'familiarity' and get upset by people being too informal with them. However, in Boyle's case he is only talking about staff in restaurants while Trollope is talking about Americans in general. Trollope is writing a book about the 'manners' of Americans so we can infer that at that time people in England behaved in a very different way. Boyle's main complaint is that phrases like 'you guys' have been 'imported from America'. He wants us to be different from them. They both use quotations in order to criticise them and amuse the reader: 'them gentlemen' and 'Listen up, guys'. Boyle is angrier than Trollope, who is just surprised by what she hears.

Section B: Writing

5. Look at the mark scheme for question 5 on page 208, decide which description is closest to your answer and then decide which mark to give yourself up to a maximum of **[40]**. The task is marked for content and organisation, and for technical accuracy.

Page 183 English Literature Paper 1 – Shakespeare and the 19th-Century Novel

Section A: Shakespeare

For all questions, look at the mark scheme below, decide which description is closest to your answer and then decide which mark to give yourself up to a maximum of **[30]**.

Marks	Skills
26–30	• You have responded to the task in an exploratory and critical way. • You have used precise, appropriate references to support your interpretation. • You have analysed the writer's methods using subject terminology appropriately. • You have explored the effects of the writer's methods. • You have explored links between text and ideas/context.
21–25	• You have responded to the task in a thoughtful, developed way. • You have used appropriate references to support your interpretation. • You have examined the writer's methods using subject terminology appropriately. • You have examined the effects of the writer's methods. • You have thoughtfully considered links between text and ideas/context.
16–20	• You have responded to the task in a clear way. • You have used references effectively to support your explanation. • You have clearly explained the writer's methods, using relevant subject terminology. • You have understood the effects of the writer's methods. • You have clearly understood links between text and ideas/context.

This question is also marked for AO4 (spelling, punctuation and grammar) up to a maximum of **[4]**.

Marks	Skills
4	• You have spelled and punctuated with consistent accuracy. • You have consistently used vocabulary and sentence structure to achieve effective control of meaning.
2–3	• You have spelled and punctuated with considerable accuracy. • You have consistently used a considerable range of vocabulary and sentence structure to achieve general control of meaning.

Your answers could include some of the following points.

1. **Macbeth**
   - Macduff's speech is broken up by caesuras.
   - He asks a series of short questions, seeming not to believe the news.
   - He accepts Malcolm's advice but asserts he must 'feel it as a man'.
   - The scene gives Macduff the personal motivation to seek revenge.
   - He gains sympathy as a family man and for showing his feelings.
   - Earlier he passed Malcolm's 'test' by showing his own integrity.
   - He is seen as loyal and brave, as Macbeth was at the start of the play.
   - He fights bravely and fiercely, and is patriotic and loyal to Malcolm.
   - Unlike Macbeth, he is honest and neither cruel nor ambitious.
   - When he kills Macbeth we learn he was 'from his mother's womb/Untimely ripped', so the witches' prophecy can be true.

2. **Romeo and Juliet**
   - Friar Laurence is surprised and shocked by Romeo saying he loves Juliet.
   - He sees Romeo (and all young men) as fickle, their love 'not truly in their hearts, but in their eyes'.
   - He recalls how love for Rosaline made Romeo miserable.
   - He distinguishes between 'doting' and 'loving', not believing Romeo truly loved Rosaline.
   - Juliet returns Romeo's love – 'Doth grace for grace and love for love allow'.
   - Friar Laurence might not be convinced but sees an opportunity for reconciling the Capulets and Montagues.
   - Romeo and Juliet's love is seen as strong and mutual when they meet.
   - Love is also complete when they marry, giving spiritual and sexual fulfilment.
   - However, it puts them in opposition to their families, leading to their deaths.

3. **The Tempest**
   - Caliban does not seem to want freedom, just a different master.
   - He is servile, not defiant as he was before.
   - All the characters are drunk and the scene is broadly comic.
   - Caliban unexpectedly speaks in verse and describes the island poetically.
   - Perhaps this shows what he could have been if Prospero had not enslaved him – or perhaps his eloquence is the result of the education Prospero gave him.
   - Caliban sings about his freedom. His joy might be genuine, but he is not actually free.
   - The play is influenced by the colonisation of places like America happening at the time, with settlers enslaving indigenous peoples.
   - Caliban and Ariel are sometimes seen as two different kinds of slave.
   - Prospero also enslaves Ferdinand to test his love.
   - In a sense, all the characters are imprisoned on the island and most are freed at the end.

4. **Much Ado About Nothing**
   - Don John is Don Pedro's brother but, as a bastard, is an outsider with no power.
   - He claims that he is honest and will not pretend to gain favour.
   - This is the first time we see him – he is talking to his confidant, Conrad, so we can take what he says as the truth.
   - Conrad urges him to co-operate now he has been defeated by Don Pedro.
   - They both use natural imagery – Conrad talks about a 'harvest' but Don John of being 'a canker in a hedge'.
   - We will see later the use he makes of his discontent as he plots against Claudio and Hero.
   - His actions provide the plot of the play, both by causing Claudio to reject Hero and, indirectly, bringing Beatrice and Benedick together.
   - His presence casts a shadow over the play. He stands apart from the happiness of the others at the end.
   - He can be seen as a 'malcontent', an unhappy character at odds with the world, common in plays of the time.

5. **The Merchant of Venice**
   - Portia is in control, telling Bassanio what she wants.
   - However, she is controlled by the will of her dead father.
   - She is obedient to her father's wishes, not wanting to be 'forsworn'.
   - Making a good marriage is important to her as well as to her father, but she wants to marry the man she loves.
   - She speaks openly of her love for Bassanio while stating that 'a maiden hath no tongue but thought', meaning she has no real power.
   - Jessica, like Portia, is controlled by her father but she asserts her independence by eloping.
   - Portia and Nerissa disguise themselves as men, which is necessary if Portia is to be taken seriously.
   - All three women express themselves openly and behave independently, following their hearts.

6. **Julius Caesar**
   - Brutus's suicide would be seen as honourable by Romans.
   - Antony makes a distinction between Brutus and the others – 'only he' had 'honest' motives.
   - Brutus is seen as a good politician, interested in 'common good to all'.
   - He is also praised as a man – he was 'gentle' and he lacked the vice of envy.
   - Antony uses rhetoric to proclaim Brutus's worth, imagining nature itself praising him.
   - Octavius echoes Antony's sentiments, wanting him treated 'according to his virtue'.
   - Their sentiments are especially important because they were his enemies.
   - In his conversations with Cassius, Brutus is shown as the idealist, an honourable man.
   - He is important to the conspiracy because of his reputation.
   - He is a brave soldier and leader who inspires love and loyalty.

Section B: The 19th-Century Novel

See mark scheme on page 210 for Section A. This question does not carry additional marks for AO4.

Your answers could include some of the following points.

7. **The Strange Case of Dr Jekyll and Mr Hyde**
   - The description of the scene at twilight creates a sad, gentle mood.
   - Jekyll is compared to a 'disconsolate prisoner', making him seem like a victim.
   - Jekyll's words about being 'low' and it 'will not last long' suggest an illness he is not in control of.
   - Jekyll is polite and pleasant when speaking to the visitors.
   - The sudden change in his look is frightening and the 'terror and despair' is like the reaction of a victim.
   - Jekyll is discussed by Utterson and Lanyon as someone who used to be a good, reasonable man but has become strange.
   - His friends are inclined to see him as a victim of Hyde and want to help him.
   - Dr Lanyon's narrative reveals the full horror of what Jekyll has become and his 'moral turpitude'.
   - Jekyll's own narrative gives us insight into his motives and his feelings about what he has done, making him sympathetic again.

8. **A Christmas Carol**
   - The Cratchits show their love for Tim and for each other after the 'death' of Tiny Tim.
   - Mrs Cratchit is anxious about Bob, not thinking of herself.
   - Bob tries to be positive, speaking of the 'green place' where Tim is to be buried, but breaks down.
   - Contrast between reactions to Scrooge's death and Tiny Tim's.

- The reaction of Scrooge's nephew contrasts with how Scrooge treats people including the Cratchits.
- The Cratchits represent decent hard-working people who find it hard to get by.
- They are the model of a loving, cheerful family, and show the true spirit of Christmas.
- Scrooge's treatment of Bob shows him to be a bad employer, in contrast with his old boss Fezziwig.
- Scrooge learns from watching the Cratchits at home. Their home life is the opposite of his.
- Sending the turkey to the Cratchits shows how much Scrooge has changed.

9. *Great Expectations*
- The setting in the graveyard makes Magwitch's first appearance terrifying and memorable.
- He is described as an intimidating figure and is clearly an escaped convict, but his cold and hunger might make him sympathetic.
- His speech, rough both in content and style, is in stark contrast to Pip's.
- Although frightening to young Pip, there is a comic element to the character brought out by the adult narrator.
- His physical strength is emphasised.
- He is absent for most of the novel and not even mentioned so that his reappearance comes as a surprise.
- Pip's reaction to discovering he is his benefactor puts Pip in an unsympathetic light – he mentions his 'abhorrence'.
- In contrast to Pip and his 'expectations', Magwitch succeeds and makes money through hard work.
- Magwitch tells his own story, making him sympathetic and correcting a lot of Pip's misunderstandings.
- The fact that he could turn Pip into a gentleman – and that he is Estella's father – questions the idea of social class and privilege.
- He is like a father to Pip and Pip comes to see that he is a 'better man'.

10. *Jane Eyre*
- Jane is included in the party but sits apart, listening and not making a contribution.
- She slips out by a side door, wanting to be as unobtrusive as possible.
- Rochester seems concerned about her but questions her abruptly.
- He also gives her orders: 'Return to the drawing-room'.
- She is conscious of not having the 'freedom' to speak to him as an equal.
- She is from an upper or upper-middle class background but is impoverished and has to earn a living.
- Her position means that she can mix with (and observe) servants as well as employers and their friends.
- She does not like the affectations of people like the snobbish Ingrams.
- Her judgments are not based on class – she can praise or condemn people regardless of their background.
- Rochester does not care about her class or background.
- Ultimately, though, she returns to her 'proper' position in life, getting an inheritance as well as a 'good' marriage.

11. *Frankenstein*
- Frankenstein compares his enthusiasm to a 'hurricane' and there is a sense of violent haste about the account.
- He admits that pride and ambition motivate him.
- There is a sense of the virtue of pursuing knowledge, bringing 'a torrent of light into our dark world'.
- However, his language betrays a desire to 'play God' by becoming a 'creator'.
- His description of the 'horrors' of his work, digging up bones, etc., conveys a sense of revulsion at odds with his ideas about doing something noble.
- This is seen as 'profane', against religion and God, in desecrating holy ground.
- After giving the creature life, Frankenstein is instantly repelled and rejects his creation.
- He makes no attempt to care for or educate the creature, which therefore has to learn from its experience.

- He becomes afraid of the creature and remorseful about his actions.
- He is punished for his act of creation by the deeds of the creature and his own misery.

12. *Pride and Prejudice*
- Austen describes Mr Collins's reaction ironically by using the kind of hyperbolic vocabulary he might have used – 'triumph', 'grandeur'.
- His 'triumph' depends on others ('his wondering visitors') being as snobbish.
- Sir William responds in the same way, showing off about his own 'situation in life', to assert his superiority to Mr Collins.
- Mr Collins assumes others will be as impressed as he is and keen that the experience does not 'overpower' them – the implication being that he hopes it does.
- His advice to Elizabeth about her dress is comic because of its inappropriateness – as a man he would not be expected to discuss such things with ladies.
- Snobbery is shown by his concern with superficial things like how people dress and how many rooms they have.
- What he says about Lady Catherine and the 'distinction of rank' proves to be true, showing that she is a snob.
- Darcy is also a snob, though not as obviously as his aunt. This is shown in his behaviour at the Meryton ball.
- Jane's romance with Bingley shows the snobbishness of his sisters and the damaging effect it can have.
- Elizabeth might also be a bit of a snob. Consider her feelings about her family's behaviour at Netherfield Park.

13. *The Sign of Four*
- Watson is excited about showing the treasure to Miss Morston and proud of being allowed to bring it.
- He may see the treasure as proof of his love for her.
- She has 'no eagerness in her voice', surprising us by her apparent 'indifference' to the treasure.
- Tension and expectation are built by the description of the box and the difficulty of opening it.
- The treasure box is exotic and incongruous in Mrs Forrester's house, the use of Mrs Forrester's poker adding some humour.
- As soon as he sees the box is empty, he feels the same, showing their mutual love.
- Finding the treasure seemed to be the point of the adventure but finding the truth is more important.
- The pursuit of it has placed Holmes, Watson and others in 'horrible peril'.
- It is the motive for the killing of Jonathan Sholto and the reason for the death of Morston.
- The story of Jonathan Small shows that the Agra treasure – or rather the desire of people to possess it – has always caused unhappiness and death.

Page 194 English Literature Paper 2 – Modern Texts and Poetry

Section A: Modern Prose or Drama

See mark scheme on page 210 for English Literature Paper 1. This question carries **[30]** marks plus **[4]** marks for AO4 to a maximum of **[34]**.
Your answers could include some of the following points.

1. *An Inspector Calls*
- Priestley presents a very unequal society – we see the rich middle-class Birlings and hear about Eva Smith.
- Eva experiences many problems, such as losing her job and getting pregnant.
- At the time the play is set, there is little help for her.
- Priestley wrote the play in the 1940s when there was a lot of discussion about the welfare state.
- Eva could be several different girls with different problems. Eva is a device for bringing them to our attention.
- Daisy Renton, the girl Gerald was involved with, could be the same girl as Eva or she could be a different person, used to show how little the Birlings value people of her class.
- Her problems can be seen in terms of socialism and/or feminism. Are they the result of her class or her gender?

- The central message is about taking responsibility for each other.

2.
- The Inspector takes charge and commands respect.
- He is an 'outsider' and does not belong to the world the Birlings move in.
- He acts like a detective in that he is investigating something and asking a lot of questions.
- He is not really investigating a crime but is looking into the reasons for Eva's act.
- He apportions blame and judges the other characters.
- He moralises about society and warns of the consequences of acting like the Birlings.
- His name, Goole, is pronounced the same as 'ghoul'. Is he a ghost from the future?
- He has come from the 1940s, the time the play was written, to examine an earlier time.
- He may be warning the audience not to return to the society of 1912.
- He can be seen as the voice of the writer.

3. *Blood Brothers*
- Mrs Johnstone makes a choice to give away (or sell) her child.
- Her choice may be justified by her economic circumstances.
- There is a sense that tragedy is inevitable, expressed by the narrator.
- Is this because of what she has done or because of class and poverty?
- Mickey is seen as the victim of social inequality.
- However, he makes bad choices throughout the play.
- The writer's (and audience's) sympathies seem to be entirely with Mrs Johnstone and Mickey.
- The two boys are not different in nature – their differences are the result of upbringing.

4.
- Linda stands up for Mickey to his brother and the other older children.
- She is one of the gang, equal to the boys in their games.
- She is protective and caring towards Mickey.
- The conversation about dying prefigures the end of the play, as does Sammy's gun.
- She is pragmatic in a comic, childish way: 'if y'dead, there's no school'.
- Here, Mickey introduces Linda to Edward for the first time. Their relationship will be crucial.
- In the park, Linda proves better than the boys at shooting: is Russell making a feminist point?
- She is outgoing and witty, and she helps to create a lighter atmosphere as she and the boys have fun together.
- She is in love with Mickey but, as his wife, is frustrated in her attempts to help him.
- She turns to Edward for help, unwittingly bringing the tragedy closer.

5. *The History Boys*
- The Headmaster sees education as a competition – the boys' success reflects on the school.
- He is not an academic high-flyer and is in awe of Oxford and Cambridge.
- He does not give away what he really thinks about issues such as Hector's 'fiddling'.
- He has a distant relationship with the teachers and pupils. Teachers call him 'Headmaster'.
- He uses the teachers and manipulates them, especially Irwin against Hector.
- In turn he is manipulated and controlled by Dakin.
- His public language is formal and authoritative (as in his last speech) while in private it is coarse.
- He could be seen as being interested in self-preservation and taking credit for others' efforts.

6.
- Mrs Lintott says Posner wants to know if Irwin has 'ceased to be a teacher and become a friend', implying you cannot be both.
- Posner is looking for personal advice, which could be seen as part of a teacher's job.

- Irwin seeks to discover more about Hector's relationship with the boys. This could be seen as crossing a professional line or as showing concern about Hector crossing lines.
- Posner notices Irwin's interest in Dakin. Dakin takes advantage of this attraction and treats Irwin as a friend.
- Hector blurs the lines between teacher/pupil relationships and friendship. Even without the 'groping', he could be seen as over-friendly.
- It could be said that a 'friendly' relationship with pupils is helpful in teaching but that is not the same as becoming friends.
- At times, the friendship between staff and pupils can seem fun and positive but it can also be harmful and manipulative (on both sides).

7. *DNA*
- All the characters are teenagers. We are in their world.
- The 'killing' of Adam is shocking and shows what they are capable of.
- Their reaction, blaming the postman, might be more shocking.
- They are part of a gang/friendship group but also belong to smaller groups.
- The interaction between them and the way they talk is typically 'teenage' – normal in spite of the abnormality of their actions.
- Their relationships with adults are not shown, only reported by them, but seem distant.
- They are distinct characters with different reactions, so not just stereotypical teenagers.
- They are dominated by strong characters and the demands of the group.

8.
- Cathy is not seen as the leader at first but takes over later in the play.
- She wants to be popular.
- It is she who gets the DNA from the postman.
- She finds the events after Adam's disappearance exciting.
- She does not feel guilty, seeming to have no sense of right and wrong.
- She enjoys the attention of the media and other people.
- She thinks about gaining materially from the situation.
- She takes control of the group and then the whole school.
- She is power-hungry, ruthless and bullying as leader.

9. *The Curious Incident of the Dog in the Night-Time*
- He finds people confusing. Christopher articulates his perspective on the world.
- He speaks differently from other characters, saying what he thinks without embellishment.
- Other characters are conscious of treating him differently, e.g. not touching him.
- His relationship with Siobhan marks him out as 'officially' different as in having special needs.
- His parents demonstrate how his 'difference' affects those close to him.
- His thoughts are presented through Siobhan reading his notes.
- The way he experiences life is presented theatrically, e.g. by the voices when he arrives at the station.

10.
- Christopher is concerned by the fact that he has been accused of killing Wellington.
- He like facts and is not willing to let this go – he needs to know the truth.
- He applies his own logic to the case, based on dogs being as important as people.
- Ed's reaction suggests to the audience (but not to literal-minded Christopher) that he is hiding something.
- Christopher's investigation will lead him to uncover the truth about other things, like his parents' marriage.
- He becomes more independent, taking the initiative and facing his fears, e.g. on the train.
- Other characters may begin to value him more, but does he value them more?
- He himself attributes his increased confidence and success to the incident, referring to how he went to London on his own.

- We are left wondering how much he can achieve.
- How much has he changed? And if he has not changed, does it matter?

11. *A Taste of Honey*
- The play's main characters are Jo and Helen, the men being incidental characters.
- Jo's relationships with men may be a reaction to her mother's attitudes.
- Helen uses men for money and sex. She depends on them but does not respect them.
- Jo's relationship with the Boy is romantic but brief.
- He lets her down, shattering her dreams.
- The Boy and Geof are outsiders (like Jo), one because of race and the other because of sexuality.
- Peter is unpleasant and overbearing.
- All the men leave Jo in the end, leaving her with Helen and facing an independent but uncertain future.

12.
- Jo shows immaturity and lack of understanding of what motherhood will mean.
- Her attitude might be a way of avoiding her true feelings.
- She does not say she wants to be a mother but refuses to consider abortion.
- She says she does not know much about love – will she be able to love the baby?
- Geof, not knowing her, assumes Helen will care because she is Jo's mother.
- Later Jo panics and says, 'I don't want to be a mother'.
- Geof tries to help her but she reacts by joking and flirting, trying to avoid the subject of motherhood.
- Helen's idea of being a mother is unconventional.
- She is selfish and shows little concern for Jo.
- She becomes sentimental about the baby but focuses on material things like the cot.
- Their love–hate relationship is the central one in both their lives.

13. *Lord of the Flies*
- Simon is the opposite of Jack. He is inherently good.
- He is gentle, and kind to the 'little 'uns'.
- He has the same sort of background as the other boys but for him ideas about morality and civilisation are not superficial.
- He understands what the 'beast' means.
- His hallucinations are almost mystical and holy.
- His murder represents the ultimate triumph of evil and savagery.
- He can be seen as a sacrificial victim, perhaps like Jesus.

14.
- Being British is a shorthand for being civilised.
- The boys' ideas of correct behaviour are entwined with ideas about being British, learned at home and at public school.
- The officer talks about British boys putting on a 'better show'.
- Being British means coping with adversity.
- At the time the novel was written, Britain's place in the world was changing, the days of Empire coming to an end.
- The sense of 'Britishness' alluded to by the officer is a male upper-class concept.
- The novel is influenced by the kind of boys' adventure stories popular in the nineteenth and early twentieth centuries, in which British boys overcame danger and adversity.
- Britain is associated with colonialism – the events of the novel undermine the idea of colonialism.
- Golding implicitly criticises all nation states, not just Britain, and their involvement in wars.

15. *Telling Tales*
- In 'Korea', the narrator at first seems to have a good relationship with his father as they go fishing together.
- They cooperate and work well together.
- Fishing is part of a disappearing way of life, reflecting the change that will come for the family.
- When he overhears his father talking about Korea, the boy realises how his father feels towards him.

- The older generation seem to think more of themselves and money than of their children.
- Compare with the distance between father and son in 'A Family Supper'.
- Compare with the discovery of cruelty and violence in the older generation in 'The Darkness Out There'.
- Compare the two narrators and their reactions in 'Korea' and 'Chemistry'.

16.
- At the beginning of 'The Darkness Out There', stories about crashed planes and girls being attacked are just rumours to Sandra, not reality.
- Her walk to the cottage in the woods is reminiscent of a fairy tale.
- Mrs Rutter's story reveals the reality of war and death.
- The young people are shocked at how Mrs Rutter and her sister behaved.
- Sandra sees Kerry differently because of his angry reaction: 'older' and 'larger'.
- She feels that her life is changed and sees the 'darkness out there'.
- Compare with the way in which the narrator learns about death and growing up in 'Chemistry'.
- Compare with the change in the narrator's feelings about his father in 'Korea'.
- Compare the change to Elizabeth's life in 'The Odour of Chrysanthemums'.

17. *Animal Farm*
- Old Major is 'wise' and respected by the other animals, so his ideas are listened to.
- He makes a logical and persuasive case against Man. He sounds reasonable.
- His 'dream' gives an almost mystical power to his ideas.
- Although he talks about rebellion, he does not make any practical plans for it and says it might not come for a long time.
- He is the equivalent of Vladimir Lenin, whose ideas shaped communism.
- He dies before the rebellion so we cannot know whether he would have remained an idealist.
- It is up to others to put his ideas into practice and interpret them.
- After the rebellion, his ideas are changed and his followers corrupted.
- This reflects the history of the USSR and other regimes based on egalitarian ideals.

18.
- Old Major blames humans for all the animals' problems.
- He states that 'we must not come to resemble them' and lists things that animals must never do.
- Even when they are putting up the commandments, the pigs give instructions to the other animals.
- The pigs learn human skills and take privileges for themselves.
- Squealer stops opposition by threatening the return of humans.
- They breed dogs to keep order; the dogs follow Napoleon as they did Mr Jones.
- The pigs start dealing with humans, using money and sleeping at the farmhouse, but have an answer for every criticism.
- The other animals change from being willing comrades and supporters to being confused and questioning, but they continue to obey the pigs.
- The pigs eventually rule by terror and are more cruel than humans.
- At the end, the pigs are indistinguishable from men, their transformation complete.
- These changes reflect the changes in the behaviour of leaders in communist and other populist regimes.

19. *Never Let Me Go*
- Kathy is a first-person narrator and we see everything through her eyes.
- She is a naïve narrator as she does not understand a lot of what is happening.

- Her tone is chatty, and she shares her feelings and reactions openly.
- She is proud of her success as a 'carer', working within the system.
- She is not quick to question but she listens to Tommy.
- Her naïvety and lack of understanding mean that we discover things gradually with her.
- She forms strong emotional relationships, demonstrating her humanity.

20.
- Ruth voices her feelings about being a clone, which no-one else has articulated.
- The word 'clone' is rarely used in the novel and for a long time the reader might not realise the characters are clones.
- Ruth feels that the others are living a fantasy, trying to make themselves feel better.
- She associates clones with 'trash' – they are even less than the worst humans.
- In spite of the clones knowing that they are different, they have human emotions and human relationships.
- Kathy feels that their 'human' behaviour is learned, with her friends imitating relationships and behaviour they see on television.
- At the end, her feelings are no different from the feelings of any human.
- We see everything through a clone's eyes, leading us to wonder what the difference is between clones and humans.
- We might ask whether it will be possible to create clones in this way and, if so, will they feel and think like humans?

21. *Anita and Me*
- Syal describes Indian dress and food in great detail.
- The narrator is very aware of her 'different' culture.
- The visits of the aunts, uncles and Nanima bring Indian culture to Tollington.
- Meena is not always happy about being different and is drawn to the culture of Tollington.
- Religion is part of the culture but it is not as important to Meena's parents as to others.
- The stories told by her family give Meena a sense of culture, tradition and history.
- At the end, when they move, she embraces Indian culture and her ethnic identity more fully.

22.
- The house is described as old-fashioned and uncomfortable.
- Meena's father gets 'sick of it' and its distance from work.
- Tollington's situation in the countryside appeals to Meena's mother.
- She likes it because it reminds her of home in the Punjab.
- She is seen as unusual and odd by other Indians who want modern houses nearer the city.
- Tollington itself is a poor, run-down village; part of its appeal to the young Meena is its size and the sense of community.
- The family is conscious of being the only Indian family and therefore the object of curiosity and prejudice.
- They are also middle class and better educated than most of their neighbours and they sometimes look down on them.
- As Meena gets older, she becomes more aware of racism and the differences between her and other Tollington residents.

23. *Pigeon English*
- The novel opens with a murder and Harrison becomes obsessed with 'the dead boy'.
- He witnesses the violent attack on Mr Frimpong and is drawn into a world of violent gangs.
- At first he is excited by violence but he comes to understand the reality of it.
- There is violence in school and among teenagers outside school.
- Aunty Sonia has harmed herself to stay in the country.
- Miquita suffers violence from her boyfriend.

- It is a world of gangs, knives and guns – even the police on the tube have guns.
- The climax, when Harrison is murdered, seems inevitable.

24.
- Mamma is a dominant character in Harrison's life.
- She is seen as hard-working and caring, perhaps a stereotypical African mother.
- Aunty Sonia is entertaining and fascinating but her self-harm is disturbing.
- Lydia is a stereotypical older sister, fighting with Harrison and bossing him around.
- Harrison's crush on Poppy gives some relief from the violence.
- Women, such as Miquita and Aunty Sonia, are seen as victims of violence.
- Although they are portrayed as strong personalities, they are largely ineffective.
- The gangs depicted are all male and the violence is mostly done by males.
- Adult males, if not violent or criminal, do not feature much in Harrison's life.

Section B: Poetry

For both questions 25 and 26, look at the mark scheme below, decide which description is closest to your answer and then decide which mark to give yourself up to a maximum of **[30]**.

Marks	Skills
26–30	• You have compared texts in an exploratory and critical way. • You have used precise, appropriate references to support your interpretation. • You have analysed the writers' methods using subject terminology appropriately. • You have explored the effects of the writers' methods. • You have explored links between text and ideas/context.
21–25	• You have made thoughtful, developed comparisons. • You have used appropriate references to support your interpretation. • You have examined the writers' methods using subject terminology appropriately. • You have examined the effects of the writers' methods. • You have thoughtfully considered links between text and ideas/context.
16–20	• You have made clear comparisons. • You have used references effectively to support your explanation. • You have explained the writers' methods using relevant subject terminology. • You have understood the effects of the writers' methods. • You have clearly considered links between text and ideas/context.

25. Your answer might include comparisons such as:
- Relationship with a parent – 'Follower', 'Eden Rock', 'Walking Away', 'Mother, any distance.'
- Memories/nostalgia – 'Follower', 'Eden Rock', 'Walking Away', 'Neutral Tones', When We Two Parted'.
- A sense of place – 'Eden Rock', 'Follower', 'Letter from Yorkshire'.
- References to popular culture, etc. to give a sense of period – 'Eden Rock', 'Walking Away'.
- Direct address to the poem's subject – 'Winter Swans', Sonnet 29, 'When We Two Parted', 'Neutral Tones', 'Love's Philosophy', 'Letters from Yorkshire', 'Walking Away'.
- Colloquial language – 'Singh Song!'.
- Division into stanzas of equal length – 'Neutral Tones', Eden Rock', 'Love's Philosophy, 'When We Two Parted'.
- Use of half-rhyme – 'Follower', 'Winter Swans'.

26. Your answer might include comparisons such as:

- Experience of a battle/war – 'The Charge of the Light Brigade', 'Exposure', 'Bayonet Charge'.
- First-person account of a life-changing experience – 'The Prelude', 'Exposure'.
- Persona adopted by the poet – 'My Last Duchess'.
- Poem based on reports/research (not personal experience) – 'The Charge of the Light Brigade', 'Bayonet Charge', 'War Photographer', contrast 'Exposure'.
- Colloquial language – 'Exposure'.
- Individual shaped/haunted by memory – 'War Photographer', 'The Emigree', 'The Prelude'.
- Violent imagery and diction – 'Exposure', 'Bayonet Charge', 'War Photographer'.
- Use of present tense – 'Exposure', contrast 'The Charge of the Light Brigade' and 'Bayonet Charge'.
- Structure – stanzas of equal length, varied line length. Change at end.
- No regular metre of rhyme scheme but some rhyme and half-rhyme – 'Exposure', 'Storm on the Island'.

Section C: Unseen Poetry

27-1. Look at the mark scheme below, decide which description is closest to your answer and then decide which mark to give yourself up to a maximum of **[24]**.

Marks	Skills
21–24	• You have explored the text critically. • You have used precise references to support your interpretation. • You have analysed the writer's methods using appropriate subject terminology. • You have explored the effects of the writer's methods on the reader.
17–20	• You have responded thoughtfully to the text. • You have used appropriate references to support your interpretation. • You have examined the writer's methods using subject terminology effectively. • You have examined the effects of the writer's methods on the reader.
13–16	• You have responded clearly to the text. • You have used references effectively to support your interpretation. • You have explained the writer's methods using relevant subject terminology. • You have understood the effects of the writer's methods on the reader.

Your answer might include comments on:

- Comparison of frost to a ghost sets the mood and makes us think of death.
- Depressing mood continues with language like 'dregs', 'desolate' and 'weakening'.
- Landscape and weather reflects the poet's mood – pathetic fallacy.
- In the second stanza, Hardy places himself in the landscape.
- He associates the landscape with passing time, as the century (nineteenth) comes to an end.

- He uses an extended metaphor of a corpse, continuing the morbid theme.
- The use of alliteration of hard 'c' gives a sharp, uncomfortable tone.
- There is a sudden change ('At once') with the sound of the thrush.
- Contrast of the 'joy' of the thrush with the death-like landscape.
- Religious imagery in 'evensong', 'soul' and 'carolings'.
- The age and weakness of the thrush makes his singing more extraordinary.
- Hardy sees the thrush as making an active choice to 'fling his soul'.
- The poet is unaware of the 'blessed Hope' but the thrush's song shows him the possibility of hope.

27-2. Look at the mark scheme below, decide which description is closest to your answer and then decide which mark to give yourself up to a maximum of **[8]**.

Marks	Skills
7–8	• You have explored comparisons of the writers' use of language, structure and form. • You have used appropriate subject terminology. • You have convincingly compared the effects of the writers' methods on the reader.
5–6	• You have thoughtfully compared the writers' use of language, structure and/or form. • You have used effective subject terminology. • You have clearly compared the effects of the writers' methods on the reader.

Your answer might include comments on:

- In both of them, the poet is alone in the landscape.
- The landscape and weather are harsh in both, reflecting the poets' moods.
- In 'The Darkling Thrush' the poet's mood is changed but in 'Spellbound' it remains the same.
- Brontë does not say what the 'tyrant spell' is, whether it is from nature or her own feelings. Similarly, Hardy does not explain his mood.
- Hardy writes about an incident in the past – Brontë writes in the present tense.
- Brontë's natural imagery is literal and simple, while Hardy uses an elaborate extended metaphor in the second stanza, as well as a simile in the first stanza.
- Brontë uses repetition and a refrain to give a sense of her situation.
- At first Brontë seems powerless but the last line suggests she is choosing to be where she is ('I will not').
- While the weather depresses Hardy and his mood is rescued by the thrush, Brontë seems to rejoice in the 'dreary' night.
- Both poems are regular in form and structure.

Acknowledgements

The author and publisher are grateful to the copyright holders for permission to use quoted materials and images.

Every effort has been made to trace copyright holders and obtain their permission for the use of copyright material. The author and publisher will gladly receive information enabling them to rectify any error or omission in subsequent editions. All facts are correct at time of going to press.

P30–31 *Nineteen-Eighty-Four* by George Orwell (Copyright © George Orwell, 1949) Bill Hamilton as the Literary Executor of the Estate of the Late Sonia Brownell Orwell. P88–89 *An Inspector Calls* by J B Priestley. P88–89 *The History Boys* by Alan Bennett (Faber and Faber Ltd). P88–89, P91 © Simon Stephens, 2004, *The Curious Incident of the Dog in the Night-Time*. Reprinted by permission of Bloomsbury Methuen Drama, an imprint of Bloomsbury Publishing Plc. P90–91 *Never Let Me Go* by Kazuo Ishiguro (Faber and Faber Ltd). P90–91 *Lord of the Flies* by William Golding (Faber and Faber Ltd). P90–91 *Anita and Me* by Meera Syal. Reprinted by permission of Bloomsbury Publishers Ltd © Meera Syal 1997. P90–91 © Willy Russell, 2001, Blood Brothers. Reprinted by permission of Bloomsbury Methuen Drama, an imprint of Bloomsbury Publishing Plc. P100 From 'Kamikaze' by Beatrice Garland:

Copyright Templar Poetry in *The Invention of Fireworks* (Templar, 2014), reproduced by permission of Beatrice Garland. P100, P101 *Singh Song!* from 'Look We Have Coming to Dover' by Daljit Nagra (Faber and Faber Ltd). P100, P101 *Checking Out Me History* copyright © John Agard 1996, reproduced by kind permission of John Agard c/o Caroline Sheldon Literary Agency Ltd. P100, P101 *Follower* from 'Death of a Naturalist' by Seamus Heaney (Faber and Faber Ltd). P116–117 'Florence' by Joyce Rackham, from *The Times* (13 October 1982). P174 *Checking Out Me History* copyright © John Agard 1996 reproduced by kind permission of John Agard c/o Caroline Sheldon Literary Agency Ltd. P174, P198-199 'Before You Were Mine' from *Mean Time* by Carol Ann Duffy. Published by Picador. Copyright © Carol Ann Duffy. Reproduced by permission of the author c/o Rogers, Coleridge & White Ltd., 20 Powis Mews, London W11 1JN. P174 *Storm on the Island* from 'Death of a Naturalist' by Seamus Heaney (Faber and Faber Ltd). P198-199 'Remains' by Simon Armitage. Copyright © Simon Armitage.

Published by Collins
An imprint of HarperCollins*Publishers* Ltd
1 London Bridge Street, London, SE1 9GF

HarperCollins*Publishers*
Macken House, 39/40 Mayor Street Upper,
Dublin 1, D01 C9W8, Ireland

© HarperCollins*Publishers* Limited 2022
ISBN 9780008534998
First published 2015
This edition published 2022
10 9 8 7 6 5 4 3 2

All rights reserved. No part of this publication may be reproduced, stored in a retrieval system, or transmitted, in any form or by any means, electronic, mechanical, photocopying, recording or otherwise, without the prior permission of Collins.

British Library Cataloguing in Publication Data.

A CIP record of this book is available from the British Library.

Author: Paul Burns
Cover Design: Kevin Robbins and Sarah Duxbury
Inside Concept Design: Sarah Duxbury and Paul Oates
Text Design and Layout: Jouve India Private limited
Printed in India by Multivista Gloal Pvt.Ltd,